The World of
Schnauzers

Illustration by Bob Groves.

The World of
Schnauzers
Standard • Giant • Miniature

Johan Gallant

Alpine
PUBLICATIONS
Loveland, Colorado

Library of Congress Cataloging-in-Publication Data

Gallant, Johan.
    The world of Schnauzers : standard, giant, miniature / Johan Gallant.
    224 p.   cm.
    Includes bibliographical references (p.   ).
    ISBN 0-931866-93-6
    1. Schnauzers.   I. Title.
SF429.S37G36 1996   96-25948
636.7'3—dc20   CIP

This book is available at special quantity discounts for breeders and for club promotions, premiums, or educational use. Write for details.

Front Cover photos:
Upper left: Ch. Feldmar Nightshade, a top winning Miniature Schnauzer owned by Marcia Feld, United States. Booth Photo.
Lower left: Australian Ch. Remporter Revel in Glory, top winning Standard Schnauzer in Australia in 1993 and 1995. Owned by J. Lee. Photo by CS Photography.
Right: Ch. Ogar v. Bartenwetzer, AD, IPO III, WMZ-3—Int. Ch., VDH-Sieger, Klubsieger PSK, and champion in Germany, Poland, Hungary, and Czechoslovakia. Giant Schnauzer owned by H. Glänznerova, Czechoslovakia.

Back Cover Photo:
The author with two Schnauzer puppies.

Cover Design: B.J. McKinney

1 2 3 4 5 6 7 8 9 0

Printed in the United States of America.

Contents

Three sizes of Schnauzers, all pepper and salt. Left to right: Kalenheim That Girl (Miniature) owned by Kathryne Heim, England; Fritz Mar-Jon (Standard) owned by Andrew Sims, England; and Jolly of the Greyguards (Giant) owned by Kathryne Heim, England.

Preface

The reader might wonder why this book was not written in an orthodox manner. Indeed, I have not emphasized the names of breeders and exhibitors who, over the years, have contributed to make up schnauzer champions. Although this is certainly important, I did not want to orient this book in that direction. Lists of breeders and their champions, their ancestors, and the number of their champion progeny is usually known by those people interested in that part of the hobby. I have also omitted the type of photograph with schnauzers in a show stance with their proud owners carrying the winner's rosette. It was my endeavor to put the accent on the schnauzer himself and not so much on the show fancier behind him. Although I consider myself in this category, I realize that we represent only 5 percent (if that much) of all people interested in schnauzers. This 5 percent usually knows what it is all about or endeavors to learn the ropes. They are members of breed clubs, read magazines, and educate themselves with regard to their hobby. I felt that by elaborating on their efforts I was not necessarily going to educate the other 95 percent about the schnauzer.

I have tried, as fairly as possible, to place the schnauzer and his origin in the limelight. I have done so because I am convinced that the breed's best publicity lies in the character and unique physical traits. Regardless of what the future may hold in store, the schnauzer's intrinsic nature and abilities will continue to guarantee the breed's success. This is, of course, subject to those people closely involved in the breed being aware of these qualities and respecting them.

The schnauzer has, even outside his native country, gained enormous popularity. The efforts and, in some cases, the breeding methods applied by "foreigners" have often contributed to the improvement of some aspects of the schnauzer. On the other hand, lack of insight and sometimes lack of awareness of fundamental points of importance allowed the foreign schnauzer to wander off on a side track.

Recent legislation within the European Community has already influenced, to a large extent, the fundamental appearance of the schnauzer that, during the breed's early years, had chosen the artificial style of cropped ears and docked tails, in accordance with the culture of the times. Believe me, if it is hard for anyone to envisage and, thereafter, accept a schnauzer with hanging ears (and now the possibility of a long tail), it is most difficult for the Germans. When the 1988 prohibition of ear cropping came into effect in Germany, the number of registrations dropped dramatically, but after only a couple of years, everything has returned to normal.

Around 1980, I predicted that Western civilization would soon refuse to accept the cropping of pups' ears to enhance beauty. For this view, I was laughed at. I did not think that the present changes would embrace the docking of the tails as well. It is a matter of fact that breed fanciers are not even consulted on those changes but are forced to abide by decisions made beyond their circle of influence.

Although these changes may shock us and the schnauzer's appearance may change dramatically, there is a consolation that it will not affect his nature. Registrations may temporarily decrease; but common sense will reign, and these numbers should revert to normal.

These measures and the foreseeable introduction of a free travelling pass for pets throughout Europe, including those countries with quarantine restrictions will, without doubt, bring British and Continental schnauzers closer together before the turn of the century. British breeding will no longer depend on local stock and imports, and a British breeder will be able to take his bitch across the Channel to have her mated anywhere on the Continent and return safely to Great Britain without being subjected to quarantine. Of course, such a travelling pass will only be issued to dogs that can be identified through microchip or tattooing and are in possession of all the required veterinary certification.

My concern for the future of the schnauzer is that, unlike the trend toward unification occurring in European dogdom, the North American scene will continue to remain distant. It cannot, however, be ignored that the number of Miniature Schnauzers bred in the United States probably exceeds the number bred in the rest of the world. The force of numbers supporting a typical American attitude will, hopefully, not constitute the wedge that could separate schnauzer ranks.

I sincerely thank the American authors who took the trouble to write their chapters. It is irrelevant if our opinion and approach sometimes differ. Ideas are there to be compared, not necessarily to be shared.

I trust, however, that the reader, throughout this book, will experience my commitment to the *wirehaired pinscher* who became the schnauzer. A breed that, in all its sizes, has been and will remain an integral and intrinsic part of my life. I will not turn my back to it, even if in the near future it should happen that I have to get used to an undocked wagging tail. Such an attribute will yet change the schnauzer's outlook but not the power of his soul. It will simply allow him to better express his mood and ease his way of communication. That is quite a comfort.

Acknowledgments

My thanks to—
Edith, my wife, for her critical eye, advice given, and drawings;
Ray Weingartz for supervising my grammar;
Seffie Princen for helping with the translation of German breed standards;
Jackie Isabell, the editor, for her patience and efficiency;
all schnauzer fanciers who spontaneously submitted photographs;
the PSK office, first in Alsdorf and later in Remscheid, for the abundant information.

About the Author

In 1974, Johan Gallant decided to undertake the descent of the Zaire River in a dugout to commemorate the centennial of Henry Morton Stanley's historic exploration into the heart of Central Africa. The photographic yield was fabulous, however three months after his return to Belgium, Johan's optical nerve inexplicably collapsed, forcing him to sell all of his photographic equipment. Shortly afterward, a friend presented Johan with a little mongrel, sparking Johan's interest in dogs. A few months later, Johan met his future wife, Edith, and together they decided to acquire a Giant Schnauzer.

"Bella" became Johan's new hobby and it wasn't long before he enthusiastically began exploring everything about Schnauzers and dogs in general. Johan's camera had previously been his medium of contact with society, but Bella surpassed all earlier interests. After Bella came "Bles," a salt and pepper Standard Schnauzer, and "Irma la Douce," a black and silver Mini. Within a few years, Johan became chief trainer at his local dog club as well as a committee member of the Belgian Pinscher and Schnauzer Club. He wrote a book on Schnauzers and another on assisting readers to make the correct choice when acquiring and educating pure-bred dogs. In 1980, Johan and Piet Duthoy, a fellow cameraman, co-produced an educational film called *Dog and Master* for Belgian national television.

In 1981, Johan and Edith Gallant decided to join Edith's family in South Africa. A new Schnauzer challenge lay ahead. The Gallant's imported "Feldmar All American Boy," the first black and silver Mini, from America. They bred all three sizes of Schnauzers, but they applied most of their attention to the Giant. In 1985, Johan founded the Giant Schnauzer Club in South Africa and has subsequently headed the club as chairman.

Since 1976, Edith and Johan have bred fifty-nine litters of Schnauzers and have exported puppies to fourteen different countries. They have personally prepared twenty-four breed champions and have qualified many of their Giant Schnauzers in international working trials. They have achieved their main goal of breeding Best in Show winners that simultaneously qualify in working trials.

After Johan retired as a physiotherapist, he concentrated all of his time on studying canine behavior, training dogs, and writing about his experiences with them.

Ch. Negus v. Hilbelinkhof at Manos Pelegri and Ch. Mocky v. d. Napoleonstock at Manso Pelegri , bred, respectively, by H. Lutjenkossink (Netherlands) and M. Loh (Germany). Owned by M. and A. Gil de Biedma (Spain). Photo © Jorgen Bak Rasmussen.

Introduction

It was in 1975 that I fell in love with Bella, a six-month-old black Giant Schnauzer bitch, who would, for the next thirteen years, share the life of my family and, thereby, change it totally. Within a few months, my wife, my children, and I became schnauzer addicts. My son acquired Bles, a pepper-and-salt Standard Schnauzer bitch, and my six-year-old daughter became the proud owner of Irma la Douce, a black-and-silver Miniature Schnauzer—a bitch, of course.

Since childhood, I have never been without a dog, owning breeds varying from a Pomeranian to a Mastiff, but Bella was something different. She opened our doors to dogdom, took us to dog shows, obedience classes, and working trials. She is also responsible for the writing of this book.

Over the years, we have developed a deep respect for the schnauzer. I don't want to discredit any other breed, but for us, the schnauzer is just something special. We discovered that the schnauzer has, above all, a keen sense of honesty. A schnauzer is a *good* dog in the real sense of the word.

In Bella's case, it was obvious to our community that, beside my wife and myself, she was the leader of the pack. She had the gift of interrupting an argument and at once stopping it from going any further. It was not only stopping arguments between dogs that was her specialty. I remember a picnic with friends where one of the fathers had to reprimand an undisciplined son. The youngster screamed his head off. Bella did not hesitate to interfere, and without hurting the father but by pushing him away and showing her teeth, Bella blocked his way to the child. She made it clear that because the child had shown submission, that was the end of the conflict.

On a nice summer evening when Bella was six years old, we were watching television with all of the windows open. Suddenly, from far away but clearly audible, an animal-like cry of distress could be heard. A few seconds later, the cry was repeated but sounded somewhat strangled. When I jumped up, Bella was already at the door. We moved quickly but cautiously in the direction of the cry, which came from a little bush about one hundred paces away on the far side of the road. There was no more screaming, but a muffled sobbing and breaking of branches and undergrowth could be heard. Bella walked on the tips of her toes, and a barely audible growl told me that there was real danger. Suddenly, in the dark, I could see two men who, without any doubt, were abusing a woman. Without thinking or weighing my chances, I took the law into my own hands and told Bella, "Get him!" She had anticipated my command which supported her own conclusions. Her attack was real and lightning fast. The men, taken by surprise, ran for their lives, one of them swearing and calling for help at the same time. When I reached the woman, I called Bella back. I don't know how much damage she had done, and actually, that was the least of my concern.

Later, when I saw Bella playing with puppies (even from another mother) or with my sister-in-law's little girls, I often thought back to that night. It is unbelievable that such a good-natured animal could be so efficient in a really dangerous situation. It is the perfect combination of an ideal nature with an inexorable efficiency that makes the schnauzer such a well-balanced breed.

I write this book as a tribute to Bella and all other schnauzers. If there was anything that Bella hated, it was injustice. Sadly enough, over the past years, I discovered that great injustice has been done to her breed. I hope this book will help to open the eyes of those people who, because of ignorance, incorrectly interfere with nature and wrongfully manipulate the breed by modifying it for fashionable reasons. Their intervention is not aimed toward improving the breed or maintaining its physical and mental standards because they have little knowledge of the breed's origin, the traits for which it has been selected, and the achievements of the breed's pioneers in its country of origin.

The rural populations in the southeastern parts of Germany have forged the schnauzers over centuries. Mentally and physically, the three schnauzer breeds fulfilled their expectations and became a useful and vital part of their society. In other words, the breeds were developed as part a cultural patrimony.

Modern times brought the schnauzer from this useful life on rural German homesteads to dog shows and popularity. The breeds migrated around the world. All too often their original heritage was forgotten or barely understood. In many cases, fashion and superficial fame has robbed them of their rusticity and functionality.

My final goal with this book is to provide a deeper and more sincere insight into the individual characteristics of this marvelous breed. Therefore, I write this book for all schnauzer fanciers—those who simply intend to share a part of their life with a companion schnauzer as well as those who, through their status in the dog world, can affect the breeds' evolution.

I honestly believe that one can appreciate and love a breed only with an understanding of its intrinsic nature and abilities as well as the willingness to protect the essence of the breed in terms of its conformation.

Johan Gallant

Ch. Jana v. Bartenwetzer, AD, SchH I and her daughter Eshta v. Bartenwetzer (Giant). Bred and owned by W. Schicker (Germany).

1

A Friend's Advice

Once upon an evening, a friend paid a visit. Knowing my interest in dogs, he came to announce his recent decision to buy a Great Dane, a harlequin, a male! Personally, I adore Great Danes, those fierce Apollos of dogs. I have even trained a few of them, and I have a deep respect for those strong fellows. But, I knew my friend as well, and I was not at all impressed with his answer to my first question: "Charles, why a Great Dane and a male on top of it?"

"At least that's a dog with which one makes an impression, and of course a male! Do you see me walking a bitch along the streets?"

His answer did not convince me at all. He probably noticed my smile when I invited him to come in and sit down.

I poured out two glasses of beer and started my explanation. "Charles, one does not acquire a dog just to make an impression. This is not a sports car, my friend, it's a live animal and above all man's best friend—even more, his oldest ally."

I told him about the primitive Stone Age men who first domesticated wild canines and later on, by selective breeding, developed and adapted them to fulfill their own needs. I explained that all through the evolution of the human species the different breeds of dogs evolved accordingly. The different breeds came into existence through man's involvement and his selection for a certain purpose or job.

From the half-wild canines wandering around the caves of prehistoric man, the first alliance was made. These canines had at their disposal a very precious organ—their nose, an unfailing help for pursuing and finding prey. The dog's nose and man's spear, together, formed a terrible team, and there was enough food for everybody. Rearing wild-born cubs who had lost their mothers was another definite step toward domestication.

In the course of history, primitive man ceased his wandering life and settled down, and a need for another type of canine arose. The homestead and the whole settlement needed protection against intruders. So, the original hunters continued to be "hounds," but from the strongest and toughest of them, guard dogs were selected. Even more, man had now domesticated some livestock, and he needed dogs to herd and protect his flock. In those early days, the dog's direct ancestor, the wolf, became his greatest foe. The flock had to be protected against hungry wolves. From dogs with the dual purpose of herding and guarding, man specialized these all-rounders toward specific shepherds and other strong, ferocious defenders of the flock. In this way, even a large flock herded by shepherd dogs and protected against intruders by surrounding guard dogs could be left alone during the night.

So you understand that already in the early days man had dominion over hounds, shepherds, guard, and protection dogs.

In his isolated settlements, man procreated, and his numbers increased. So arose tribes, nations, and cultures. Rivalry between these cultures caused the first wars. From the mastiff-like guard dogs able to protect the flock and homestead, ferocious war dogs were selected. Historians have proven that the Sumerians, four thousand years ago, used ferocious fighting dogs in their armies, as did the later Assyrians, Medes, and Persians.

The Greek conqueror Alexander the Great was very impressed by the armored Persian war dogs. After defeating their armies, he brought specimens of those Middle East fighting dogs as spoils of war to his homeland. From the Persian war dogs, ancient Greek breeders developed other strong molossian (large, mastiff-like hound) types.

The Greek civilization held dogs in great esteem and even built a city in their honor. The ancient Greek people were already so civilized that small dog breeds were selected as companions for the ladies. Aristotle give us a fine description of the ancestors of our modern Maltese and Bolognese.

With the decline of the Greek empire, the Romans took over the helm. The Greek molossian shifted to Rome, and from them, new breeds were developed; in particular, the vicious dogs performing in the arenas became notorious. The Romans conquered all that in those days was the known world. Their fighting legions brought the Pax Romana (Roman peace) and their war dogs. The soldiers were followed by the Roman settlers, users of more docile dog types. Caesar was very surprised when he was resisted by Britons using, just as he did, terrible war dogs. This proves that the dog's role in human lives was not limited to the primitive settlements and ancient cultures around the Mediterranean Basin.

Indeed, elsewhere on our globe, excavations proved the existence of domesticated dogs. The oldest findings go back to 8,500–10,000 years before Christ. There are not only the important nuclei in Turkey, Persia, and Israel but also, of even greater consequence, are the findings in Germany, Denmark, and England. In North America, similar discoveries were made in Idaho and Arizona. It's a fact that before Rome, the ancient cultures of the Middle East favored the rising of a diversity of dog breeds.

The Celts also developed their own breeds and later improved them by means of Roman imports and vice versa. So, tied to local circumstances and environment, we notice the development of well-known mountain guards such as

Ch. Epoche von den Munteren Gesellen—fifteen championship titles (Standard). Bred and owned by G. Gerth (Germany).

Ch. Dicky vom Grafen zu Moers—*Bundesjugendsieger* (Standard). Bred by M. Welge and R. Backhaus; owned by R. Steltzer (Germany).

the Pyrenean Mountain Dog on the French side of the Pyrenees and the Mastin de los Pyreneos on the Spanish side of the range. Isolated in the Alps, the Saint Bernard came into existence. In lower Swiss valleys, famous cattle dogs such as the Appenzeller, Entlebucher, and Berner Sennenhund evolved. A little further in Germany, Rottweilers, with a Roman molossian background, showed their working abilities.

After six centuries of dominion, the Roman reign in Gaul was toppled by a flood of barbarians from the East. Wild hordes of Huns, Vandals, Goths, Alans, and others ousted one another all over the European hinterland in the direction of the coast. The Alans, in particular, were renowned for their huge, swift, ferocious dogs. From these various breeds, other strong breeds developed in the region that is presently known as Germany. The later ones were the predecessors of the modern Great Dane, whose most important and direct ancestor is the Ulmer Dogge.

In the ninth and tenth centuries, at the beginning of the Middle Ages in western Europe, our forefathers possessed a variety of dog breeds. It was the era of convents and castles, of lords and venery (hunting) with packs of hounds. Hundreds of different types of hounds were selected in Belgium, France, Germany, Switzerland, Italy, and Britain—each destined to hunt a particular game, adapted to a particular landscape. There were the *lymers* (on-lead trackers), followed by the pack to approach, the pack to attack, and the killers. For hunting birds with throwing nets, the first spaniels were developed, the predecessors of the early setters and pointers. The terriers became the poachers for the ordinary man.

With the eighteenth-century invention of the musket as a hunting arm, hunting practices changed completely, and the gundog, in all its different varieties, became man's most precious helper. Dogfighting, bullbaiting, and ratcatching were betting sports for ordinary men. Around the farms and on the heath, shepherd dogs and cattle drivers were very popular. The butchers had their own strong fellows; modest farmers and traders used cart dogs as a source of cheap draft power. There were tens of other examples of dog breeds serving man.

When in the second part of the nineteenth century, a mere 120 years ago, modern man wanted to open a registry for dog breeds, to classify them, to develop purebred dogs, and to show them, it was from the collection of "dogs with a job" that he had to make his choice. So, all our modern purebred dogs have a background of ancestors created for a specific purpose. And whether we like it or not, each of our 350 recognized breeds carries more or less a certain amount of natural qualities typical of that particular breed. This is a natural heritage, and that is exactly what we have to take into account and what we have to respect when choosing a particular dog breed.

"From this, two questions arise. First, what is a specific dog breed able to give you? Second, what does the breed require, or what must you be able to give him? The answers to both questions can be weighed. If the scale balances, your breed choice is correct! Charles, as far as the Great Dane is concerned, if we analyze these questions, and if then, your answer remains yes, without any doubt the problem is solved!"

Charles, who had listened very attentively to my long monologue seemed impressed. He postponed my last suggestion by proposing that I spend an evening at his place and to resolve the problem in the company of his wife. I had to smile, because by Charles wanting to make a correct choice together with his wife, I felt I had scored a bull's-eye, and I enjoyed the idea of spending an evening with Charles and his lovely wife, Pamela.

Ch. Faust van de Havenstad—*Europasieger, VDHsieger, Weltsieger,* and champion in Germany, Luxemburg, and the Netherlands (Giant). Bred and owned by C. de Meulenaer (Belgium).

"Friendly with children, reasonably trainable, and not a lapdog." A family portrait at Argenta Kennel (Sweden).

2

After Careful Consideration

A few days later, I stopped my car at Number 23 in Grosvenor Street. Charles and Pam had recently moved in, and this was my first visit. At first sight, I saw a lovely home placed in a neatly fenced garden. I pushed open the iron gate and walked up the path to the front door. What an ideal place for a Great Dane! In my imagination, I could see the fierce harlequin, like a porcelain statue, sitting next to the fish pond. From the kitchen, Pam had probably watched my arrival, and she now opened the front door with a friendly "Welcome."

Immediately, she added, "As you know, John, my husband wants to buy a big dog. Since we got married and especially since I am pregnant, he has lost interest in his football and his football friends. Nearly every weekend, we drive to the countryside, and we enjoy long walks. I like the idea of a dog because I love animals, and anyway, when I was a child, we always had dogs at home. But I realize that, just as for our canary, I will have to care for it. Moreover, I know that an average dog's life is about twelve years, and I want to make the right choice so that we can enjoy each other—the longer the better."

"Pam, you are a clever girl. Don't worry, tonight we will sort that out!"

At this stage, Charles came out of the inside garage door, and we all settled down in a fully carpeted cozy corner. What a lovely place for a Great Dane! I could see him hogging the whole sofa, his head reposing on the armrest. After a little small talk, I opened the discussion.

"I understand that both of you want to add a dog to your lives. This being agreed, we can go ahead. Let us make a list of all your requirements, all your expectations, all your conditions toward your future friend. What must be his qualities?"

Pam opened the list with friendly with children, reasonably trainable, not a lapdog you have to push from your knees toward another cushion, not interested in a long coat that leaves hair on carpets and clothes, a reasonable size but not dragging her and the children's buggy around town. Congenital garden diggers to be avoided.

At this moment, Charles took over, adding able to guard the property, sportive type able to accompany him on jogging jaunts, rather a rare breed that makes an impression.

As the enumeration now faltered a bit, I seized the opportunity of taking over. "All right, at present I know more or less what your requirements are. Out of these, I believe I can advise you on a number of breeds. However, before we get to the point, let us find out what you can offer your future dog. First of all, I must ask if you are prepared and can you afford to spend a fair amount of money on the purchase of a good quality puppy? Do you realize that feeding and caring is an ever-present cost?"

Pam and Charles, without hesitation, nodded positively.

"Good! Now arises the question of where to house your future dog. Will you give him a full-time place in the house, will you build him a decent kennel, or will you combine house and kennel?"

Charles had probably not thought about this, but Pam reacted very positively, saying, "I don't object to having the dog in the house because I just want his company. I will teach him how to behave. My only restriction is a breed that sheds on my carpets. On the other hand, I believe it's desirable to build a good wooden kennel in the garden where the dog feels at home—for example, when we have to go out without him or in other circumstances."

This time it was my turn to nod my head approvingly, before I carried on with," I understand you intend taking your dog on your weekend trips, Pam wants to take him along for walks in town and Charles on his jogging jaunts, but do you also intend taking him to dog-training classes?"

Now Charles was the first to reply with the story of a friend at work who had a German Shepherd Dog that he was taking twice a week to a club where they trained for obedience and protection work. He aimed, if possible, to do the same, but for some personal reason, he was not interested in that breed.

At this point, I knew enough. I had to deal with two young people who really wanted a dog and were prepared to share their lives with him. Moreover, I had obtained enough information to help and advise them with the choice of the right breed. "From what you have told me of your likes and dislikes, I would exclude nearly all the toys and hounds as well as most of the gundogs and terriers. Honestly, I believe we must concentrate on the working group. However, before carrying on, I must tell Pam that not only longhaired breeds lose their coats but also short-haired varieties leave their hairs on carpets and pants. With daily brushing, you can reduce this nuisance to a minimum. However, if Pam is reluctant on this point, then we must select from the curly or wirehaired breeds. These dogs do not lose their hair, but they need a regular clipping or grooming. The Poodle is the best example of the curly-coated breeds."

Here, I was interrupted by Pam. A Poodle, with all respect, was not exactly the dog they were looking for, and Jessy, a friend of hers, brushed her Labrador and Keeshond every day and there was always hair on her carpets, even in her car. As Pam was absolutely adamant on this point, we had to concentrate on the middle-sized wirehaired breeds, friendly with children, rather a rare "executive" breed,

Ch. Florence van Masatina and Ch. Dapper van Masatina (Standards). Bred and owned by C. Vaes (Belgium).

Ch. Dapper van Masatina—Int. Ch., *VDH-sieger, Bundessieger, Europasieger, Klubsieger PSK, Weltsieger.* Winner Amsterdam, and champion in Luxemburg, Denmark, France, Hungary, Belgium, Germany, and the Netherlands (Standard). Bred and owned by Mr. and Mrs. C. Vaes (Belgium).

Ch. Jandumin Hasse—*Klubsieger PSK* and champion in Finland, Sweden, and Norway (Standard). Bred by R. Latvala; owned by A. Hahtonen (Finland)

Ch. Argentos Akki—*Klubsieger PSK, VDHsg,* and champion in Germany (Miniature). Owned by A. W. Kogzmann (Germany).

easily trainable, and, eventually, as a watchdog suitable for protection dog training.

At this moment, I dug out of my bag an illustrated dog encyclopedia, and ignoring their last request, I started to show them a gundog—the German Wirehaired Pointer, a rare and magnificent breed, fulfilling almost all the demands but failing when touching the point of protection dog and corresponding training. My next picture showed a terrier, the Airedale. At this place in the book, we left a paper strip in order to come back to this dog later on. Then followed the Laekenois (rough-haired Belgian Shepherd), the Picardy Sheepdog (rough-haired French Shepherd), and the Bouvier des Flandres.

When I turned the page featuring the three schnauzer varieties, Pam put her hand on mine and stopped further skimming by telling us, "In the park, I often meet a lady taking a walk with two of these small creatures. They are tough little things, well built, alert, and consider her their property. Two weeks ago, she came and sat on the other end of the bench. It took her quite a while to persuade her doggies that, obviously, I was not dangerous. It took even more time before the little male, very self-confident, came to sniff me and say hello. I did not know these miniatures had bigger cousins. Do they have the same vigorousness? And are you sure they don't leave their harsh coat all over the house?"

"Pam, besides the Miniature Schnauzer, there are also the Standard and Giant Schnauzers, respectively, with an average size of thirteen, nineteen, and twenty-seven inches at the withers. In the old days, the Miniature Schnauzers were ratcatchers, the Standards were active in horse stables and alongside carts, and the Giants were developed from the beginning as protection dogs. As far as their coats are concerned, when these dogs are properly bred, according to the breed standard, they will have a wiry topcoat covering a short soft undercoat. This combination, when regularly brushed and stripped twice a year, will really leave a minimum of hair in your house."

Now, following the paper strips left in the book, Pam quickly turned back to the Bouvier and the Airedale. She had a long look at the last one and then came back to the page where she had kept her index finger, and with typical feminine intuition decided, "Charles, we must go and have a look at these schnauzers and find an excellent breeder. Personally, I prefer the Standard one. If you want, you can go for the Giant, but you must promise to give me a hand with his education."

I was honestly convinced that Pam had made a good choice. A schnauzer should definitely be happy in these surroundings and, if properly trained, should fulfill all expectations. The problem of size and gender could be left for later, but I felt I had now to tell them the story of the schnauzer.

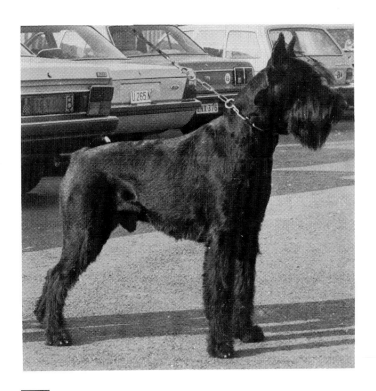

Djim van't Wareheim (Giant). Bred by J. and E. Gallant; owned by Jolibois (France).

The wirehaired pinscher. Reproduced from Jean Bungartz, *Handbuch zur Beurteilung der Rassenreinheit des Hundes*, 1884.

3

Early History of
the Schnauzer

"So Pam," I continued, *"I explained to your husband that all over the world where prehistoric excavations were done and the testimony of Stone Age man was uncovered, one usually also discovered evidence of dogs sharing man's life. One of these excavations, which occurred in an area not far from the region where the schnauzer took root, could be of particular importance in the breeds' history."*

When in 1854, for some natural reason, the water level in the mountain lakes in the Swiss Jura drastically lowered, very important prehistoric findings were made in the peat layers that emerged. Near the remains of lake dwellings, archaeologists found skeletons of men and dogs together. Scientists classified the dogs as *Canis familiaris palustris,* more commonly known as peat dogs. These discoveries have been dated at the end of the Stone Age period (circa 3000–2000 B.C.). This leaves no doubt that the neolithic Swiss reared a considerable number of dogs of an average height of 0.5 meters (1.6 feet).

The Swiss zoologist Theodor Studer (1845–1922) made an in-depth study of the Swiss peat dogs and explains his findings in a paper *"Beiträge zur Geschichte unserer Hunderassen."*[1] He gathered a famous cynologic collection that was transmitted to the Albert-Heim-Foundation, which continues the research work. *(Cynology*—the scientific study of dogs, especially their natural science.)

The oldest skulls of peat dogs were found in Wetzikon excavations (circa 3000 B.C.), and Rutimeyer reconstructed one of them. The peat dog remains from the Lattringen excavations are dated about 2000 B.C. During the thousand year interval, there is a clear differentiation toward two or three different skull types, which indicates that some type of selection—either natural or human—took place.

The evolution of the peat dog throughout the neolithic period is important in that a differentiation toward two or three main structures can be detected. W. Tchudy, in his *Geschichte des Hundes*[2] contends that the structure of one particular peat dog corresponds with the structures of our modern keeshond and spitz families and has to be considered their ancestor. The skulls found in Lattringen are, in structure, the nearest to our schnauzers and terriers and have to be considered their link with prehistory.

Early Art and Literature

"Of course, it's a long way from the Stone Age man in Lattringen with his primitive companions to our recent show schnauzer specimens. You will understand, Pam and Charles, that it is naturally impossible to follow this evolution over thousands of years. However, the rare points of contact one could find are worth mentioning because they give us a clearer insight into this breed."

The first writings that could refer to our schnauzers are from the hand of the Merovingian King Dagobert (r. A.D. 628–638). In his *Lex Baiuvariorum,* Dagobert states that penalties were enforced on Germans for the death—by negligence during the hunt or in other circumstances—of a bibarhund, a terrier-type breed used by some German tribes to hunt beaver.

The French noble Gaston de Foix (also called Gaston Phoebus), in his famous treatise *Le Livre de la Chasse,*[3] circa 1387, describes the hunting practices of those medieval days. He does not restrict himself to France but clearly mentions the rough-haired terrier-like tanner that was frequently used for hunting in Germany, a descendent of the bibarhund.

Albrecht Dürer owned a schnauzer-type dog between 1492 and 1504. Several of his works during this period show us in one or another way a clear representation of a dog that, without any doubt, shows a good likeness to our modern schnauzer.

Lucas Cranach, Jr., was an artist who created tapestries. On a piece produced in 1501, we clearly recognize a schnauzer-like figure.

Between 1758 and 1836, the Frenchman Charles Vernet painted *Le Départ du Chasseur.*[4] In between the horses, we recognize the likeness of an eighteenth-century pinscher.

It is a matter of fact that much written evidence concerning our breed remains hidden. Today's schnauzer fans interested in history still discover, from time to time, some interesting information. Herbert Hirschfelder from Erlangen is one example. In the Number 1 and 5 1985 issues of the German *Pinscher-Schnauzer Zeitung,* the official monthly magazine of the Pinscher-Schnauzer Klub, he tells about his latest findings. He recently discovered a 1863 book by Conrad Jahn called *Das Werk von Johann Adam Klein.*[5] This book represents a collection of Klein's etchings. Number 79, signed by Klein in 1812, bears the following comment by Jahn: "The two Pinschers with broad collars, the one is wirehaired seen ¾ from the front, sitting on a wall on which the inscription Klein, fec. [made in] 1812 can be read. The smooth haired one lies next to him facing in the opposite direction." (The identification pinscher may sound confusing in this schnauzer context; however, old literature used this term when speaking about the forefathers of our modern schnauzer.)

Let us have a look at this very good likeness. There is a definite distinction between the wirehaired and smooth-haired dog, though not so pronounced as in our modern schnauzer and pinscher. Both dogs are cropped (very short) and docked. The wirehaired one shows some beard and eye-

FIGURE 3-1

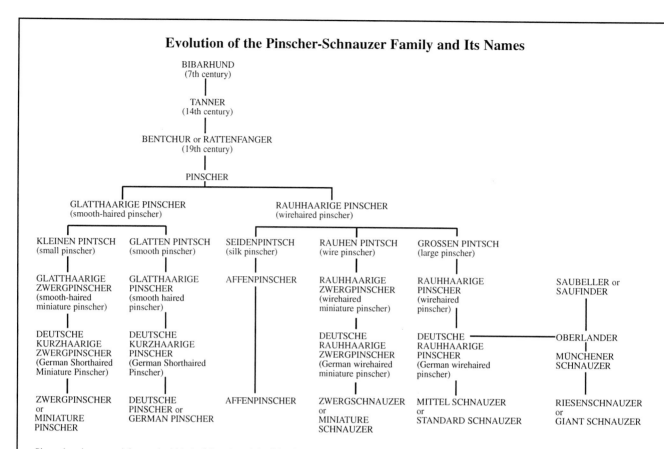

Since time immemorial, a typical kind of dog shared the life of the southern German rural population. The species was about nineteen inches tall, had either a smooth or wiry coat of an inconspicuous color ranging from brown over gray to black. Known as the bentchur or rattenfänger, they were mainly used as watchdogs and vermin killers in and around the homesteads. From this primal stock, modern cynology has developed well-defined pinschers and schnauzers of different sizes, coats, and colors..

brows; the eye is dark; the forechest is pronounced; front quarters are straight, strong, and have cat feet. From the size of the thistle leaf in the painting, we may conclude that the dog's size is between 40 and 50 centimeters (16 and 20 inches).

One question remains. Did Klein, in 1812, give the name pinscher, or was it Jahn who, in 1863, added this caption? This is important, in a way, because one cannot identify with certainty when the English-sounding term *pinscher* was introduced into the German language. Research into old books will not give a straight and easy answer to this question, but let us see what we can find.

In 1833, F. W. Riemer collected and studied the correspondence between Professor Zelter and Goethe between 1796 and 1832. In one letter, Zelter mentions "docked horses and pinschers." Further, we find another contribution, "Poets and artists seem to have the same destiny as horses and dogs, which are transformed to Englishmen or pinschers."[6]

Herbert Hirschfelder recently discovered a 1832 book about dogs, which can be considered the oldest in the German language. Written by Johann Wilhelm Baumeister, *Die Jagd- und Andere Hunde in Allen Ihren Verhaltnissen*[7] describes and classifies the different dog breeds. It is interesting that Baumeister was born (Augsburg or Schwäbisch Gmünd, 1804), lived, and died (Stuttgart, 1846) in southern Germany, the region of our breeds' origin. A country veterinarian, Baumeister must have known these rural breeds very well. Under Class II in his enumeration and description of breeds, he mentions the bentchur or rattenfänger. Although he gives no illustration of the breed, his description is full of details and portrays a dog similar to the one in Klein's 1812 etching. He states:

The dog has a rather round head with lively eyes, an excellent bite, and a snout covered with rough-haired whiskers. His legs are strongly muscled and equipped with strong nails. His body is short, and his tail is usually docked. The topcoat is not too long but wiry etc.

Table 3-1. The Pinscher-Schnauzer Family and Its Names

Year	Source	Name					
1832	Baumeister	Bentchur-Rattenfänger					
1833	Riemer	Gestützten Pinschern					
1834	Götz	Pinscher					
1834	Reichenbach	Glatthaarige Pinscher			Rauhhaarige Pinscher		Saubeller Saufinder
1852	Weiss	Pinscher-Terrier					
1863	Jahn	The Two Pinschers					
1876	Fitzinger	Seidenpintsch	Kleinen Pintsch	Glatten Pintsch	Rauhen Pintsch	Grossen Pintsch	
1884	Von Schmiedeberg	Kurzhaarige Pinscher			Rauhhaarige Pinscher		
1886	Bungartz		Glatthaarige Zwergpinscher	Glatthaarige Pinscher	Rauhhaarige Zwergpinscher	Rauhhaarige Pinscher	
1891	Reul				Griffon Terrier Allemand Sans Queue		
1895	Pinscher Klub	Affenpinscher or Rauhhaarige Zwergpinscher	Glatthaarige Zwergpinscher	Glatthaarige Pinscher		Rauhhaarige Pinscher	
1897	Van Bylandt	Affenpinscher	Deutsche Kurzhaarige Zwergpinscher	Deutsche Kurzhaarige Pinscher	Deutsche Rauhhaarige Zwergpinscher *or* Pinscher Schnauzer	Deutsche Rauhhaarige Pinscher *or* Schnauzer *or* Rattler	
1907	Schnauzer Klub				Schnauzer		
1890-1920	Varia						Oberlander Russen Schnauzer Münchener Schnauzer Bier Schnauzer Grosser Münchener Schnauzer
1923	PSK	Affenpinscher	Zwergpinscher *or* Miniature Pinscher	Deutsche Pinscher *or* German Pinscher	Zwergschnauzer *or* Miniature Schnauzer	Mittel Schnauzer *or* Standard Schnauzer	Riesenschnauzer *or* Giant Schnauzer
		(black)	(black and tan *or* red)	(black and tan *or* red)	(salt & pepper *or* black)	(salt & pepper *or* black)	(salt & pepper *or* black)
1968					(black & silver *or* white)		

The Pinscher-Schnauzer Klub is the international parent breed club for the six breeds shown here: Giant Schnauzer, Standard Schnauzer, Miniature Schnauzer, German Pinscher, Miniature Pinscher, and Affenpinscher.

The first published illustration of a wirehaired pinscher. Reproduced from
H. G. L. Reichenbach, *Der Hund in Seinen Haupt-und Nebenrassen,* 1834.

This etching by J. A. Klein, dated 1812 and representing a wirehaired and a smooth-haired pinscher, is part of the Luthardt Collection, owned by the University Library of Erlangen
(Germany).

Der Pinscherhund. Reproduced from Theodor Götz, *Hunde-Gallerie,* 1838.

Der Pinscherhund. Reproduced from Theodor Götz, *Monographie des Hundes,* 1834.

In its main points, this description fits our modern breed standard.

In the same period, Theodor Götz published the *Monographie des Hundes*[8] in 1834 and *Hunde-Gallerie*[9] in 1838. He vaguely introduced the theory that the shorthaired pinscher variety made its way from England to Germany.

In 1834, *Der Hund in Seinen Haupt- und Nebenrassen*[10] by H. G. L. Reichenbach was the first to give a description as well as a reproduction of the rauhhaarige pinscher (wirehaired pinscher) and the glatthaarige pinscher (smoothhaired pinscher). In a note, he clearly states that pinscher is not an English term indicating a breed. The picture of the wirehaired variety shows an uncropped dog, light in color, and a face with a slight beard and a darker mask. Reichenbach also mentions a saubeller or saufinder. *Sau* is the German term for pig or boar, *beller* means barker, and *finder* has the same significance in English as in German. This "barker at boar" is a middle-sized dog with a dark, wiry coat and, though he is bigger than the wirehaired pinscher, shows plenty of resemblance to the last one.

When C. F. H. Weiss published his 1852 German translation of William Youatts' *The Dog,* he generalized the term *pinscher* and used it as a translation of the term *terrier*—for example, Schottischer pinscher instead of Scottish Terrier. This is probably the reason why, for the next thirty years, most German dog literature used the word *pinscher* where terrier is meant.

We may conclude that many smaller terrier-like dogs existed in Germany. Some of them have smooth and others have wiry coats. At the same time there was a slightly bigger dog showing a good likeness to the wirehaired type spread over the southern German hinterland (Württemberg, Swabia, and Bavaria). The smaller ones, because of their terrier-like character, were mostly used as vermin killers. The bigger specimens were strong enough to herd pigs and cattle on the farms and even to be used in driving wild boar. Whereas the ordinary man called these dogs bentchur, rattler, or saubeller, the early authors introduced the term pinscher, which would continue to create some confusion in the second half of the nineteenth century.

A New Era in Cynology

When someone in England decided to found the kennel club in 1873 and to introduce a studbook for purebred dogs, history took a turn. Within twenty years, all Continental countries had followed the British example, and each country created its own national kennel organization. As the British had taken a strong lead by selecting and unifying their national breeds, it is not surprising that, at the earliest Continental shows, most purebred dogs were pointers, setters, spaniels, collies, and various terriers imported from across the Channel. Very quickly, Continental nationalists called upon the people to do something about their own dog heritage and to make up for lost time.

Of course, it was first the hunting dogs of the aristocracy who found their place in studbooks and special breeding clubs, but in those days as the dog became "in," selective breeding toward a particular type or breed also took place with the types of dogs belonging to the rural populations. That was the reason why the most typical direct ancestors of our modern schnauzers left their humble homesteads in southern Germany and came into the hands of dog breeders making their way to the early dog shows and set out the basis of a modern purebred breed.

Let us have a look at the general appearance. In Dr. L. J. Fitzinger's 1876 book *Der Hund und Seine Racen,*[11] he describes a whole collection of pinscher varieties. First of all, he mentions the seidenpintsch or silk pinscher, whose description corresponds with the modern Affenpinscher. Related are the kleinen pintsch and rauhen pintsch, respectively the modern Miniature Pinscher and Miniature Schnauzer. Important for us are his descriptions of the glatten pintsch (modern German Pinscher) and, even more, that of the grossen pintsch, corresponding to today's Standard Schnauzer. He states that the grossen pintsch, commonly called rattler (ratcatcher), is a brisk, lively dog who enjoys himself in the house as well as in the horse stables; he is courageous and, besides killing rats, can be used to hunt foxes and badgers.

The year 1876 is even more important—for the first time, a wirehaired pinscher was entered in a dog show at Hamburg. There was not yet any question of systematic breeding, and although the rattlers were well-known by the rural population in Swabia and Württemberg, they created some confusion between the elite purebred dog fans when arriving at a show. A letter by R. von Schmiedeberg in the magazine *Der Hund*[12] on 17 July 1879 illustrates the problem. The letter is headed "What Is a Pinscher?"

This question—what is a Pinscher?—was asked by an English reporter in Hannover, and I answered as well as I could. It would certainly be of great interest that we ourselves should create more and more clarity about this breed that has been included in the show program of Hannover, and an exhaustive answer to this question would be received thankfully. In my humble opinion, we can demonstrate a race in our pinscher that is analogous to that of the English terrier. About whether we possess an independent breed of shorthaired pinschers analogous to the so-called Manchester terrier (black with brown markings) or whether the specimens we meet hail originally from England, I am still unsure. It does, however, appear to be a certainty to me that we cannot deny that the wirehaired pinscher has a highly original and characteristic nature, which differs completely from that of all the English terriers, and I would almost like to state that we are, in this case, confronted with a specific

Peter, Vetter, and Souris. Zwergschnauzers. Reproduced from Count Henri van Bylandt, *Les Races de Chiens,* 1894.

Zwergschnauzer. Reproduced from Count Henri van Bylandt, *Les Races de Chiens,* 1894.

Pfefferle and Pfeff. Rauhhaarige pinschers. Reproduced from Count Henri van Bylandt, *Les Races de Chiens,* 1894.

Zwergschnauzer. Reproduced from Count Henri van Bylandt, *Les Races de Chiens,* 1894.

Rauhhaarige pinscher. Reproduced from Count Henri van Bylandt, *Les Races de Chiens,* 1894.

The wirehaired pinscher. Reproduced from Jean Bungartz, *Handbuch zur Beurteilung der Rassenreinheit des Hundes,* 1884.

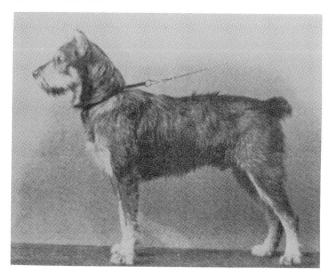

breed because its characteristics constantly reappear and will not be bastardized in spite of the complete absence of rational breeding.

When I speak of the wirehaired German pinscher, I am thinking of a very specific type, similar to the type being displayed at all Dutch shows in a specific class, namely the smoushond. *We also find this breed illustrated and described in the* Book of Points *of the Dutch Nimrod club. It would be very desirable that the pinscher breed should be discussed and defined more fully before the next international exhibition so that we may find it represented in greater numbers than was the case in Hannover. There, we only found wirehaired pinschers of German breeding, but in such a variety of types that the unbiased observer would soon understand how few of the characteristics of this breed really are consistent.*

Nobody gave him an answer because, in 1879, there existed no special club and the breed was not yet recognized by the German Kennel Club, and von Schmiedeberg took the reins in hand himself. Based on the technical terminology of an English dog manual by W. Gordon Stables, he published the *Rassekenzeichen von Pinschern*[13] in 1884. He stated that these dogs have a typical German patrimony. Concerning their ancestors, different views were supported and that, from his side and at that moment, he was not able to find out when the pinscher breed had split into wirehaired and smooth-haired varieties. After this introduction followed a fairly accurate description of the kurzhaarige pinscher and rauhhaarige pinscher or rattler (shorthaired and wirehaired pinscher or ratcatcher). This first breed standard was accepted and published by the Delegate Commission of the German Kennel Club. It read as follows:

The Rauhhaarige Pinscher or Rattler

Has an average weight of 3.5 to 10 kg (8 to 22 English pounds) and beyond. He is light, sinewy, and elastic. He has a harsh, wiry coat and carries his tail upward. His attitude is inquisitive and audacious. He has a restless temperament, is continuously vigilant without making unnecessary noise, full of courage without being quarrelsome or rapacious. He is attached to his master, loves horses and has stamina on long tours. A skilled ratcatcher and mouser and, consequently, is in great demand as a stable dog. His head is not too heavy, rather long. Flat skull slightly narrowing to the front. Pronounced stop. The bite is close fitting. Ears are cropped. The neck is of medium length, strong, well-arched, the skin fitting tightly at the throat. His coat is as wiry as possible. On the snout are moustaches, whiskers, and bushy eyebrows.

Color: red-yellowish or gray-yellowish. His feet and underline usually lighter or gray-white.

Further also allowed blackish, metal-gray, or silver-gray.

Either unicolored or with yellow-brown marks on the eyes, the snout, and the legs. Also unicolored flaxen or gray-white or white with black spots.

Nose is always black; eyes and nails are dark.

Von Schmiedeberg concludes the description of the breed as follows:

So beloved this breed may be, it does not know great dispersion, probably to be ascribed to the present fashion of predilection for Pugs. The breeding is restricted to a few good dealers in Württemberg.

The recognition of this breed standard by the *Verein zur Veredlung von Hundenrassen für Deutschland* (Union for Ennoblement of Dog Breeds in Germany) ushers in a definite breakthrough for the rattler. Breeders who, until then, had spent their efforts on more popular breeds, understood the importance of this valuable indigenous breed. They started breeding in an appropriate way, showed their dogs, and—most importantly—registered their puppies with the German Kennel Club. The best-known breeders from those early days were Mr. Burger and Mr. Essig from Leonberg, Max Hartenstein from Plauen, Mr. Schilbach from Greiz, Mr. Göller and Mr. Siegel from Stuttgart, Mr. Köhn from Ravensburg, and Dr. Mulzer from Dietmansried.

That cynology was progressing in Germany is proven by the 1884 publication of a wonderful book by Jean Bungartz, an animal draftsman. In his *Handbuch zur Beurteilung der Racenreinheit des Hundes,*[14] we find exact drawings and descriptions of fifty-six different breeds. He mentions the glatthaarige pinscher, the rauhhaarige pinscher, the glatthaarige zwergpinscher and the rauhhaarige zwergpinscher. These correspond with the modern German Pinscher, Standard Schnauzer, Miniature Pinscher, and Miniature Schnauzer. The breed particulars given are those established by von Schmiedeberg and accepted by the German Delegate Commission. Roughly sketched, they correspond with the modern breed standards. The most important aberrations are to be found where size and weight are concerned. Also, for the color of the coat, a wider variety of tones was allowed, going from black to silver-gray and reddish-brown.

Those first breed enthusiasts were definitely not sleeping; at a show in Stuttgart in 1890, nearly one hundred smooth- and wirehaired pinschers were shown. Not only in Germany were the pinschers gaining in popularity and reputation but also foreign authors refer to them.

In 1891, the Belgian A. Reul mentioned the German griffon terrier without a tail in his book *Cynotechnie, Les Races de Chiens.*[15]

In 1893, the Belgian magazine *Chasse et Pêche*[16] published an article relating to a dog show in Munich. The Belgian visitor reports that "besides the usual breeds, my attention was attracted by the German Shepherd Dogs and the Griffon d'Ecurie and their reductions." Griffon d'ecurie means horse stable griffon, which was, in the old days, the French name for wirehaired pinscher.

The most important Continental contribution to be is the monumental dog encyclopedia of Count Henri van Bylandt (1894). In his *Les Races de Chiens,*[17] he describes all the breeds—common and less common—in those days. The rauhhaarige pinscher (wirehaired pinscher) is represented in thirteen drawings. He stipulates that the dog's size is between 30 and 50 centimeters (11¾ and 19½ inches) and the weight ranges from 8 to 16 kilograms (18 to 36 English pounds). He mentions that now in Germany one has the tendency to call these dogs rattlers or schnauzers, and the smaller edition of the breed is called zwergschnauzer (dwarf schnauzer). This is the first time that the term *schnauzer* is mentioned in a book.

What's in a Name?

One may ask where the early nineteenth-century Germans got the name pinscher or pintscher. This even brought some authors to suggest that *pin(s)cher* could be related to the English verb *pinch* and, as such, that the breed and its name could actually have been imported from over the Channel and be of English origin.

I wanted to investigate this matter and, therefore, consulted a few British books written during the early cynologic period. J. H. Walsh does not mention the existence of such in *The Dogs of the British Islands* (1862). Then follows, in 1866, *Researches into the History of the British Dog* (a huge work in two volumes) by George R. Jesse, and again, no reference to the term pinscher is to be found. Also, Stonehenge, in 1887, does not refer to a pinscher. Then, in a 1899 book, *A History and Description of the Modern Dogs of Great Britain and Ireland* (four volumes) by Rawdon L. Lee, I found something interesting. One volume concentrates on terriers, and there I noted the words *Pincer, Pincers,* and *Pincher.* However, these expressions are used not to indicate a breed but as call names, respectively, for a Bedlington, Fox, Elterwater, Wire Hair, and Bull terrier. In 1904, *The Twentieth Century Dog,* four volumes by Herbert Compton, makes no mention about a pinscher. Finally, in the *Kennel Encyclopedia* (1910), I found an article about the Wire Haired Pinscher or German Terrier or Schnauger. Of course, Schnauger is a typographical error that can only be explained as follows: the writer of the article was the Continental Henri Sodenkamp, and his handwritten article about the *schnauzer* was read and printed by the editor as schnauger.

After this, I concluded that neither the shorthaired pinscher nor the wirehaired pinscher were breeds of British origin; otherwise, mention would have been made in those illustrious cynological works. However, as far as the term pinscher is concerned, this may have a British origin.

I dare presume that the name rattler or bentchur was used by the southern German owners of these dogs but that authors, officials, and breeders easily made the step from bentchur toward the more sophisticated and English-sounding pintscher or pinscher. Indeed, the German pronunciation of bentchur and pinscher is almost identical. This could mean that in the old days, the name bentchur was commonly used in the German dialect as it was spoken by the villagers in the south and became pintscher or pinscher in the *Hochdeutsch* (officially spoken and written German). Further, I believe that in 1879 it was not only the wirehaired specimen shown in Hannover who listened to the call name

the call name "Schnauzer." The typical schnauze or snout with whiskers and brows must have inspired other owners of these rattlers. It is logical that one finally, to better separate the breeds by their names, would adopt the term schnauzer for the wirehaired ones and pinscher for the shorthaired.

---

[1] Contribution to the History of Our Dog Breeds.
[2] *History of Dogs.*
[3] *Manual of the Hunt.*
[4] *The Start of the Hunter.*
[5] *The Work of Johann Adam Klein.*
[6] The originals read as follows: *"gestützten Pferden und Pinschern";* and *"Mit Poeten und Künstlern, flegt es zu geschehen wie mit Pferden und Hunden, die man zu Engländern oder Pinschern macht."*
[7] *Hunting and Other Dogs in All Their Relationships.*
[8] *The Dogs Monography.*
[9] *Dogs Gallery.*
[10] *The Dog in His Main and Additional Breeds.*
[11] *The Dog and His Different Breeds.*
[12] *The Dog.*
[13] *The Breed Particulars for Pinschers.*
[14] *Manual for Judging the Breed Pureness of Dogs.*
[15] *The Dog Breeds.*
[16] *Hunting and Fishing.*
[17] *The Dog Breeds.*

Wirehaired and smooth-haired pinschers. Reproduced from Jean Bungartz, *Handbuch zur Beurteilung der Rassenreinheit des Hundes,* 1884.

„Morro II".
Bes.: Herr J. BERTA, Erfurt.

Morro II. This beautiful Standard Schnauzer belonged to Josef Berta, who founded the first club for this breed.

4

The First German Specialty Clubs

I wondered if my exposé was becoming too technical, but Pam and Charles were such attentive and interested listeners. It was encouraging to realize that two future fanciers were so eager to "know." When Charles asked about the early organizations dealing with schnauzers, it was easy to continue.

The wirehaired pinscher and the wirehaired dwarf or miniature pinscher, together with their smooth-haired counterparts, attained some popularity over the last two decades of the nineteenth century. One of the old German rural dog breeds had found its way to the show ring and steadily made its reputation known beyond the borders of its native southern German region.

Although the breed belonged to the ordinary rural population and not to the nobility, it had a German heritage worthy of attention. This was the reason, in the beginning of 1895, that Josef Berta called upon all breed fanciers to concentrate their efforts in order to select and improve all the different pinscher varieties. This pioneering work could only be achieved in the bosom of a governing club.

On 3 March 1895, a preliminary meeting was held in Nordhausen. Two months later, on 23 May at the inaugural meeting in Seesen am Harz, a committee was chosen and a breed standard, as published some years before by the German Delegate Commission was accepted. At the age of forty, Josef Berta was elected chairman. With the exception of one year (1901) he governed the club until 1921. In 1900, the club had fifty-nine members; by 1902, Berta had succeeded in doubling the membership. At the end of 1902, the first studbook, covering the period from 1895 to 1902, was published. Josef Berta's foreword to this studbook puts us in the picture:

> When the signatory called for the charter of a pinscher club in spring 1895, there were very few breeders and lovers of our worthy native dog to be found. The schnauzer, the foremost representative of the pinscher family, was a cynologic stepchild and endured a lowly existence compared to the aristocratic, highly esteemed foreigners.
>
> Lack of planning and confusion ruled in his ranks; the observer was not yet greeted by uniformity in his breed, there was no tangible type to enthuse the sportsman to spend his experience and fervor on such a hopeless character. The situation concerning his short-haired cousin was even worse. He had been completely forgotten and forlorn while the colorful assortment of multifaceted Miniatures left much to be desired, even unto this day.
>
> During this time, when a plethora of highly developed foreign breeds stood unassailably in the foreground of German cynology, it was not an easy task for the pinscher club to give our own backward dog his due respect and recognition. This was indeed a slow process.
>
> Each inch of the way had to be fought for with weak and inadequate means. But, supported by a small group of persistent fans and enthusiasts, the club was enabled to progress step by step, to increase its membership, and thus to expand in might and influence, which are indispensable for successful work toward its goals and aims.
>
> For him, the foremost and most effective means to achieve his aims was the establishment of a comprehensive studbook, a compendium of everything that breed selection and experience had tried and reached. Thus, it now fills him with great satisfaction to be able to publish the first edition after long and strenuous research.
>
> For the thinking breeder, this book will be a valuable source of prerequisites, hints, and inspiration, and it is hoped that it will save him from experiencing many disappointments. May it also contribute to lifting our excellent native dog onto the highest rungs of the ladder of perfection, which it has all the right to do.
>
> With these convictions and wishes, we would like to combine the expression of thanks and appreciation for the keeper of the breed register, Mr. Karl Knaus, Heidelberg, who in true sporting spirit, with joyful sacrifice, with hard work and experience served the club and the breed so excellently.

This first studbook is full of valuable information. Besides all the registered dogs for the period 1895–1902, other items such as minutes of the annual general meetings, judges reports, rules and regulations concerning championships, and so forth are inserted.

Not only the regular litters are registered but also dogs with a previous registration in the Swiss or Austrian studbook are taken over. Even specimens from unknown parents who had achieved recognition at shows had their chance.

In 1902, the club had 114 members, among which were 30 breeders. There are a total of 353 registrations, with birth dates going back to 1880. The different breeds are represented as follows:

Standard Schnauzer	248
Miniature Schnauzer	14
German Pinscher	8
Miniature Pinscher	83

From the judges reports, we learn that show entries are progressing, but only a few dogs meet the requirements of the breed ideal. The rare champions will become the pillars of the breed.

The national German kennel organization was reorganized in 1906 under the name *Kartell für das Deutsche*

FIGURE 4-2

The First Breed Standard for the Schnauzer (1907)

1. Nature, Utility, and General Appearance. The Schnauzer owns his nickname "Rattler" or "Ratcatcher" to his real occupation as an exterminator of nasty rodents, rats, and mice, which since memory have caused damage to man's property in his house or farm, in his stables and garden. In this sphere, the Schnauzer also proves himself as an unbeatable watchdog because of his perceptivity, his integrity, and his natural suspiciousness toward strangers. He is a friend of the family and a companion of children; in other words, a specific example of a family and house dog. This because he is not demanding with regard to food and care, he is good natured and shows incorruptible reliability. These facts provided him with a character which simultaneously demonstrates liveliness coupled with cautious composure and excluding the nervosity of other temperamental breeds. On the strength of his cleverness, his attachment and endurance, he is the ideal companion for his master be it by foot, bicycle, or cart and horse. He is a cheerful high-spirited fellow, whose lively eyes always ask for action and business. He is a keen retriever on land or water. He is a courageous opponent even for bigger and stronger dogs, and because of his pluck and speed, a reliable protector of his master. As such, the Schnauzer shows himself in every aspect as a real working dog (never a fashion or luxury dog). His looks emphasize this statement: a sinewy, compact, and square body of a working-oriented medium-sized dog, with firm legs and feet, a powerful jaw carrying a healthy bite, lively dark eyes and black nose, bushy eyebrows and harsh whiskers, a water-resistant wiry coat, inconspicuous in color. The Schnauzer's appearance, which is enhanced by his inherent moral and physical abilities, inspires a perfect balance of power and nobility.

2. Head. Strong and elongated, narrowing from ears to eyes and then gradually forward to tip of nose. In harmony with the substance of the body and in length (from tip of nose to occiput) in a 1:3 ratio proportion to the length of the back (from first dorsal vertebrae to set of the tail). The upper part of the head (occiput to the base of the forehead) moderately broad between the ears—not broader than ⅔ of its total length—with flat unwrinkled forehead; well muscled but not too strongly developed cheeks. Ears symmetrically cropped, set high, and carried erect under excitement. Eyes of medium size, oval, directed forward, overarched by bushy eyebrows. The powerful muzzle (from stop to tip of nose), carrying a full bite, is in a 4:5 proportion to the length of the skull; it ends in a moderately blunt wedge and is covered with bristly whiskers. The muzzle with bridge of nose runs parallel to the extension of the line formed by the forehead. The tip of the nose is full and black. The lips are tight, not overhanging. A strong and healthy scissors bite with well-developed canines and pure white teeth.

3. Neck. Not too short, skin fitting tight to throat (dry neck). Nape powerful and slightly arched.

4. Forequarters. Shoulders flat, well laid back and well muscled. Forelegs (upper and underarm) straight, without any bow when viewed from any side.

5. Forechest. Moderately broad with visible, strong sternum. The brisket is deep and descends at least to the elbow and ascends gradually to the rear. The ribs are well sprung. Back firm and straight, with short, well-developed loin. Square built: length of body equal to height at withers. Belly moderately drawn up.

6. Tail. Set high, carried erect, and docked to 3 or 4 joints.

7. Hindquarters. Thighs slanting and flat but well muscled. Hind legs (upper and lower thighs) at first vertical to the stifle; from stifle to hock in line with the extension of the upper neck line (from occiput to withers); from hocks vertical to ground.

8. Feet. Short, round; the toes are closed and arched (cat feet); dark nails and firm pads.

9. Coat. Dense, hard, and wiry on the back—when viewed against the course of the hair—rather upward standing, neither short nor lying flat. Shorter on the ears, forehead, legs, and feet.

10. Size. About 40 cm (15¾ inches) to maximum 50 cm (19½ inches) at the withers.

11. Color. All salt-and-pepper color shades or similar bristly equal color mixtures, and solid black.

12. Faults. Body too light, too high, or too low on the legs. Too coarse or too round skull, wrinkled forehead, sideward carried or badly cropped ears. Eyes too light (with light-yellowish or light-grayish rings. Strong, protruding cheekbones. Dewlap. Overshot and undershot bite. Short, pointed, or narrow muzzle. Back too long, roached, humped, or too soft. Barrel chest. Steep, falling croup. Loose elbows, cow hocked. Steep hindquarters (overbuilt). Spread toes and too long, flat feet. Coat too short, smooth, too long, soft, silky, wavy, or shaggy. All white, speckled, brindled, red, or bran colors. A small white spot or stripe on the chest must only be considered as a beauty fault and not as a breed fault.

Hundewesen (Cartel for German Dogdom). Like most German breed clubs, Berta's Pinscher-Klub became an affiliate of the national club and, as such, became and remained the only representative club for all pinscher varieties. This meant that when the Munich lawyer G. Zurhellen founded a Schnauzer-Klub in 1907, this organization could not be recognized by the national kennel club. Zurhellen, thus, started to keep his own (semiofficial) studbook for his Bavarian schnauzer members. In the context of this book, it is relevant to provide the breed standard which was laid down by this first specialty club in 1907 and expresses the point of view and the concept of the breed's pioneers.

Rivalry and even legal action ensued. The Bavarian Schnauzer Club published its first studbook in 1910. It's constitution clearly stipulates that the goal of the club consists of the pure breeding, grading up, and propagation of the wirehaired Pinscher (Schnauzer). This is different from the constitution of the Pinscher Klub, whose goal it was to foster all pinscher varieties—that is, the wirehaired pinscher, the smooth-haired pinscher, and the miniature wire-haired and smooth-haired pinscher.

World War I was more than a bit of bad luck, and after the war, everything had to be reorganized. Berta and Zurhellen agreed to join forces and to bring the two prewar clubs under one banner. So in 1918, the *Pinscher-Schnauzer Verband* (Pinscher-Schnauzer Association) was inaugurated. In 1921, the club received the new official name of *Pinscher-Schnauzer Klub, 1895 e.V.,* (PSK) which it has maintained over the years.

Of course, all registrations are now entered in one and the same studbook. The first "coalition" edition appeared in 1924 and totalled 13,474 entries.

Ch. Russ II Pfeff and Ch. Donata van Antwerpen (Standards). Owned by P. Sassen, Antwerp. (1905)

Morro. Owned by Robert Schilbach, Greiz.

Hexe Plavia. Owned by Max Hartenstein, Plauen.

Dampf Pfeff. Owned by Robert Schilbach,
Greiz.

Russ. Owned by Mr. Göller, Stuttgart.

Nante. Owned by M. Thilo, Heilbronn.

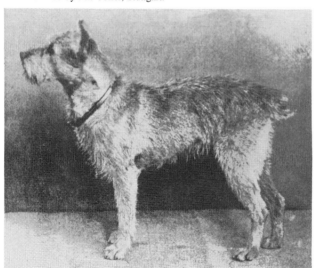

Peter Sonnenberg. Owned by J. Hübner, Amsterdam.

Gourko Pfeff and Fanny Bidlingmayer (Standards).
Owned by P. Sassen, Antwerp.

Souris. Owned by J. Kneppelhout,
Warnsveld.

Ch. Russ II Pfeff (Standard). Owned by P. Sassen, Antwerp.

Mascar's Medoc. Bred by A. Radberg and owned by M. Jacobsson (Sweden).

5

Genesis of the Standards and Miniatures

At this point, it was Pam who wanted to know how the different sizes came about.

It is evident that in the early days of schnauzers there was no clear separation between a Miniature and a Standard Schnauzer as we understand them today. Moreover, there was no mention at all of a Giant Schnauzer. After what various authors have expressed, it might be interesting to examine what the first breed standards say on the subject.

Josef Berta's Pinscher Club version of the standard, in 1902, stipulates the following for size and weight: The size varies according to local types and lies between 30 and 45 cm (11¾ and 17½ in) at the withers, with a corresponding weight of 8 to 10 kg (17½ to 35 English pounds). Preference should be given to a uniform and work-oriented medium size.

The specifications of the Dr. Zurhellen's Bavarian Schnauzer Club's breed standard, in 1907, is even more specific, with a size of 40 cm (15¾ in) to a *maximum* of 50 cm (19½ in). This, together with the description of the dog's abilities, does not make provision for a miniature variety.

The 1895 constitution of the Pinscher Club even stipulates that the club shall foster the well-being of the wire-haired pinscher, the smooth-haired pinscher, and the miniature smooth-haired pinscher, ignoring, as such, a smaller wirehaired type.

It is, therefore, important, that at present we understand that the real and original schnauzer is the medium-sized or Standard Schnauzer.

The Standard Schnauzer

From a total of 353 registrations in the first (1902) studbook of the Pinscher Club, 248 were rauhhaarige pinschers (Standard Schnauzers), representing a strong majority.

Records show that the very foundation of selective breeding was laid by Max Hartenstein from Plauen who, in his Plavia kennel, began breeding schnauzers in 1880. Contemporary breeders included Robert Schilbach (Pfeff)

from Greiz and Mr. M. Thilo (Arnswalde) from Heilbronn. Around the turn of the century, we may add Gartner (Fidelitas) from Karlsruhe, Schwan (Harthof) from Giessen, Köhn (Schussental) from Ravensburg, and Zurhellen (Schwabing) from Munich. Of course, there were other outstanding breeders who made significant contributions before the First World War.

It is a matter of fact that the selective breeding of the schnauzer was progressing in those days. The very simple proof being the fact that the old von Schmiedeberg breed standard for the schnauzer was updated by the Pinscher Club and published in its first studbook (1902). The changes put emphasis on a more elongated head, a straight back, and a powerful appearance. The size changed to from 30 to 45 cm (11¾ to 17½ in), with preference for the work-oriented upper size. Salt-and-pepper color is preferred to second-choice solid black, but red-brown and yellow-brown are still acceptable. Dogs with faded colors, white dogs, and those with white markings are now considered faulty.

The judges' records from those days show a definite preference for and tendency toward evenly distributed salt-and-pepper in different shades, next to solid black. To amplify this, let me quote Josef Berta in his report on a 1901 Heidelberg championship show when he comments on Ch. Max Kismet Harthof, born in 1897, who was entered under the color description dark salt-and-pepper with yellow markings. Berta wrote, "Bone, structure, expression, texture of coat, and type are fabulous. I don't like his color, but I must tolerate it."

Another judge's report from the hand of Mr. Gartner and relating to a show held in Munich in 1900, put the accent on the problems that breeders encountered during the early selection. Gartner writes: "I would like to see that over- and undershots are strictly put back, that dogs with soft hair on the head, those who are too cheeky and with a sharp muzzle are refused. Further, we must improve the neck, especially, by discrediting dogs with a mane."

Although the schnauzers pictured in the first studbook are mostly of good quality, they represent dogs of different type as far as structure, color, and coat are concerned. However, a few of them are close to our present breed standard. Moreover, it must be stressed that these dogs were not trimmed or groomed but shown in a natural condition. In general, the beard was shorter but harder, a fact that did not harm the typical schnauzer expression.

With regard to color, a definite improvement was made from 1900 to the beginning of the First World War in 1914. However, real success was achieved when, after the war, the Schnauzer Club and the Pinscher Club amalgamated. The fact that one unified club now fully represented the breed and that the pioneers and connoisseurs from Munich joined the ranks of the committee in Cologne was a real boost for the schnauzer. It was Felix Ebner from Munich who, on 31

December 1923, was responsible for publishing the first joint studbook. It comprised 697 pages and totalled 13,474 entries. As a proof of the enormous progress that had been made, this book also included a completely reworked breed standard for the Schnauzer, the Zwergschnauzer, the Riesenschnauzer, the Pinscher, the Zwergpinscher, and the Affenpinscher, all breeds that have since been represented by the club. This indicates that the club, especially since its unification, had achieved in bringing a clear stand in the old pinscher jumble. It was now able to give definite instructions indicating in which direction selection should take place.

It is absolutely relevant to study the new breed standard for the schnauzer. The hallmarks of the breed, especially with regard to general appearance remained unchanged. However, there are a few amendments that will be of significance for the further development of the breed. The permitted colors were restricted to salt-and-pepper and to solid black. The size is defined between 40 and a maximum of 50 cm (15¾ and 19½ in). The length of the head from the tip of the nose to the occiput must now be in a 1 : 3 ratio to the length of the body. The neck must remain strong but should not be too short. The hindquarters, from stifle to hock, must be in line with the extension of the upper neckline. The belly has to be tucked up. These amended particularities did not affect the type. They were improvements, simply aimed at the refinement of the breed.

The 1920s and 1930s were a climax. From 1924 to 1934, more than 10,000 schnauzers were registered in the Pinscher-Schnauzer Klub (PSK) studbook. Some championship shows totalled more than 300 schnauzer entries. The most famous and typical schnauzer of that period was Ch./Int. Ch. Gauner v. Egelsee, bred by Mr. Rapp in 1926. Without doubt, still today, he would be able to compete against the best opposition.

In spite of World War II and its disastrous effect on man and his best friend, the breeding of schnauzers recovered remarkably well by the end of the 1940s.

Next to a few prewar breeders who continued, we may now add some more leading kennels: Mrs. Hartman (v. Silberhal), Mrs. Haidle (v. Hühnerhof-Ruit), Mrs. Walter (v. Hartzloh), Mrs. Gerth (v. d. Munteren Gesellen) and Mr. and Mrs. Rothe (v. Hahlweg).

The Rothe's breeding started with Pfeffer v. Volken, who was bred in the United States and whose ancestors can be traced back to Lümpli Arnswalde and Flott Pfeff. Mr. Rothe is a world famous photographer who possesses the most beautiful, unique collection of schnauzer pictures.

Mrs. G. Gerth has collected, over the years, a complete and extremely important data bank of information on Schnauzers and Riesenschnauzers.

While writing about schnauzers, it is relevant to investigate where and when the black variety entered the field. We know that Max Hartenstein owned and bred black schnauzers before the foundation of the Pinscher Club in 1895. The earliest breed description mentions black as a recognized color. From old registration books, we learn that black pups sporadically appeared in litters from salt-and-pepper parents.

It is, however, only in the 1930s that a few breeders endeavor the systematic breeding of black schnauzers. We may say that all black schnauzers can be traced to the kennels v. Muldental, v. Ahorntal, and v. Hagenstein, who were leading in those days. Their efforts would be continued after the war.

To have an idea of the trend, let us compare the PSK schnauzer registrations of the two colors:

1945—244, of which 24 (10 percent) were black
1959—700, of which 204 (30 percent) were black
1969—807, of which 256 (over 30 percent) were black
1990—962, of which 419 (about 40 percent) were black

This proportion is more or less maintained at present. Moreover, we might say that the black schnauzers that have been shown on the European continent during the last decade undeniably prove that the breed is recovering from a thirty-years arrears on the salt-and-pepper variety.

In 1956, the description of the breed was again reworked. The details that are changed were already often present in the best prewar dogs. We may say that after seventy-five years of selective breeding, we have reached a stage of perfection. The dog described in the revised standard has improved in general appearance. The conformation, structure, and coat is in perfect harmony with mental and physical abilities, whose description has not been altered over the years. This means that although the schnauzer became more refined and uniform, the responsible authorities did not allow the breed to become fashion dogs, disregarding their rustic heritage and their mental and physical abilities.

Let us have a quick look at the changes since Felix Ebner published the 1923 standard. In the 1956 revision, the head to back ratio is now 1 : 2. Emphasis is placed on the square proportions of the schnauzer—that is, the height at the withers is to be equal to the length of the body. The neck must be nobly crested and, while blending into the shoulders, must give an impression of power. The back is not an absolutely straight rod but is the flowing continuation of the crested curve of the neck nobly blending into the withers. It continues in a straight part toward the *slightly* rounded croup to end at the high-set tail carried at 2 o'clock. The fore and hindquarters are well angulated. The colors are now limited to solid black and to salt-and-pepper with corresponding dark mask. The ideal for the salt-and-pepper color is a topcoat of medium tone, evenly distributed with grayish undercoat. The size is restricted between 45 and 50 cm (17½ and 19½ in).

The Miniature Schnauzer

It is clear that the Miniature Schnauzer did not walk into modern cynology as a fait accompli. Indeed, the old German literature mentions that smaller wirehaired pinschers occurred. However, the authors are somewhat contradictory and definitely don't provide a clear view of the situation. Some speak about a smaller wirehaired pinscher with an apple head and an undershot jaw. Others give a similar description but specify that the dog should be called Affenpinscher, emphasizing the monkeylike face of the breed. Still others simply stipulate that there were wirehaired pinschers measuring around 30 cm (11¾ in) or less.

The very first breed description for pinschers that was recognized by the German national kennel organization in the 1880s mentions a dwarflike variety of the wirehaired pinscher and links them together—"the miniature wirehaired pinscher or Affenpinscher."

We know that Schilbach, under the kennel name Pfeff, started selective breeding of wirehaired pinscher before the foundation of the Pinscher Club in 1895. When the club was established, the committee was not keen on taking a stand with regard to a smaller wirehaired pinscher and rather ignored what had been published about the Affenpinscher. It probably felt that this was a situation of neither fish nor good red herring.

With the smooth-haired pinschers, the committee did not seem to have a problem as they split them straightaway into a standard variety of about 45 cm (17½ in) and a toy variety of 28 cm (11 in) or less. This can be explained by the mere fact that this split in sizes had already come about in a natural way.

It was probably based on this example that some of the early wirehaired pinscher breeders endeavored to select for a toy schnauzer measuring 28 cm (11 in) or less. They bred a kind of toy dog that, indeed, no longer had the aspect of a schnauzer. From 1900 on, the small wirehaired pinschers were shown in two different classes—one for the Affenpinschers, with their undershot jaws and monkeylike faces, and one for the smaller version of the wirehaired pinscher.

In 1903, the studbook first registered Affenpinschers separately from the other wirehaired pinschers. It was Josef Berta who cut the knot by stressing that, in his opinion, the miniature wirehaired pinscher should correspond with the standard-sized breed in conformation, head, coat, and nature. In other words, they could be smaller but otherwise identical and definitely not a toy. As a typical example, Berta mentions Ch. Jocco-Fulda-Lilliput, born in 1898, who had the correct type but, pity enough, did not pass it to his descendents.

By 1910, the separation was formalized, and the smaller wirehaired pinschers were registered as two separate breeds—the Miniature Schnauzer and the Affenpinscher. The famous first studbook produced by Felix Ebner in 1923, after the unification of the German clubs, included a detailed Miniature Schnauzer standard.

The pioneer breeders who may be credited for making the breed popular were Schilbach (Pfeff), Stache (Chemnitz-Plauen), Miss Zitzelmann (Zitzelmann), Martin (Lehrte), and Wach (Werneburg).

Precisely like their larger counterparts, the color spectrum of these first Miniature Schnauzers varied from solid black to black-and-tan, red-yellow, gray-yellow, and salt-and-pepper.

The cornerstones on which the breed has been based and to which most of our Miniature Schnauzers go back are originally the dark-gray Cito v. d. Werneburg and his black son Peter v. d. Westerberg (born in 1902); further, the black-and-yellow Prinz v. Rheinstein (born 1903), a son of Gift v. Chemnitz-Plauen. To them, we may add the salt-and-pepper Rudi v. Lohr, bred by Weber in Frankfurt in 1912.

The studbooks from 1916 and 1923, respectively, show 353 and 1,505 registered Miniature Schnauzers. The new 1923 breed standard makes it clear that Berta's ideal had materialized, for it states that the Miniature Schnauzer must be the smaller version of the Schnauzer, under the condition that the quality of its nature and excellence are maintained. This breeding aim was further pursued after the First World War by upcoming kennels that, without doubt, left their mark on the breed. The most important were Countess Kanitz (Abbagamba), Dr. Frommer (Baltischort), and Riehl (v. Dornbusch).

Countess Kanitz and Dr. Frommer, both breeders living in East Prussia, must have bred remarkable dogs, as Josef Berta wrote after a 1927 show in Elbing: "The Miniature Schnauzer is the biggest trump that East Prussia can play. The products of the kennels Baltischort and Abbagamba can count for all what the rest of the country is producing."

In the 1930s, it was Herman Walter who, in his kennel Heinzelmännchen, obstinately pursued the double goal of correct size and correct salt-and-pepper color. The breed standard of 1923, in spite of the stipulation that the Miniature Schnauzer must be a smaller version of the Schnauzer, still mentioned a size of 28 cm (11 in) at the withers. Herman Walter proclaimed that such a size tended to dwarf the Miniature Schnauzer, with all the consequences thereof. At the same time, he warned against an intermediate size that would bring the miniature too close to the Standard Schnauzer. His point of view—that the ideal size for a miniature should lie between 30 cm (11¾ in) and a *maximum* of 35 cm (13¾ in) in order to allow the miniature to look like and also to behave like a Standard Schnauzer—would prove to be correct and became generally accepted. Impure colors, which in Baltischort days had been tolerated and whose heritage the Heinzelmännchen partially carried, were eliminated through selective breeding of Herman Walter and his supporters.

By 1956, the revised breed standard places the Miniature Schnauzer, as far as color is concerned, completely in line with the Standard Schnauzer. In other words, only solid black and salt-and-pepper remained acceptable. These two varieties are now strictly bred and shown separately and, in the show ring, receive separate CACs *(Certificat d´Aptitude au Championnat)*.

It is worth mentioning that the Countess von Kanitz came across a few black-and-white speckled puppies in the 1920s. She bred them together and was able to fix a strain to a certain degree. The committee of the PSK, at the time, did not feel fit to encourage her endeavors and to consider the recognition of a separate variety.

It is also important to note that, in spite of all the efforts to maintain separate solid black and salt-and-pepper color strains, black-and-silver pups sporadically appeared in litters from salt-and-pepper parents. These occurred even more frequently in countries where it was permitted to mate black to salt-and-pepper.

After long discussion, it was only in 1968 that the PSK committee agreed to give some consideration to the black-and-silver color. They agreed to allow experimental breeding of locally born black-and-silver Miniature Schnauzers with similar imports from the United States, Denmark, and Israel. Frieda Steiger from Switzerland, supported and advised by Dr. Hans Räber, definitely contributed a great deal to the establishment of the Continental black-and-silver Miniature Schnauzer. By 1977, the black-and-silver variety obtained official recognition by the Fédération Cynologique Internationale (FCI) and was granted Certificat d´ Aptitude au Championnat International de Beauté (CACIB) with the possibility of obtaining international championship status.

I believe that it is relevant to go back to the mid-1960s when the reintroduction of the black-and-silver variety was discussed by the PSK committee. Many committee members, at that time, were still aware of the panoply of colors that had prevailed in the past and of the efforts of many dedicated breeders to obtain the correct salt-and-pepper and the solid black color. It was by bearing this in mind that they made the strict recommendation that, if the black-and-silver variety had to be recognized, it should be *fixed* as soon as possible by strictly mating only individuals of that color. In spite of this warning and the directives given by the breed authorities in Germany, the future would prove that next to many magnificent black-and-silver specimens, a wide range of washed-out and impure-colored Miniature Schnauzers would reappear. It has been experienced that often the black-and-silver color, though correct in tone at a young age, starts to fade away after the age of one year. This has incited some fanciers to commit irregularities such as dying their dog's coat for the show ring.

The black-and-silver Miniature Schnauzer has, at present, definitely obtained a first-class place in the world of Miniature Schnauzers. However, if the fanciers want to maintain such a solid position and the reputation as a pure-bred dog, this can only be achieved by breeding black-and-silver to black-and-silver dogs. It is wrong to believe that only the show-quality dog should be black-and-silver and that littermates sold as pet quality may be of any color. Such a principle may favor the show fancier but is of no benefit to the breed as a whole. To fight such indiscriminate actions, the judges, acting under FCI regulations, have the right to take a sample of the coat of any suspect black-and-silver Miniature Schnauzer presented and to have it analyzed for artificial coloring.

When the PSK committee was confronted with the problem of the black-and-silver variety in 1968, it was also faced with the demand for recognition of the white color variety. As this was purely a German request based on the success of a couple of German breeders who had interbred white Miniature Schnauzers born from black parents, this matter was treated as an internal affair. Provision was made for the registration of white Miniature Schnauzers in the PSK studbook. As such, the development of a separate variety could start under perfect control of the parent breed club in Germany. The nomenclature of dog breeds issued by the FCI in July 1990 mentions four varieties of the Miniature Schnauzer—black, salt-and-pepper, black-and-silver, and white. However, the white variety may be shown in international shows sponsored by the FCI, but it cannot yet be awarded with a CACIB. As such, this variety is still in the process of becoming internationally recognized. In my opinion, based on the number of white Miniature Schnauzer that have been bred since 1968 and the extensive control exercised by the breed wardens of the club and its committee, I dare believe that FCI recognition is not far away. One may dislike the color, but no one can deny that the enthusiastic breeders, who have been sculpturing the white Miniature Schnauzer over the years, have done this on a scientific basis that was duly controlled by the breed's authorities. It must absolutely be stressed that in the case of the white Miniature Schnauzer we are *not* faced with the albino phenomenon. Although the coat is solid white, the skin is flesh colored, the eyes are dark, and the nose, lips, eye rims, nails, and pads are black.

To conclude this section and while still on the subject of color, it is relevant to explain why, during the early process of selection of the schnauzer, colors such as yellow, brown, red, black and tan, and their related mixtures were eliminated. These colors were a heritage from the days when the wirehaired and the smooth-haired rattlers were interbred by the rural people of southern Germany. Colors and even size were of no direct importance to them, whereas function and a balanced temperament were primordial. Modern cynology with selective breeding has provided descendents of the rattlers that have maintained their nature but have been split into pinschers and schnauzers. The pinschers have a red or black-and-tan smooth-haired coat, while the wirehaired schnauzers coat originates from the old salt-and-pepper strains.

Early Interest from Over the Borders

Of course, the schnauzer is a German breed, and the main regions of origin are Baden, Bavaria, and Württemberg in the southern part of the country. But it is understandable that the schnauzer's presence on farms and in rural homesteads was not circumscribed by provincial borders. It is a fact that even before the schnauzer was recognized as a breed, he had migrated into neighboring Swiss and Austrian regions. This is the reason we find schnauzers already registered in the earliest studbook editions of the Swiss and Austrian kennel clubs. This does not have to be considered an export but rather a natural expansion of the breed and extension of its homeland.

As far as it is known, the first schnauzer that left Germany and can be considered a true export was called Mauss. The actual Namibia was in 1894 a German colony called German South West Africa. In 1894, Captain Volkmann decided to embark for Keetmanshoop, together with his young schnauzer bitch Mauss. For six years, she would be in active service and twice traverse the immense country while trotting next to her master's horse. In his notes, Captain Volkmann writes that they once covered 130 kilometers (90 miles) in twenty-four hours. For more than six hundred nights, Mauss slept under the open sky, guarding her master and his company. She was an excellent help during the hunt, her specialty being to drive jackals and porcupines out of their lairs. Captain Volkmann also relates that his dog's size and coat were great advantages. Her wiry coat protected Mauss against the burning desert sun. On long trips, heavier dogs suffered from blisters on their pads, and one had to carry an additional quantity of drinking water to quench their thirst.

Another German officer, who was stationed in Swakopmund, imported Puck in 1898. Mauss was mated with Puck, and their children, like the parents, were truly appreciated for their services to the colony.

In the same period, other exports are noted. Breeders in the Netherlands and Belgium bought outstanding specimens, showed them, and started to breed the first schnauzers outside Germany.

Mr. Rogmans, Mr. Woltman-Elpers, and Mr. Hubner—all living in Amsterdam—were the first Dutch breeders and registered their first litters in 1897. The Dutch schnauzer club was inaugurated in 1922 and has continued without interruption.

The first Belgian-born schnauzer litter was registered in 1902. The same year, Mr. Lacroix from Liège imported Ch. Moritz Harthof (born 1 July 1898, forty-one first prizes) and Ch. Hilde Harthof (born 15 March 1898, fifty-three first

prizes). He also bought Lümpli Arnswalde (born 3 May 1897, thirty-eight honor and first prizes); this beautiful salt-and-pepper male was of outstanding quality, and German judges mention him as a typical example of the breed. Prosper Sassen from Antwerp bought a few outstanding dogs from Robert Schilbach in Greiz.

In 1905, Sassen laid the foundations of the Pinscher-Club Belge. In spite of this very strong start, the Belgian club did not survive the First World War. Of course, there were further scattered efforts and interest in the breed in Belgium, but it was only after the Second World War, in 1954, that a new and strong Belgian schnauzer and pinscher club was recreated.

France, Italy, Denmark, Sweden, Norway, Finland, and other continental countries showed an early interest in schnauzers. Breed specialty clubs were formed, and very soon, excellent specimens were bred in these countries.

In 1905, the first schnauzer was exported to the United States, but it was only after the first World War that real interest started and a significant number reached the states.

The Duchess of Montrose imported the first schnauzer puppy in Britain in 1924. The Miniature Schnauzer, especially, gained an important popularity in this country.

Vetter. Owned by J. Kneppelhout, Warnsveld.

Ch. Telchines Appolo-n, Apt, BWT, IPO-I (Giant), bred by M. Ambrosi (Italy), owned by J. & E. Gallant, was Best Giant Schnauzer in South Africa in 1995. He is a multiple Best in Show winner as well as a qualifier in International Working Trials.

6

What About the Giant?

While I interrupted my speech with a sip of coffee, Charles took the opportunity to ask, "John, there is something that bothers me. I am constantly thinking about a Giant Schnauzer, and nowhere in your historical survey do you mention such a dog. You always speak about sizes from 12 to 16 inches weighing from 10 to 30 pounds. I am sure the big black fellow you showed us in your book a while ago is taller and heavier! Now, where do you place this dog in your story?"

"Charles, this is a forthright question. It is more than time to come to your point—the Giant or Riesenschnauzer. The reason I omitted the Giant is very simple. In fact, his history is as old but more vague than that of the Miniature and the Standard. His real entry into modern cynology occurred more recently."

The Roots of the Giant Schnauzer

In the 1830s, Baumeister and Reichenbach mentioned saubeller, saufinder, and saurüden in their books—all terms for a strong, wirehaired dog with a fair resemblance to the wirehaired pinscher but definitely bigger and more impressive. Dogs of this type were hidden on isolated farms of the Bavarian highlands and have, therefore, been known as *oberlanders*. We know nothing with certainty about their origin. It might go back to the strains of molossians imported by the Roman invaders of 2,000 years ago. It is generally accepted that the different Swiss Sennenhunds and also the Rottweiler are descendents of the molossians that developed in specific areas. This could also be the case with the red-brown-black dogs specifically found in the Bavarian highlands.

About the oberlander's uses, we may conclude that on these big farms he was an all-rounder. Guarding the premises in all weather was certainly his most important night duty. The prefix *Sau* in the different name combinations indicates an association with pigs and boars. We all know that Germans like pork and bacon, and the huge Bavarian farms were big producers. There were herds of pigs and also cattle to be driven in spring and summer to the mountain meadows. The same dog was used in autumn and early winter in wild boar drives in the Alpine forests.

We know that the Bavarian highlanders were very proud of their big farm dogs and jealously kept them apart for their own purposes. A proof of this theory is to be found in an oil painting dated 1850 that portrays Princess Elizabeth of Bavaria, later empress of Austria, in the company of a big, fierce, red-brown-black oberlander dog with a most impressive head and snout.

So, we know that in the precynologic period the forefather of the later Giant Schnauzer existed. Over the years and by natural selection, he obtained and maintained a certain identity and led his tough and isolated life on the farms of the Bavarian highland.

It is also suspected that, in addition to the molossian, a more wolflike type of dog migrated to the same area and could have played a role in the natural selection of the oberlander.

Historians mention that, during the mass migrations of the people of central Europe, western Russian tribes left the Russian-Finland border area and moved toward the southern part of Germany where they settled. They not only brought their architectural style but also their aftcharka-type dogs. This could be the link to the frequently used call names of Russ, Russelo, Russine, and so forth. Even the designation Russen schnauzer was used before and around the turn of the twentieth century, when some Munich dog fanciers obtained some oberlander dogs and Munich became the breed's second home.

Mr. Steinhaber from Aidenbach recalled those days:

Already in 1898 I possessed nine black breeding bitches with forty-five puppies. These dogs were then generally called Russen schnauzer. When I entered my bitch Fedora in a show in Regensburg, the judge, Mr. Merl, quickly put us off saying "There is no such thing as a Russen schnauzer. There is no such breed and schnauzers of such a size!"

The way from isolated farms to popularity and fame was not simple.

From the same period date the names bierschnauzer (beer schnauzer) and Münchener schnauzer (Munich schnauzer). Both names reflect the increasing presence in Munich and the dogs' occupation in the breweries. It became a common sight to see these big wirehaired dogs escorting the huge horse-drawn carts loaded with barrels of beer.

It was also in that period that in southern Germany the name wirehaired pinscher lost its significance and was generally replaced by the term *schnauzer*. That was indeed the reason why on 18 December 1907, Zurhellen, in Munich, called his new club Bavarian *Schnauzer* Club.

The First Attempt of the Giant Schnauzer

When some grosser Münchener schnauzers (big Munich schnauzers) were entered in an official 1909 show in Munich, they received full attention and were no longer excluded like the Russen schnauzer in Regensburg. This can be considered the first recognition of the breed.

Ch. Roland Rolandsheim. Owned by Mr. Pankok, Düsseldorf. The first Giant Schnauzer ever entered in a show—Munich, 1909.

Aftcharka. This old Russian sheepdog breed is believed to be one of the ancestors of the oberlanders.

More significant is the recording of 6 + 3 Munich schnauzer puppies in the third pinscher studbook, edited in 1910 by the Pinscher-Klub in Cologne. The fact that under the general heading German Pinscher we find in a first paragraph the registration of the Munich schnauzer indicates that not only in Munich but also in Cologne the name schnauzer was taking over from rauhhaariger pinscher. On the one hand, dog breeders were intervening in the oberlanders' business, and on the other hand, the Pinscher-Klub was mostly interested in the exterior of the Munich schnauzer and wanted him as close as possible to the rauhhaariger pinscher.

It was logical that oversized rauhhaariger pinscher (Standard Schnauzers) would be crossed with original oberlanders. That is also the reason why, in this early period of selective breeding of the Giant, two tendencies arose. The first used the oberlanders (good or bad) that were available—the farmers did not sell their best dogs! The second tendency developed away from Munich, more in the Stuttgart and central German area, and crossed the oberlanders with oversized salt-and-pepper Standard Schnauzers. This method was applied by breeders with some previous dog-breeding experience, with the intention of obtaining, as fast as possible, uniformity in a bigger schnauzer-type dog. This explains why some of the first Giant Schnauzers showed in Munich in 1909 were salt-and-pepper specimens.

It is also interesting to note that of the first nine registered Giant Schnauzer puppies, four were salt-and-pepper, three were black (one with a white spot on the chest), and one was brown-yellow, and one was gray-yellow.

The sire of this first registered litter was Ch. Roland Rolandsheim, owned by Mr. Pankok from Düsseldorf. He was a powerful dog, dark wolf-gray in color, and 55 cm (21¾ in) at the withers. He had a good head with a strong beard and typical schnauzer expression. His coat was harsh. His back was rather long, his ears very short and badly cropped. Although he was a result of unknown parents, he was admired by the earliest Giant Schnauzer fans and considered a good specimen. In fact, he was a nice-looking by-chance-produced dog who later proved to be a poor and inconsistent producer. So, his career as a stud dog was short, and a real Rhineland type never developed.

In the old *Pinscher Blätter*,[1] we find a report written by Josef Berta relating to the 1909 show organized by the Bavarian Schnauzer Club in which twenty-three Munich schnauzers were entered. He writes: "It was a medley of types, colors, coat varieties, and sizes!" This meant that those rather haphazardly produced Giant Schnauzers shown in Munich should not be taken too seriously. They were brought together by the earliest amateur breeders. They lacked the size and the strength of the real oberlander. Of all the dogs present, Judge Boppel Cannstadt found only the wirehaired-black Bitru v. Weinberg worthy of breeding.

There was a general feeling that the oberlander should form the basis of the future Giant Schnauzer; however, he had to be improved and selected. So, a winner as this Bitru v. Weinberg was important: Crossed with the Munich type and the central German type, Bitru produced Giant Schnauzers such as Bazi v. Wetterstein (born 1914), the cornerstones of a uniform type. The old oberlander and the Munich type were necessary to give size and power. The central German type was necessary to procure schnauzer expression, compactness, correct angulation and movement that were already available in the Standard Schnauzer.

To give an idea of the difference in size, compare the Rhineland Ch. Roland Rolandsheim, standing 55 cm (21¾ in) at the withers to the oberlander Baldur v. Fuchspark-Potzhaus, standing 76 cm (30 in) tall. It took many generations to achieve uniformity and this is also the reason the modern breed standard still allows a range from 60 to 70 cm (23¾ to 27½ in) of height.

The following are the major Giant Schnauzer breeders just before the outbreak of World War I:
- Rhineland: Pankok (Düsseldorf) had Ch. Roland Rolands heim but was less successful with his progeny
- Central Germany: O. Leps—v. Fischbach; W. Schmerwitz—v. Conze
- Munich: Beitler—v. Taufkirchen (the first to register a litter in 1913); Hastreiter—v. Sendling; K. Kluftinger—v. Wetterstein

There were also scattered breeders who did not take pains to register their puppies. Although the few kennels had produced some good dogs, a shortage of guidance and the outbreak of World War I hampered further development.

In all, during the first ten years of the existence of the Munich Schnauzer, only forty-four entries in the studbook were noted. Most of the first breeders lost interest due to the war. When in 1918 the situation returned to normal, only a few good Munich schnauzers were available.

The Definite Breakthrough of the Giant Schnauzer

C. Calaminus (from Langendiebach near Hanau am Main) was interested in the fate of the Munich schnauzer, and in 1914, he decided to concentrate on the task of breeding the real Giant Schnauzer. He had a solid background of breeding experience. With the eye of a connoisseur, he went in search of oberlanders suitable for his plans. He crossed these dogs with the Munich schnauzer type and probably with other strains as well. He wanted a black Giant Schnauzer with correct conformation. Calaminus was a persevering man who refused to disclose his breeding technique to the public. One supposes that besides the oberlander and the Munich schnauzer he used a black Great Dane, but no evidence of this was left behind. His breeding system was based on an inexorable selection. In spite of the diffi-

Bazi v. Wetterstein. A magnificent black Giant Schnauzer whelped in 1914.

Felz v. Kinzigtal. Bred by Dr. C. Calaminus.

FIGURE 6-4

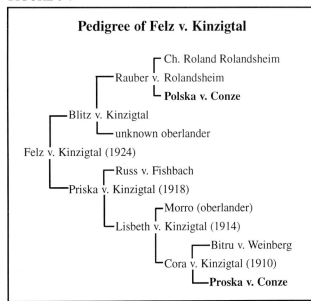

Pedigree of Felz v. Kinzigtal

```
                                  ┌ Ch. Roland Rolandsheim
                    ┌ Rauber v. Rolandsheim
                    │             └ Polska v. Conze
       ┌ Blitz v. Kinzigtal
       │            └ unknown oberlander
Felz v. Kinzigtal (1924)
       │            ┌ Russ v. Fishbach
       └ Priska v. Kinzigtal (1918)
                    │             ┌ Morro (oberlander)
                    └ Lisbeth v. Kinzigtal (1914)
                                  │           ┌ Bitru v. Weinberg
                                  └ Cora v. Kinzigtal (1910)
                                              └ Proska v. Conze
```

cult war years, he persevered, and the peace of 1918 opened the doors of the kennel von Kinzigtal to success.

At the same time, Dr. Priemel, director of the zoo in Frankfurt decided to exert his knowledge and enthusiasm on the welfare of the breed. His kennel v. d. Pfingstweide played an important role.

In Saxony, the tradition of the old v. Conze kennel was continued by Baron v. Lülsdort under the name v. Stichelsdorf. In Chemnitz, v. Schönau was rising. In Munich, K. Kluftinger's v. Wetterstein was persevering, and this reticent man finally, under pressure from club and breed authorities, released his famous Bazi v. Wetterstein for stud use with bitches outside his kennel. In Worms, the tradition of Pankok (Rolandsheim) was taken over by Mr. Oberle's v. Alt-Worms.

From 1918 to 1921, 567 Giant Schnauzers were registered. The 1922 decision of the national kennel club to ban all unregistered dogs from shows definitely stimulated registration and led the dog sport into proper channels.

There was no more doubt. The Giant Schnauzer was a reality and now needed the full attention of the Pinscher-Schnauzer Klub 1895 e. V., renamed in 1921.

In 1923, the elaborated breed standard sealed the future of the Giant Schnauzer. The first breed standard states: "The Giant Schnauzer will be the best possible, considerably enlarged and strengthened copy of the Standard Schnauzer." (This means, if he wants to be called 'Giant Schnauzer' he has to add to the power of his oberlander body the exterior and expression of the schnauzer.)

The height of the withers was fixed, in 1923, to between 55 and 65 cm (21½ and 25½ in). (This means that oversized, too heavy specimens, unsuitable as working dogs were not desirable.)

The conclusion of the description of mental characteristics states: "All these destine the Giant Schnauzer to the hard and strenuous life of a working dog. As such, he has to be confirmed and further developed by selective breeding." This puts it very clearly, without any doubt, that the Giant Schnauzer was developed in modern times to suit modern working purposes.

Before proceeding any further, it is worthwhile to return to 1923 and the breeding efforts of Dr. Calaminus. One of his first bitches was Cora v. Kinzigtal, born in 1910, a daughter of Bitru v. Weinberg and Proska v. Conze. In this way, she carried both Munich and central German blood. In 1914, he mated Cora with an unknown pure oberlander called Morro, and from this combination he kept Lisbeth v. Kinzigtal. In 1918, Lisbeth was mated to Russ v. Fischbach; in 1924, their daughter Priska v. Kinzigtal was bred to Blitz v. Kinzigtal and produced the famous Felz v. Kinzigtal. Notice that the occasional oberlander influx shown in the pedigree is stabilized by using two litter sisters: Polska and Proska v. Conze, one in the dam's line, the other on the sire's side. This proves that from the limited bloodlines available, Calaminus, as an accomplished breeder, succeeded in obtaining the best results.

At the end of his life, Calaminus partially lifted the veil on his breeding program. He admitted to three crosses to dogs of another breed: the first for dominant black color, the second for a well-crested neck and correct head proportions, the third for overall correct coat. His reserve and secretiveness on one hand and jealousy on the other were the source of criticism and backbiting.

As a Fleming, I believe one story about Calaminus is worth relating and commenting on. During the terrible inflation following the First World War, a beautiful male, Michael v. Kinzigtal, was exported to the Netherlands. He achieved great success in shows and, after winning four CCs, returned to Germany. During one of these shows, he was seen by the Belgian judge Theo Meunier, and I found his report in a 1922 Belgian magazine *Chasse et Pêche*.[2] He states that in The Hague he saw a beautiful Giant Schnauzer bred by Dr. Calaminus, the man who laid the basis for this breed. Meunier continues: "When I had a look at the Giant Schnauzer, I could not deny an enormous resemblance to our Bouvier des Flandres. Although the Giant Schnauzer's head is more elegant and has unquestionably the skull of the schnauzer." Meunier then asked Mr. Proessler, a German all-round judge who was at the show, for more information about the Giant Schnauzer. Proessler, who admitted knowing Dr. Calaminus and his dogs very well, said the Giant Schnauzer was a result of oversized Standard Schnauzers crossed with another type of dog that Dr. Calaminus refused to divulge.

Postwar articles like this tempted some persons to conclude that bouviers requisitioned by the Germans had been used in the development of the Giant Schnauzer. Let us have a closer look at this. First of all, what was the position of the bouvier in those days?

Just as the Giant Schnauzer tried around the turn of the century and the prewar period to make his way from the Bavarian farms to the show ring, the bouvier was struggling on the same kind of path. He was active as a cattle and general farm dog in the Flemish lowlands as well as on the French and Belgian side of the border. We have seen that as far as the Giant Schnauzer is concerned we identified a Munich, a central German, and a Rhineland type. Well, exactly the same thing happened to the bouvier. In 1912, at a meeting in Kortrijk (West Flanders), one officially accepted two types and worked out a breed standard for each of them. The first was called Bouvier (Belge) des Flandres, representing the type of dog from the border farms; the second received the name of Bouvier de Roulers, indicating the town Roulers, situated forty kilometers inland from the French-Belgian border, where a certain Mr. Moerman was concentrating on this type of bouvier. The Bouvier de Roulers was heavier and stronger than the border type, pitch black, and about 65–70 cm (25½ to 27½ in) at the withers.

Washington Bonaparte. A famous bouvier of the typical border type that evolved into the Bouvier des Flandres.

Bouvier de Roulers, around 1914-1918.

The coat was wiry, about 5 cm (2 in) long, with longer eyebrows, moustaches, and beard. Quite an impressive animal but still very rustic in appearance.

When the German army walked over Belgium in 1914, it stopped at the Yser, a river beyond which the most typical border-farm bouviers were to be found. Roulers was in occupied country and remained as such until 1918. Certainly, from 1914 to 1918, the Germans had a chance to make the bouvier's acquaintance. From this, to conclude that requisitioned bouviers were crossed with Giant Schnauzers is pure speculation. If one should consider the possibility that a bouvier was used at a certain moment during the development of the Giant Schnauzer, then it must definitely have been a Bouvier de Roulers and not the Washington Bonaparte (as suggested by some authors), a famous bouvier of the typical border type. To conclude this intermezzo, in 1923, at the moment that the Giant Schnauzer officially obtained a breed standard, the Bouvier de Roulers fell into discredit. The Belgian Société Royale Saint Hubert and the French Société Canine Centrale decided to give priority to the French-Belgian border-bouvier type and to recognize only one bouvier—that is, the Bouvier des Flandres. Thus, the Bouvier de Roulers was no longer registered as recognized breed on the FCI breed list. Although a dissident kennel organization recognized the breed, the Bouvier de Roulers slowly disappeared. Today, one can still trace him in old Dutch working lines.

If, at a certain moment, a Bouvier de Roulers had been introduced in the development of the Giant Schnauzer (an act that cannot be proven!), one should not blame the early breeder; one should rather praise him for his good choice. All our modern breeds are made up from different components. If a man like Calaminus wanted to improve a detail in his line and used another breed carrying this trait, he cannot be blamed. Certainly not if his choice should have been a Bouvier de Roulers, because this dog had the same cattle-farm-dog background, more or less the same conformation and size, a wiry pitch-black coat, and other similar points.

We know that the main components of the Giant Schnauzer were the oberlander to which oversized Standard Schnauzers were added. If Dr. Calaminus or other pioneers had to add some "spices" in order to obtain a pure black color or wiry coat, it is a pity they did not divulge their secret, but this is not important in itself. Only the achievement of their aim, as such, is important. If we can now enjoy and train our magnificent Giants, then we have to thank the pioneer breeders for it.

The Giant Schnauzer a Working Dog

In 1923, the authors of the Giant Schnauzer breed standard concluded the description of mental qualities as follows: "This destines the Giant Schnauzer to the hard and strenuous life of a working dog. As such he has to be confirmed and further developed by selective breeding." This puts it very clearly and leaves no doubt of how the creators of the breed felt about the Giant Schnauzer and the breed's future development.

In my opinion, two elements lay on the basis of this decision.

First of all, if one considers the mental qualities belonging to the different components of the Giant, one has to conclude that the result cannot just be a gentle lapdog. The oberlander carried a tradition of all-round work on and around the farm. Most of the time, he was under man's control and had to follow instructions, but it happened also that he had to work on his own, show some initiative, and make up his own mind. Contact with people, contact with other animals, an indoor life in the stables, an outdoor life in the tough climate of the Bavarian highlands—over the years, an environment that forged a reliable and active dog. To these basic qualities, some schnauzer spices were added, and the result could only be a fierce dog, keen to work for a handler who was a leader; otherwise, this type of dog would take the initiative.

Second, World War I opened a market and created a demand for, let us call them, police dogs. The vanishing flocks and the fact that cattle were no longer driven to the markets released a number of shepherd and cattle dogs, who were on the point of losing their ancestral jobs. Owing to centuries of selective breeding for hard work, these dogs were—with adequate training—perfectly suitable to undergo a transition to police work. The first Giant Schnauzer to obtain the *Polizei Hund* (P.H., police dog) working certificate was Helfried v. Schnonau (P.Z. 237), a son of Bazi v. Wetterstein (P.Z. 30). (P.Z. refers to the *Pinscher Zuchtbuch*—that is, the PSK studbook).

In the early 1920s, the leading kennel organizations worked out rules and regulations for tests and competition for dogs. The Germans called their program *Schutzhund* (protection dog). It consists of tracking, adaptability, and protection work with three different levels of difficulty. In order to be allowed to participate in these tests and working trials, each parent breed club had to apply to the German Kennel Club for recognition of their breed as a *Gebrauchshund*—loosely translated means utility dog, which has created some confusion in countries with a utility group. A more accurate translation of *Gebrauchshund* (or its German synonym *Diensthund*) is a dog to be used by and to serve man—that means an active working dog to be classified in the working group.

In the early 1920s, because of the popularization of the *Gebrauchshund* in Germany, several governmental training centers were established, including one in Grünheide under the management of Colonel Schönherr, a Giant Schnauzer enthusiast and member of the Pinscher-Schnauzer Klub. Peter Burtzik of Schleswig-Holstein, a former president of this club, has been a successor of Colonel Schönherr. Peter

A group of Giant Schnauzer fanciers in 1931.

Prewar Giant Schnauzers.

Peter. At the 1936 German national championship working trial for all breeds, this Giant Schnauzer won the event and four gold medals for his handler, Mr. Irrgang.

Pascha v. Haumananshof, AD, FH, SchH III. Owned by Peter Noetlichs. Pictured at the age of ten years, Pascha demonstrates perfect nose work on track. The team competed for six consecutive years in the German national championship working trial.

Here, Pascha demonstrates the "Send away!"

Burtzik knew Schönherr very well, and in the jubilee edition of the PSK (1895–1985), he recalls this in detail. Schönherr told him that in the old days up to sixty Giant Schnauzers at a time were trained in Grünheide.

Burtzik also gives a very interesting report about the Giant Schnauzer Binz (P.Z. 468), who started his training with the first course in 1922 and remained on active duty with the Berlin police until 1929. The parents of Binz were Lux (breeder Beil-Nürnberg) and Flora (breeder Seipfert-Nürnberg). Binz was a powerful, black-brown male measuring 62 cm (24½ in) at the withers, with good movement but somewhat soft in coat. He was a character-firm dog possessing all the qualities required of a good police dog. Binz distinguished himself in 1925 when a sex murder took place at the tower in Berlin. Binz was put on the track of the murderer and brought his handler to the culprit. Arrest followed! At a Berlin show that year, the judge, Mr. Best, commented upon Binz (P.Z. 468 P.H.) as follows: "Very good in conformation, a little straight in front, but with perfectly angulated hindquarters. His head is full of expression. He is the right size and has supple movement. The coat could be harsher. Vorzüglich I [excellent 1]."

The training and breeding center in Grünheide is near Berlin, and the fact that Siemens A. G., a well-known business firm, actively used twenty Giant Schnauzers as security dogs also made this breed very renowned in the German capitol.

In June 1925, at a specialty show in Berlin, sixteen Giants were present. To conclude the show, a demonstration was given by Binz, Helfried v. Schnonau, and Dussia v. Lichterode. They made such an impression that recognition of the Giant Schnauzer as a *Gebrauchshund* (working dog) followed in August the same year. The next year (1926), twenty Giants qualified as working dogs; seven of them came from the training center in Grünheide.

There followed a steady progression toward the zenith of success in 1936. Handler Irrgang and his Giant Schnauzer Peter were delegated to represent Grünheide at the national championships in Bohndorf for all working-dog breeds. Peter won the competition, leaving the elite of German working dogs behind him, and took four gold medals home.

Of course, the German Pinscher-Schnauzer Klub paid the necessary attention to the Giant Schnauzer as a working dog. From 1927, the club annually organized the *Bundesleistungssiegerprüfung* (national championship working trials) for Giant Schnauzers. As only the twenty best selected giants are allowed to participate, it is a great honour to be invited.

On 1 January 1937, the working dog class was introduced in breed shows in the FCI affiliated countries. This class is reserved for dogs belonging to a recognized working breed and which previously have obtained a recognized working certificate such as SchH I (Schutzhund) or IPO I (*Internationale Prüfungsordnung*). This measure was taken to stimulate the working fans to show their dogs and, at the same time, to stimulate the breed ring fans to work their dogs. In other words, to promote the idea of beauty and brains.

In 1938, more than seven hundred Giants were shown in Germany. The Second World War not only interrupted all activities but also dramatically thinned out all Giant Schnauzer ranks. From what was left in 1945, the Germans started all over again.

The national Schutzhund Championship was cancelled in 1939, but the PSK was in a position to reinstate this competition in 1953. It went from strength to strength, and in 1985, the title was won for the first time by a lady handler when Christa Urginus and Basko von Granitfelsen beat Bosko v. Zöllnerkoppel, the 1984 winner. Basko repeated his success in 1986.

In 1987, two competitors scored exactly the same points. Both had 99/100 for tracking, 96/100 for obedience, and 98/100 for defense work. As such, Walter Herz with Ambros v. d. Wolfseiche and Wolfgang Maurer with Eric v. Chattenhof were both placed first. Since then, Wolfgang Maurer has repeated his success by winning in both 1988 and 1989, resulting in a magnificent hat trick. Werner Brand, with Lux v. d. Frankenhöhe won in 1990. Pascha v. Herzogenhof, handled by A. Seggewisz, was the winner in 1991. The 1992 edition was won by Hans Berg with Ingo v. Schwarzen Lot, and Klaus Hüfer with Gerry v. d. Wolfseiche took the *Bundesleistungssieger* title in 1993. It is remarkable that in 1993 the 8th, 9th, 10th, and 11th places also came from the v. d. Wolfseiche kennel.

In addition, on 26–27 September 1992, the first ISPU world championship, based on IPO rules, was organized in Switzerland. Giant Schnauzers from five different countries took part, and Horst Böthig (Germany) with Zito v. Tanneneck were the winners.

The 1993 edition brought thirty-eight entries from seven countries. The first day, Storm Bergin with Iro v. Sandokan (representing the American Working Schnauzer Federation) and the Belgian Clement Distelmans with Flair v. d. Wolfseiche astonished the crowd with a stunning 100/100 score for tracking. The final winner was Roswitha Krüger with Enzo v. Zigeunereck.

In the monthly *Pinscher und Schnauzer* magazine, the number of Giants succeeding in working tests is conspicuous. Each time a list of 30–50 successful Giants is published.

If one considers all this, there can be no shadow of doubt that the Giant Schnauzer was conceived and further developed by the Germans as a working dog.
- The first breed standard of 1923 states it clearly
- The recognition as such in 1925 proves it
- The successes and performances over the years confirm it.

Ch. Cora van't Wareheim, CQN, CACIB/IPO—Int. Ch., *Klubsiegerin PSK,* and champion in Belgium, France, Germany, and the Netherlands (Giant). Cora proves that beauty and performance can go hand in hand. In just twenty-five shows, she had twenty-three best-of-breed wins and one best-in-show win. Cora is the mother of forty-two pups in five litters (ten champions), and her son Ch. Farouk van't Wareheim is the first Giant Schnauzer in South Africa to earn the IPO III title. At the age of ten, she still enjoys going to the training field with her handler.

At the age of three.

Training for the IPO (FCI working certificate) at fifteen months.

Decked out for tracking.

Hot on the track.

A six-foot wall can be negotiated.

Retrieving over an A-frame is a mere trifle for a Giant with sound hips.

It is not only my opinion but rather a logical conviction that the aim of the creators and the work of the promoters—that is, the parent breed club in the country of origin—must be respected and adhered to. Nobody has the right to redesign a breed or to adapt it to local fashion or trend. The breed standard as elaborated by the breed specialists in the country of origin should be an immovable guideline. Every breeder has, of course, the duty to improve the breed. To improve means to bring the progeny as close as possible to the ideal image as described in the breed standard. Pity enough, outside its native country, changes in the Giant Schnauzer standard occurred and usually the working capabilities were affected. It is a matter of fact that outside his native country the Giant Schnauzer is less considered as a police dog and worked as such.

Why must there be a German Giant Schnauzer, an American type, a British type, a breed-ring type, or a working type? All common sense implies a one and only one type—a Giant Schnauzer with brains, who is put together in such a way that enables him in the best possible way to perform the work for which he was developed. Too many breeders don't bother or totally ignore the brains and don't realize that by changing the exterior they diminish the working capacity that is the natural heritage of the breed.

To conclude and to prove that I am not the lonely voice crying in the desert, I want to cite Werner Jung who in 1959 formulated the breeding aims for the Giant Schnauzer as follows: "Nobility-Beauty-Performance."

In his contribution to the PSK jubilee edition, Peter Burtzik wants to add "Health" and "Surrounding-friend-liness" to the breeding goals that any Giant Schnauzer breeder should bear in mind. With "Health," he wants to emphasize the breeder's duty to eradicate hereditary diseases such as hip dysplasia. "Nobility and Beauty" is what one can expect from any well-bred purebred dog. "Performance" undoubtedly reflects on the working ability, which should never be neglected. "Surrounding-friendliness" is an essential quality required of any well-adjusted working dog. In other words, in our hectic modern way of life, a sound Giant Schnauzer should never display fear or viciousness.

I probably needed a little breath and paused in my long speech.

Pam took the opportunity to put her hand on my shoulder and said, "John, what you told us tonight is tremendous. I can see the fire in your eyes when you speak about the Giant Schnauzer. There must be other people who want to learn all this. Why don't you write all your experiences in a book? Let us put it otherwise, you better promise me to do so."

I agreed with Pam, and although I realized very quickly that writing a story is a different matter than telling a story, I never regretted my promise.

---

[1] *Pinscher Pages.*
[2] *Fishing and Hunting.*

Pascha v. Haumananshof, AD, FH, SchH III. Owned by Peter Noetlichs. Pascha demonstrates one way to stop an escaping criminal.

↑
Snob v. Bartenwetzer (Giant), a qualified search-and-rescue dog, at work with the army in Switzerland. Bred by W. Schicker (Germany).
↓

Ch. Idris van't Wareheim (Giant).

A Standard Schnauzer that belonged to Max Kamp.

Swimming and retrieving are favorite sports. Out for the stick.

Wotan (Standard). Owned by Rob Wilmsen (Belgium). Scaling a 2.1 m vertical wall presents no problem.

Back again, with the stick.

Wotan (Standard). Owned by Rob Wilmsen (Belgium). Wotan easily catapults himself over a 4 m long jump on an agility course.

Family situations often affect one's choice of dog. *Photo by H. Höller.*

7

Acquiring a Schnauzer

The Nature of the Schnauzer

Now that Pam and Charles knew about the history of the schnauzer, I did not want them to buy a pig in a poke, and therefore, I felt I had to tell them some more about the schnauzer nature.

The best way to analyze and better understand the nature of the schnauzer is to look back to the aims for which the rural population in southern Germany bred them.

Stable dog, ratcatcher, vermin killer in general, pig herder, highly appreciated aide in drive hunts for wild boar, homestead and premises guard, cart escort, cattle drover, children's playmate. In other words, playing a useful role in every aspect of life in the countryside. Most of these jobs were executed under man's control or management, but there were often situations in which the schnauzer was alone and had to prove his own initiative and determination. We must understand that all these activities took place in summer as well as in winter, on sunny, rainy, snowy, or freezing days: that one moment the schnauzer enjoyed the coziness of the fireplace in the living room, the humid heat of the horse stables, and—the next moment—joyful trotting in a miserable rain. We definitely understand the schnauzer is not a cosseted lapdog.

From this background, we may conclude that the main characteristics of the schnauzer nature are happiness, determination, and loyalty. He is a *happy* dog because he enjoys all that he does, because he only does what he enjoys. He is a *determined* dog; once he has put his mind to something, he will persevere to the point of stubborness. He is a *loyal* dog, not to be confounded with slavish submissiveness, which he definitely is not; in the schnauzer's case, loyalty must be understood in the noble sense of the word.

In all honesty, I must conclude that the schnauzer is a fantastic dog but don't expect to program him like a computer or expect him to be a slave. A schnauzer is a freebooter who will only give you his true heart and soul, if he finds you worthy. A schnauzer is devoted to his owner and family. Not that he ignores other people, but at first approach, he will rather show suspicion. When strangers show their good intentions, he will accept them after a while.

When opponents threaten, he will fight like hell. When the opponents are other schnauzers or other strange dogs, the threshold of the threat is easily exceeded. The schnauzer will grow up with other dogs, and the hierarchy of the pack will be established. Once the pack is formed, it is very hard for a schnauzer to accept an intruder, especially when the intruder does not demonstrate the usual signs of submissive courtesy. So be warned—a well-educated schnauzer will not be the first to start a fight, but he needs only a spark to detonate his pugnacity.

To close the subject, I would like to mention Marga Höller's description of the schnauzer: The schnauzer's exterior and nature are of an exceptional harmony, because his general appearance clearly demonstrates what he is and what he can do. His rough exterior symbolizes his resistance. His sturdy structure embodies his pluck. His expressive head reveals his intelligence, and his eyes reflect the big soul deep down in him. His sound composure is no sluggish phlegm. His temperament is no nervous exaggeration. His spunk is no blind frenzy. He is neither a spruced parlor beauty nor a bully body builder; he is not a spoiled fashion plate and not a bloodthirsty carnivore—but he is a real and jolly fellow.

Your Choice—A Miniature, a Standard, or a Giant Schnauzer

Does the above description of the schnauzer's nature apply to the Miniature, the Standard, and the Giant Schnauzer?

My answer is yes, and let me explain. One must not forget that the average size, in the olden days, varied between the present Miniature and Standard schnauzers. Depending on one's particular needs, one chose the smaller or bigger size. When a breed standard later divided Miniatures and Standards and "fixed" their sizes, this had no influence on their natures. Later on, when the Giant Schnauzer was developed from the Bavarian oberlanders and oversized Standard Schnauzers, very similar natures were combined so that the final result can be considered unaltered. A future dog owner who has made up his mind and likes the schnauzer exterior and nature, will now, depending on certain circumstances, have to decide upon the size of his schnauzer.

Although all schnauzers like outdoor life and activity, it is logical that a Miniature can fit in an apartment or a smaller house as long as he is given the opportunity to exercise his athletic little body daily in the garden or park. He is an ideal vigilant companion for all kinds of families, and even elderly people can manage these lively little characters.

The Standard Schnauzer is a good guard dog with a convenient size. He is a keen watchdog and a clown, all at the same time, and he enjoys sharing an owner's most foolish escapades. However, in order to fulfill all the expectations of modern society, he needs training and some gentle guidance. If you are not prepared to provide this, forget about a Standard Schnauzer!

A winsome litter of Miniatures. Bred by Roger and Yo Coucke.

Edith Gallant with Bhima van't Wareheim.

Ch. Jana v. Bartenwetzer, AD, SchH I—Int. Ch. *Bundesjugendsieger, Klubsieger PSK, Jahresseniorensieger,* and champion in Germany and Luxembourg (Giant). Bred and owned by W. Schicker (Germany).

Orein van't Groeningheheem at seven weeks. Breeders, Y. and R. Coucke (Belgium).

The author and his spouse with a litter of four-week-old standard puppies.

The Giant needs space and action. He may achieve this in your garden or his surroundings, but you will still have to take him to the training field, where he will be able to develop and enjoy (with his handler) his natural qualities. A Giant Schnauzer must be worked. By this, I don't mean that he needs soul-destroying drill. It is, however, essential that he can perform in the company of his handler to forge the link that he expects with his pack leader. As a pup, he will yearn to play with you. As a youngster and as an adult, he will be longing for a run next to your bicycle, a tracking session in the veld, or a good workout on the training field. All schnauzer obedience training must be based on stimulating natural keenness and awakening natural drives, never on the basis of slavish submission. This would destroy the schnauzer's nature and result in a dull and introverted dog.

A Dog or a Bitch?

This question may seem unimportant, and one could think that the ideal answer depends on personal preferences. Let us leave breeders and professionals out of consideration for the moment and concentrate on the average dog lover who has decided upon the choice of a particular breed (in this case a schnauzer) and now has to decide upon a dog or a bitch.

Arguments such as "I want a male because he is more impressive" or "I don't want a bitch because of her seasons" only take into account a part of the problem and shouldn't be decisive.

Let us list the specific differences.

Schnauzer male.
- Bigger, stronger, physically more impressive (even the Miniature)
- Temperament rather sharper, more pugnacious, greater tendency to independence
- Sexual life (like all dogs): marks his territory in a demonstrative and sometimes profuse manner; sexual desire does not depend on certain periods and can always be stimulated

Schnauzer bitch.
- Exterior more elegant, more feminine, smaller, and more graceful in her movements
- Temperament typical schnauzer and typical bitch; the threshold for aggression may be a little higher, but once in action, there is as much determination as the male; sentimentally and jealously attached to her handler
- Like other dogs, she normally comes in season every six months for twenty-one days; with precautions, this creates only minor problems

Where Do I Buy My Schnauzer

I believe I must give some general advice. To find a schnauzer that meets specific criteria, you must "plan" your puppy, see the parents or at least the mother, and find out about their qualities and abilities in order to have as much in your favor as possible.

Look for a dedicated and experienced specialist breeder. Even better, visit several breeders. When you find the breeder whose dogs are reared in a family (pack) situation (not puppy mill mothers producing litters in isolated, individual kennels), a breeder who initially shows more interest in selecting *you* to find out if you will be a worthy owner for what he has bred with care, then you are at the right address. The best way to find such discerning breeders is to contact the secretary of the local schnauzer specialty club. He or she will provide addresses of affiliated breeders who can be recommended by the club. Some of them may have puppies available, and others will give the date they expect pups from a particular sire-dam combination.

The national kennel club can provide the addresses of local schnauzer club secretaries, or similar information can be found in a good dog magazine. A good breeder will not be afraid to show you his dogs. He will be proud to exhibit the trophies won in the breed ring, obedience classes, or working trials. If you are interested in a Giant Schnauzer puppy, the latter are very important. It is my humble conviction—and I will come back to this later in my story—that a breeder who does not "work" his Giants can't make a clear judgment about the working abilities or natural qualities of his breeding stock.

In order to find out if the exterior of his breeding stock measures up to the breed standard, the breeder takes his dogs to breed shows where they can be judged by connoisseurs.

To help eradicate disabling hereditary diseases and to ensure that the parents don't have such diseases, the breeder will have them certified free of diseases such as hip dysplasia, congenital juvenile cataract, and progressive retinal atrophy. I will return to these diseases shortly, not because they are inherent to schnauzers but because, just like all other breeds, they can occur in schnauzers.

To ensure that the sires and dams have the correct schnauzer nature and temperament, the breeder will avoid the use of any timid, lethargic, or vicious schnauzer.

What about the Parents?

Once you have decided upon a breeder in whom you can place your trust and this feeling is reciprocated by the breeder, who estimates that you will be a worthy owner, the human conditions are met.

It now becomes important to explain the criteria that will ensure that the puppy will fulfill your expectations. These are criteria for the average fancier who wants a good-quality companion, not for the fancier looking for specific qualities related to show, obedience, and working trials.

First of all, ask to see the parents, or at least the mother of your potential puppy. (Some breeders send their bitches to outside studs, in which case, you won't be able to meet the father.) If the parents are not the kind of schnauzer that you would like to take home, don't expect their puppy to surpass their qualities.

Even before seeing the parents, make sure that the breeder shows you their certificates of registration and certificates that they are free of hereditary disorders. At the same time, the breeder can show their certificates of performance in the show ring, temperament tests, obedience and working trials, and so forth. As such, you will be well-informed about the *health* and *performance* of the parents. A problem that is present in the sire and dam might be transmitted to their puppies. If the desired traits are not present in the parents, don't expect them to appear miraculously in their puppies.

Now is the time to meet the parents to find out about their nature and exterior. It is perfectly normal for any schnauzer to be a little wary when a stranger approaches home territory, even when the stranger is accompanied by the owner. Such distrust should, however, disappear quickly, especially when the owner assures the dog and the stranger behaves in a normal friendly way by speaking to the dog and trying to make contact. Once the ice is broken by this greeting ceremonial, any schnauzer should interact freely with a visitor. This means, he will allow you to touch him, will show an interest when you call his name, and will even be prepared to play with you. In other words, normal social behavior within a dog-man pack relationship. If a sire or dam should be anxious and refuse contact or—worse—show a desire to bite, there is something wrong, and I would say, stay away from that strain.

If you are happy with the nature of the parents, it becomes, thereafter, essential that you have a look at the most important part of a schnauzer's exterior—the coat. You must make sure that your puppy's parents have the correct coat texture. The dog's coat must, as a primary insulator, consist of a soft, short undercoat covered by a straight, harsh wiry topcoat that does not lie tight to the body but stands out slightly. While making friends with the schnauzer and stroking the neck and back, you must feel a certain resistance between your fingers when trying to bend the topcoat. The hair on the legs should virtually be of the same structure and not longer than the hair on the body. If this is not the case, it means that the wooly undercoat has overgrown the upper layer. While wearing a weather-resistant jacket, such a schnauzer will drag four water-absorbing mops over the street and through your garden, then wipe those mops in your home. I am adamant on this matter, not merely because a wiry coat is a hallmark of the breed but rather because it is a practical coat for that dog that will, at the same time, save you time and grooming money.

The parents should be sturdily built, with a well-developed chest, strong legs, look square in proportions, and have a keen expression in their dark eyes. Of course, there are many more details that show-going fanciers look for, which will be described in the chapter on the breed standards.

Before going further, let me tell you how Pam and Charles acquired their schnauzer.

Pam and Charles were, somehow, in a privileged position. They did not have to consult the specialty clubs as I could advise them of several good Giant Schnauzer breeders. We phoned a few of them. The third one had a five-week-old litter that, pity enough, was completely sold out. However, he had another bitch that was due to have puppies in three weeks. He said that we were very welcome to come and have a look and a chat. We made arrangements for the coming weekend.

The breeder had given us correct directions to the kennel. His house was situated at the outskirts of the village, and we stopped the car at the gateway, which was closed. We did not need to step out and ring the bell because, at the moment of our arrival, we were clamorously greeted by two black devils on the other side of the gate. The owner must have been used to this signal because he appeared very soon, calmed the dogs, and invited us to come in. We were thoroughly sniffed at while walking down the drive.

In the meantime, the breeder explained that Tascha, the well-proportioned lady that vigilantly jumped around us, was nearly three years old and due to have puppies in three weeks. This would be her second litter. The young male that kept her company was her one-year-old son. The breeder was very happy with this youngster, not only because of a couple of outstanding results in the puppy class at breed shows but also because of his keenness to work on the training field. He did quite well in the obedience sessions, was already a good tracker, and had recently proven to possess the necessary drive and courage to enjoy elementary defense work.

As we turned the corner of the garage, a chorus of canine voices protested our entry into their territory. The breeder invited us into his office, accompanied by Tascha and her son. They were convinced by now of our good intentions, and their wet noses pushed into our hands to make friends. The breeder explained that he had four bitches and two males. Three bitches had had puppies already, and the fourth one, now fifteen months old, was due to be mated at her next heat. Duke, the oldest male, was now five years old, free of hip dysplasia, a breed champion, and an ideal trialist. His son, whose head was now resting on my knees, was very much like his father. For a few months, however, they had been kept apart as Duke dominated the son too much, which did not give his personality a chance to develop properly. Since the breeder had decided to let them run free alternately, war had been declared. As far as the bitches were concerned, the breeder

An early introduction to other "critters" is important for good future relationships with other family pets.

Miniatures and their Vizsla companion on holiday.

explained that he only used bitches that had been proven in the show ring, were free of hip dysplasia, and most important, had proven their working talent and stable character.

The breeder's wife came in to greet us and to offer a cup of coffee. She promised to take us to the puppies in a while. They were now six weeks old and sired by Duke.

Tascha, the bitch in whelp, had been shipped to and was mated by another outstanding champion named Thor, whose pictures were also in the family photo album. He was, indeed, a very impressive male, head held high and proudly, a broad and deep chest, and four straight and strongly muscled legs. There were also two pictures of Thor in full action with a decoy. Thor had obtained his Schutzhund II degree and was now training for the most advanced degree. He did not belong to a breeder. As the only dog, he shared the family life of his handler with four children. He was a handsome dog with an outstanding personality, and the breeder had big expectations for the offspring of Thor and Tascha.

While sipping our coffee, we were told that all litters were born and reared in the house until the age of three weeks, when the pups started to climb out of the whelping box. At that stage, they moved to the puppy kennel. It was now time to go and visit them.

Notwithstanding the barking in adjacent kennels, a bunch of five fat puppies showed their interest in strangers. When the lady opened the door of the puppy kennel, a black mass rushed up and bit our trouser legs and shoelaces. Not one showed timidity. Then the breeder shook an old cloth, the pups lost interest in our presence and dashed up to him and the toy. While they continued their wild rush over the lawn, the lady also released their mother, who had realized that we had no evil intentions toward her puppies. She came to smell us, then greeted us and allowed us to stroke her while keeping an eye on her children. Suddenly, two of the young warriors noticed their mother, lost interest in the game, and as fast as their toddling legs allowed, rushed in her direction. Their little snouts each grabbed a teat, and the smacking noise were the signal to alert and call the rest of the bunch over. Most unfortunately, all these pups were sold.

Charles, Pam, and myself were impressed with the whole set up. Beautiful dogs, well looked after and reared with love, talent, and idealism. While the owners returned the mother and her offspring to the kennel, I confidentially advised Charles to discuss the matter further and to book a puppy from Tascha's coming litter. When we left, Charles had the copy of a contract in his pocket by which he would eventually become the owner of a registered, fully inoculated and wormed female puppy out of Tascha and Thor. On his side, the breeder did not hesitate to reserve a puppy for Charles and Pam as from their conversation he realized that the pup would go to an ideal home.

About Hereditary Diseases

Hip Dysplasia

All Standard and Giant Schnauzers used for breeding should be certified free of hip dysplasia, which is common in the larger breeds, less common in smaller breeds such as the Miniature Schnauzer.

If one analyzes the word *dysplasia*, one must consider the two Greek words from which it is derived: *dys* stands for bad or difficult, and *plasis* means formation. As such, the medical term *hip dysplasia* (HD) is defined as a malformed hip joint. The hip joint is a typical ball-and-socket joint, with the head of the femur being the ball and the acetabulum being the pelvic socket into which the femoral head should fit perfectly to allow a wide range of smooth movement.

In dogs, HD became notorious about thirty years ago. Studies based on X-ray examinations showed that there were different degrees of malformation, with the higher grades being crippling at an early age. The following is a commonly used grading system.

- *Free or HD-0-.* The femoral head and the acetabulum are congruent, and the femoral head is deeply seated in the socket. The cranial-effective acetabular rim appears sharp or slightly rounded. The joint space is narrow and even.
- *Transitional or HD-1-.* The femoral head and the acetabulum are slightly incongruent, and the femoral head is deeply seated in the acetabulum; or, the femoral head and acetabulum are congruent, but the femoral head is not so deeply seated in the acetabulum. Minor irregularities in the acetabular edges may be present.
- *Mild or HD-2-.* The femoral head and the acetabulum are incongruent, and the acetabulum is shallow, and/or there is a slightly flattened cranio-lateral rim. Irregularities or no more than slight signs of osteoarthritic changes of the acetabular edges and femoral neck may be present.
- *Moderate or HD-3-.* Obvious incongruency between the femoral head and the acetabulum, with subluxation. The acetabulum is moderately shallow. Flattening of the cranio-lateral rim and/or osteoarthritic signs are present.
- *Severe or HD-4-.* Marked dysplastic changes of the hip joints (such as luxation or distinct subluxation), very shallow acetabulum, obvious flattening of the cranial acetabular edge, malformation of the femoral head and/or other signs of osteoarthritis.

This indicates that the parents' *phenotype* does not equal their *genotype*. In other words, even if the parents of a particular litter are certified free of hip dysplasia based on an X-ray examination, this only refers to their *phenotype*, and this does not guarantee that their offspring, as a result of their *genotype*, will necessarily inherit their perfect hips. Of

Table 7-1. PSK Records of Hip X-Rays: Percent of Each Grade, 1980–1989

	1980	1981	1982	1983	1984	1985	1986	1987	1988	1989
Giant Schnauzers										
Number X-Rayed					514	518	526	462	392	402
HD-0	51.50	55.22	61.15	60.15	66.15	66.34	61.78	68.40	69.94	66.92
HD-1	27.00	22.25	19.22	22.31	16.93	16.94	22.43	18.61	22.05	18.41
HD-2	14.00	16.21	13.89	12.79	12.26	12.95	11.21	8.01	6.67	7.71
HD-3	7.00	6.32	4.17	4.52	4.48	3.59	4.56	4.98	1.28	6.72
HD-4	0.00	0.00	0.24	0.25	0.20	0.20	0.00	0.00	0.26	0.25
Standard Schnauzers										
Number X-Rayed					277		239	215	202	218
HD-0	73.30	79.50	79.50	78.99	78.34	73.71	74.05	71.30	72.91	75.23
HD-1	11.80	13.94	11.58	11.60	15.17	14.35	17.15	17.59	19.21	16.97
HD-2	11.10	4.92	7.02	6.53	5.42	9.17	5.85	8.33	7.39	6.42
HD-3	3.70	1.64	1.41	2.54	1.09	2.79	2.92	2.31	0.49	0.92
HD-4	0.00	0.00	0.00	0.00	0.00	0.00	0.00	0.00	0.00	0.46

course, the odds of getting good hips are much better from certified parents.

When the initial belief that HD was a recessive trait fell before evidence that it did not respond to selective breeding as expected, new theories of the hereditary factors that caused HD popped up with regularity. Theories of a neuromuscular disorder of the pectineus muscle and of a hormone imbalance attracted substantial followings. For a while, many breeders gave megadoses of Vitamin C as a HD preventive.

It is now well established that HD is a polygenic trait, which is influenced by a combination of genetic and environmental factors. The modifiers appear to be additive—that is, when breeders keep stacking the deck in favor of good hips, they produce a higher percentage of puppies with good hips. The more severely the parents are affected, the higher the frequency and severity in the offspring; the higher the proportion of normal ancestors and siblings of parents, the higher the proportion of normal offspring. Control programs in many countries with many breeds have proven that using normal x normal or normal x near normal matings significantly increases the percentage of normal hips.

*Although HD is definitely hereditary, several environmental factors contribute to its frequency and severity. In general, the age of onset and severity of symptoms is higher in heavier, more rapidly growing puppies. F. W. Nicholas (*Veterinary Genetics, *1987) states: "Restricted feeding during the growth phase can reduce the liability to hip dysplasia." Therefore, during the period of rapid growth, puppies should be kept slightly underweight, with the ribs just barely showing.*

Limiting exercise during the growing phase also decreases injury and stress to vulnerable, rapidly growing hips, especially between the ages of 4 and 6 months. Although studies have shown that extreme confinement of puppies substantially reduces the incidence of HD, the early social deprivation produces adverse effects on temperament and trainability. As with most things, moderation and common sense help.[1]

In the schnauzer's homeland, all Giants and Standards used for breeding must be certified free of HD, and many other countries also have this requirement. Statistics prove that slow but positive progress is being made.

Concerned breeders have contracts that all buyers will have their dog x-rayed after the age of 12 months and inform the breeder of the results. I am convinced that breeding without HD control can be detrimental to an expanding breed to such an extent that, although X-ray control programs improve the statistics slowly, lack of control leaves the doors open for disaster.

Congenital Juvenile Cataract

Since 1969, cases of a hereditary cataract have been recorded in Miniature Schnauzers in the United States.

Congenital juvenile cataract (CJC) is described as a symmetrical and bilateral opacity of the lens that affects dogs at a few months of age, with the cataract progressing to complete lens opacity and blindness. It was established that its inheritance is due to a simple autosomal recessive gene.

The fact that the symptoms can be identified with the simple help of an ophthalmoscope by the age of eight weeks makes it relatively easy to carry out a test-breeding program. If, for example, a clear male is mated to an affected bitch and they produce a litter of at least four puppies of which all are clear, one may certify the male as genetically free of CJC. Such test-breeding programs have been encouraged and controlled by specialty clubs. In fact, if it were not for unscrupulous backyard breeding, the problem could have been fully under control and virtually eradicated. It is, therefore, important that, when buying a Miniature Schnauzer, you request proof that the parents are free of CJC.

Progressive Retinal Atrophy

Miniature Schnauzers are among the breeds in which progressive retinal atrophy (PRA) has been diagnosed.

The retina is the photosensitive part of the eye. The iris and the lens adjust the influx of light impressions. The retina, through a system of light-sensitive cells, registers them before sending the information along the optic nerve to the brain.

PRA is a progressive degeneration of these light-sensitive cells of the retina. Unlike CJC, the onset of PRA usually occurs at a later age. The degenerative process is slow but gradually progresses to blindness. It first affects the cells for night vision, and owners usually notice the onset when their dog starts to bump obstacles in his way during twilight. Due to the slowness of the degenerative process, most dogs adapt to the weakening vision, and they usually continue to move about without difficulty in familiar surroundings.

It is essential that Miniature Schnauzers are examined annually by a veterinary ophthalmologist. Once the degenerative process starts, PRA can be diagnosed with an ophthalmoscope. An electroretinogram (ERG) can detect the disease at an earlier age, before the onset of symptoms. Any Miniature Schnauzer coming from an affected line should be tested before being used in a breeding program.

Ch. Sofar's Foolish Affair—a champion in Canada and the United States (Giant). Owned by J. and N. Keay (Canada). Where did those squirrels go?

Rhapsodie de Bacara (Miniature) at the age of eight months. Bred by J. Tonossi; owned by F. Meneghello (Italy).

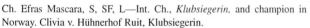

Ch. Efras Mascara, S, SF, L—Int. Ch., *Klubsiegerin,* and champion in Norway. Clivia v. Hühnerhof Ruit, Klubsiegerin.

Miniature puppies at van't Groeningheheem. Roger and Yo Coucke (Belgium).

Miniature puppies at van't Groeningheheem. Roger and Yo Coucke (Belgium).

Gunner Caprice Geistvoll and Argenta's Melville owned by Boel and Mikael Niklasson (Sweden) with Garbiella and Caroline.

Sibling play aids species identification and pack-dominance relationships.

8

Psychosocial Development

I felt that Pam and Charles—as two intelligent, potential future schnauzer owners—needed to learn something about the psychosocial development of the canine. The understanding of this process is absolutely essential for a good human-canine relationship.

The Pack—A Canine Phenomenon, and Its Impact on the Schnauzer

Over the last two or three decades, some very important research has been accomplished in dog behavior as well as that of his direct ancestor, the wolf. The way of life of the wolf, in natural surroundings, is a fascinating phenomenon of social relationships and behavior. In fact, the whole cycle is geared toward survival and maintaining the species. The key to success is, therefore, drastic natural selection. Only the best animal is good enough to procreate, and in spite of this, out of these select offspring, only the strongest and most intelligent will survive. This is the reason why wolves, in spite of thousands of years of existence in the harshest climatic conditions, while mercilessly hunted by human predators, still survive in strong family packs.

Studies have proven that after thousands of years of domestication, our dogs' way of live, their inner drives and habits, are still ruled and coordinated by the laws that are binding in the pack. Precisely like the wolf, our schnauzer is, by nature, a pack animal and behaves as such. As far as our domestic dogs are concerned, we must, however, accept a slight difference caused by domestication. The wolves' social relationship is strictly prescribed by peers, and the interaction is directed toward the pack members. The domestic dog has found a place in man's world. He no longer exclusively shares life with his own species. This means that in a dog's mind, his pack is not just restricted to dogs but includes other mammals with the same social tendencies, and they can, therefore, be part of his pack.

The domestication of dogs is a logical consequence of parallel tendencies in the social behavior of primitive man and primitive canine. Without this parallelism, the dog would never have become man's best friend and ally in all kinds of circumstances and jobs.

If we understand and accept this fact, it will be easy for a man, as a rational creature, to profit from this situation and to be respected as the pack leader. This is the key to success with your schnauzer.

Comparative research has been done on the social behavior of wolves and dingoes on one side and domestic dogs or hybrids of domestic and wild canines on the other. The conclusion was that all canines, wild or domestic, pass through a series of well-defined "formative" periods in their youth, during which their social behavior is developed step by step. The final result is a youngster that understands his place in the pack thoroughly and that clearly knows what the pack leader expects from him. At the age of eight months, a cub has been taught by the pack leader and older pack members how to behave within the group. He is now ready to go and hunt with the pack. He knows exactly how to behave, how to apply collective hunting techniques, and what he is allowed to do once the prey is captured and killed. He now needs only experience to become an adult and an accomplished wolf.

In the case of a schnauzer, and assuming that the humans who are in contact with a pup behave like adult pack members, a puppy will have the opportunity to develop all the inherent qualities received from his parents, given the right atmosphere. At the age of eight months, he will have grown up to be a youngster that understands perfectly how to behave in man's society, and a sound basis will have been laid.

The *inherent qualities* have developed under *man's guidance* and in *man's surroundings*. These three components are collectively responsible for the final result: a socially well-balanced dog, eager for activity and fearless when confronted; a dog that is ready to experience further training and events in man's life and, as such, ready to become a perfect companion to his handler and family during adulthood.

Eberhard Trumler, a disciple of Konrad Lorenz, relates his experiences and conclusions with regard to the different determining and formative stages in a young dog's life in his books *Mit dem Hund auf Du* (1971) and *Hunde Ernst Genommen* (1974). After I read his books and tested his findings on several litters born in my house, I decided, in 1978, to visit Mr. Trumler at Wolfswinkel, his experimental center in Germany. Although already convinced of his theories, this visit and discussion with Trumler dramatically reinforced my approach to and understanding of my schnauzer's behavior.

I was completely convinced of what could be destroyed in young dogs by their relationships with humans if the humans were unaware of the fundamental critical stages that each young dog will, by law of nature, pass through.

It suddenly became clear to me, especially where our schnauzers are concerned when some cosmetic operations are performed during these critical stages, that such interventions could have a detrimental effect on the young dog's mental development. It is for these reasons that one must

Just twenty-four hours old, Giant Schnauzer pups happily gathered at the source of life.

Ears and eyes sealed, a newborn pup looks unfinished.

A miniature mother with six healthy puppies, aged two weeks.

Ch. Idris van't Wareheim and her family.

Björn and Boas v. d. Schipbeek at the age of six weeks. Bred by J. Beeftink (Netherlands).

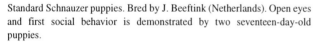

Standard Schnauzer puppies. Bred by J. Beeftink (Netherlands). Open eyes and first social behavior is demonstrated by two seventeen-day-old puppies.

Table 8-1. Critical Stages of Development

Stage and Period	Days	Weeks	Months
1 *Vegetative*	1–14	1–2	
2 *Transition*	15–21	3	
3 *Imprinting and Socialization*		4–11	
a Basic Imprinting — Submission	22–28	4	
b Further Imprinting and Socialization	29–49	5–7	
c Puppy Testing, Tattooing, and Transfer	50–57	8	
d Fear Imprinting	58–77	9–11	
4 *Rank-Order*		12–24	4–6
5 *Puberty*		25–52	7–11

consider the cosmetic interventions in direct relationship with the stages of life in which they are performed.

It was not only Trumler but also other canine behaviorists such as Scott and Fuller at Bar Harbor in the United States who, in the light of their research, described the critical stages and emphasized the importance of a correct man-puppy relationship during these periods. Based on what I learned from Trumler, read from Scott and Fuller, and personally *experienced* with many litters of schnauzers born in my kennels, I summarized the *critical stages* in Table 8-1.

Let us now have a closer look at each of these periods and try to explain how they are linked in a right chronological order with the natural aim of obtaining a canine ready for adulthood at the age of one year.

Stage 1—Vegetative Period

A schnauzer bitch, just like all other canines, gives birth after an average gestation period of sixty-three days. Sometimes, birth can take place from the sixtieth day, especially when it involves a large litter. By experience, we know that birth before the fifty-ninth day, because of the short period of gestation, is less viable and usually gives problems. The same applies to bitches that after sixty-five days do not show sufficient, or any, labor.

Luckily, our schnauzers are a sound breed with few complications at birth. Most of them still show the primitive canine instinct of preparing a natural lair. It is a clear indication of approaching birth when a schnauzer bitch—just like the she-wolf—starts to dig a hole in the garden at about her sixtieth day of gestation. An inattentive breeder could be surprised and find the pups born in this lair under a shrub in a peaceful place in the garden. When your bitch is due to have puppies and starts digging, then it is best to bring her to the whelping box and keep her there. She will continue her destructive work in this artificial lair by tearing up all the cloths, paper, or straw that you carefully prepared. This is an ideal exercise for her abdominal muscles.

If, when the waters break, the firstborn is not right there, he is definitely making his way. Normally, it needs another three to five contractions of the uterus to push the slick bag containing the puppy into the outside world. If the membranous bag is not yet broken, you will see a dedicated mother using her incisors to open the bag. She will chew through the umbilical cord with her premolars. The first cry of her baby will not disturb her. With a careful tongue, she will thoroughly clean her offspring of all the sticky mucus.

After the relatively short gestation period of sixty-three days, the newborn puppy appears unfinished. His eyes and ears are closed. He uses his little limbs to push, crawling over the surface. In other words, the nervous system needs perfection. This will happen in the first two weeks, and this is why it is called the vegetative period.

Biotonus, hypothermia, and fading puppy syndrome. I must digress here on a phenomenon that, during the past few years has received more and more attention in canine and veterinary literature and that, for the lay man, is sometimes confusing.

I recently read that a survey reported that from 10 to 30 percent of puppies are lost before weaning. Of these, approximately 16 percent are reputedly due to exposure and 13 percent to crushing. The death rate due to exposure is said to result from the newborn pup's inability to control his own body temperature. Therefore, treatment is advised as follows:

- Artificial heat to bring the environmental temperature to 29–30° C (84.2–86° F)
- Glucose at regular short intervals
- Appropriate antibiotics, Vitamin C, lots of fluids, and so forth

This article puzzled me. I have been involved in dog breeding for many years—initially on the European continent where several litters were born in winter. I remember, in particular, the January of 1978, when the temperature dropped to -15° C (5° F) overnight. A little worried, I went to check the temperature in the kennel building and inside the completely closed and insulated wooden whelping box. In the building, I measured -5° C (23° F). In the enclosure of the whelping box, and because of the draft inhibitor through which no draft could penetrate, I found a happy Giant Schnauzer bitch with eight healthy, suckling pups cuddling together in a temperature of 12° C (53.6° F) without any form of artificial heat. In the confinement of this artificial wooden lair, the warmth radiated by the bodies of mother and pups, cuddling together, was kept inside. The weather remained cold for weeks, and nobody faded away. Instead, three weeks later, all eight pups were happily playing together in the snow-covered garden. I had never seen pups fading away from exposure or heard about the fading puppy syndrome until 1986, in December, during the hot African summer with an average temperature of 25° C (77° F), when I heard a veterinarian advise somebody to put artificial heat above his puppies and to give them antibiotics, glucose, and so forth. When I queried this, he said, "Yes, these pups are fading away, and this is the only way to stop it!" I suspect that the vet—without making a differential diagnosis between fading puppy syndrome and hypothermia—intended to catch two birds with one stone.

Fading puppy syndrome or neonatal septicemia is usually caused by a *Streptococcus* infection acquired from a genital tract infection of the dam during delivery, through the milk, or an infection of the naval; *Staphylococcus* and other organisms have also been identified. Puppies are vigorous and nurse well after birth, but about 12–18 hours later, they suddenly fade away quietly. The highest onset occurs at 3–4 days, but deaths may occur up to 8 days.

Whereas fading puppy syndrome is caused by an infection resulting in the fading away of pups, hypothermia (or subnormal body temperature) is caused by external conditions and, in my opinion, also by internal factors, and it results in the same fading away of chilled pups.

The incident at the vet's surgery and the above-mentioned article cast my memory back to 1978 when, after having read his books, I visited Eberhard Trumler in his survey center in Germany. Before Trumler, G. Ewald coined the term *biotonus*. However, Trumler observed and studied the phenomenon in wolves, dingoes, several dog breeds, and hybrids of wild and domestic canines. He has proven that *all* normal pups and cubs are born with the same series of inherent drives; although in each individual there are differences in potential, they are all aimed at survival and activated by the instinct to survive.

The biotonus (or expression of the urge to live) demonstrated by a newborn puppy is the first manifestation of the survival imperative. Let me explain with an example. The newborn pup that—still sopping wet and dirty—squeaks terribly and desperately, attempts to follow his "heat detector," crawls toward the mother's breast, swallows a teat deep in his throat, and greedily starts to suck manifests a 100 percent biotonus. When newborn pups are dispersed in a circle around a warm water bag serving as a surrogate mother, they will start to move toward the heat source. Some of them are faster and crawl with more determination than others, depending on the intensity of their individual biotonus.

Pups and cubs are born with an incomplete nervous system that will develop further during their vegetative period. During these first days of life, they have no control of their body temperature. However, their bodies or a particular tactile-sensitive part of their bodies is sensitive to heat. Heat triggers the biotonus as a first demonstration of this complex instinctive system that aims to guarantee the survival of the species as an entirety and not the individual as such.

The schnauzer breeder must realize that during this vegetative period the pup, above all, needs his mother and the food and body warmth that she provides. Bruce Fogle, in *The Dog's Mind* (1990), also describes the pup's heat detector that instinctively directs him to the mother's teats and simultaneously to the safe and cozy warmth of a litter that flocks together. Regulating their individual body temperature is not yet possible; therefore, the instinctive "packing" together is essential and guarantees the necessary warmth. The breeder should observe and keep record of the early biotonus of each pup as this is a first indication of his future activity potential.

I am convinced that in some cases hypothermia resulting in pups who fade away is Mother Nature's early way of euthanasia with the purpose of combating a weak link in the chain of survival of the species. That is in my opinion the reason nature did not provide newborn pups with the ability to control their body temperature. If the combination of genes does not provide them with the necessary heat detection and the corresponding biotonus, they are doomed to fade away and die from exposure as they will not even be good enough to play a domestic role in the pack society.

In humans, it is hard to understand the above law of nature, let alone stand to apply it when we interfere with nature while breeding domesticated dogs. We should, however, learn that it is essential that we provide our pregnant domesticated canine with a kind of lair that gives the same comfort and coziness as the enclosure of a wild canine's den. A soft bed with a heating blanket or with infrared lamps hanging above it may, to human standards, evoke perfection. It is not, because in a den the dogs' body heat maintains the warm temperature, whereas heat simply disperses away from the luxurious bed. The ideal whelping bed is a type of covered, four-poster bed, with an adjustable curtain hanging over the entrance. Such an alcove provides the mother with coziness and the tranquility of semidarkness. At the same time, it gathers and keeps the natural body warmth produced by all the inhabitants. The adjustable curtain allows easy access to the mother and, at the same time, makes it possible to virtually close the entrance during the coolness of the night. After three weeks, the canopy can (subject to temperature conditions) be totally or semidismantled. I have applied this system for more than 500 puppies born in my house. I *never* used an infrared lamp nor a heating blanket, irrespective of the season or the country where the puppies were born. I never lost a single puppy through exposure.

Breeders interested in working breeds in the broad sense of the term should not even consider keeping pups alive artificially that under the above-described conditions and because of hypothermia desire to fade away and are disregarded by their mother. If such fading pups are artificially supported and do survive to become very docile and pleasant pets, they should be spayed or neutered and definitely *never* used for breeding purposes in order to avoid the spread of a basic and most principal lack of a natural instinct. In my opinion, a lack of biotonus implements a further lack of the drive to catch prey, an instinct that is not only essential for the wild canine but also of the same importance in view of the learning ability of the domesticated dog.

Stage 2—Transition Period

This period lasts only one week, the third week of life. During this time, the nervous system is being completed. The little eyes start opening individually, and a passage to the inner ear also appears. At the end of the week, we notice that the pups start to sniff and touch each other on purpose, showing the beginning of social behavior. Just as in a wild pack (when at the end of the third week the cubs demonstrate the desire to leave their lair for the first time) our pups will try to climb over the board of their whelping box. If the one that first shows the most determination to succeed is the same pup that demonstrated the highest biotonus, please keep an eye on that little individual (male or female)—that one will surprise you even more in the future. What we have to remember from the transition period is not only who made the greatest effort for an early social contact but also, especially, who was the first to tumble over the side panel of the whelping box to explore new territory.

Stage 3—Imprinting and Socialization Period

This is a very decisive period in a young dog's life. It starts at the beginning of the fourth week and ends at the end of the eleventh. In our case, *imprint* means exactly what the Oxford dictionary states: "impress on or in mind or memory." This period can be divided into substages.

Basic imprinting—submission. In order to ensure correct behavior within the pack, therefore guaranteeing the survival of the pack system, the golden rule—a submissive attitude toward the pack leader—must be indelibly imprinted at a very young age, the fourth week. This is why at this stage the pack leader initiates the formal education of his future co-hunters. He sometimes plays in such a rough manner with the young cubs that those that lack the natural instinct to adopt the *submissive position on their backs* or are not physically strong or fast enough to seek shelter in the den will not even survive the game. This is a crucial rule of natural selection: physical disability or weak elements are a burden in the pack. In addition, cubs that resist the natural inherent behavior of submission will cause future problems and have to be eliminated.

As far as schnauzers and all other domestic dogs are concerned, most will, unfortunately, not have a chance to play with their father as he is often not present. I have observed that *any sound adult male* will play the father's role if given the opportunity, and from the fourth week on, the mother will allow him to play with the pups. Ever since my understanding of the importance of this ritual, I have always allowed the father or a surrogate male to do so.

Further imprinting and socialization. The basic bond with peers is imprinted through social contact during the fourth through eighth weeks. The specific aim is that a pup should understand that he is a social pack animal that cannot survive as an individual. At the end of Week 7, the pup's brain is neurogically complete. Hopefully, he has not yet been damaged or conditioned by a bad environment.

Puppy testing, tattooing, and transfer. At this precise period in time—the eighth week—the puppy can be tested with the Personality Profile (discussed later in detail). It is also the ideal time to join his new family and home so that during further socialization he can transfer his loyalty to the permanent human pack partners.

Fear imprinting. The ninth, tenth, and eleventh weeks are the fear-imprinting period. Cubs in the wild are now old enough to leave the play area round the den where they were born. At the beginning of their wandering life with the pack, they have to be imprinted about the objects or subjects that they must fear and, therefore, must avoid—for example, man with his rifle or other predators.

The consequences of incorrect management. In the case of our schnauzers, any traumatic experience should be avoided during this period. For example, cropping or healing of cropped ears, careless shipping, and so forth. Above all, one must bear in mind that a genetically sound puppy, which has received the necessary and correct attention from the breeder, can during these early weeks be ruined for life by the new owners. For example, if one unconsciously *hits* a puppy during this period, he will remain wary of your hand, newspaper, or stick for the rest of his life.

To summarize, one must understand that littermates and pack members play a fundamental role in the socialization process. However, in the case of our schnauzers and all domestic dog breeds, socialization with humans and their crazy twentieth-century world is of paramount importance.

Let us consider the following question: What about the litter of schnauzers born and kept isolated in a backyard? They don't experience any *positive* imprinting! Instead, they have their ears chopped off at the age of six weeks.

The dam clarifies the pack hierarchy.

Loving attention begins human bonding.

Sibling play aids species identification and pack-dominance relationships.

They can't play—that is, socialize—properly with their brothers and sisters because their healing ear stumps are very sensitive. The only human they have seen is the person who feeds them. If they have tried to greet him by jumping against his trousers, he shouts and kicks at them. With this poor grounding, the memory of aching ears and the unfriendly man, they arrive at the age of eight weeks in a family with children, another dog, a cat, a motor car, a TV, a hi-fi set, and so forth. Luckily, there are four weeks of the imprinting and socialization period still to come.

If the new owners are understanding people with the feeling and necessary tact to educate the new arrival, this will partially make up for the past. However, if on the contrary, the new owners are as stupid as the breeder and kick the "stupid" puppy because of his clumsiness, then you have a perfect psychopath in the making.

The pup may have been born with the best inherent qualities; however, poor environment and an inadequate approach by man will prevent any possibility of this pup maturing as a well-adjusted schnauzer. The dog—or alternatively, the breed—will be blamed. Such a breeder will never admit that he is interfering with nature whilst lacking the most elementary knowledge of canine behavior and psychology.

The new owner, on his part, believes that the pedigree revealing illustrious parents is enough to guarantee a superior dog. He forgets that correct education is also of paramount importance. He should understand that whatever is put into the puppy will be harvested a hundredfold. He must make the input result in an output that satisfies his expectations. Never forget the magic formula: Heredity + Environment + Training = Final Result.

Early introduction to other animals is important for good future relationships.

Stage 4—Rank-Order Period

Cubs and pups—at the age of four, five, and six months—pass through their rank-order period, during which, depending on their inherent personalities, they develop a particular attitude, allowing them at a later stage a particular position on the social ladder of the pack. It is a period of sham fights with and intimidation of littermates or other dogs. It is the ideal way to find out if the latter is a coward or a chap that one will have to reckon with.

A good schnauzer should, during this period of life, try (at least a couple of times) to deliberately disobey and challenge his handler. I'm not joking! I'm very serious, because a schnauzer that does not behave in this way lacks the true schnauzer temperament. So, if your youngster at one stage or another raises his hackles, growls, and shows his teeth, it does not mean that he is a revolutionary—he just wants to test you. Under these circumstances, there is only one way to react, and that is the way of the pack leader: grab the subordinate by his neck and growl "No!" If you omit doing so or, even worse, if you are afraid to do so, your youngster will conclude that he is not your subordinate and will develop ambitions to become the pack leader. In particular, do not make this mistake when you are dealing with a dominant schnauzer male.

It is not only the potentially *dominant* schnauzer that will challenge the handler. The less dominant pup will also try. If in such a case *your attitude* is also that of a loser, you will really confuse the young dog. This youngster, which has not inherited the gifts of a pack leader and is by nature destined to play a subordinate role in the pack hierarchy, suddenly finds himself in a position without a pack leader. From a psychological point of view, this is a disaster, leaving you with an unstable dog, which in conflict situations will react in an unexpected or unfavorable way such as flight or fear biting.

Stage 5—Puberty Period

The puberty period runs from the seventh to the twelfth months of life. It is a further evolution of the rank-order period but with the accent on sexual behavior.

You should understand that throughout the periods of socialization, rank-order, and puberty, the accent is laid on

Let's go and greet Daddy.

Enak is embarrassed by so much recognition from his family.

He can't resist a kiss from his favorite son.

relationships and the development of natural qualities. Bearing this in mind and adapting the educational program of our schnauzer to these natural laws, we have every opportunity to succeed.

Once the household bylaws have been imprinted, it becomes time, already during the rank-order period, at the age of 5–6 months to start his formal training. There, he will experience and contact other dogs and people, contact that is absolutely necessary for a balanced social development at that age.

Owners who opt for working trials with their Giant Schnauzer should now start to develop the dog's nose work by elementary tracking. Don't forget that a six-month-old wolf is able to track prey. A schnauzer that is properly taught will be able to follow a human track at the age of six to seven months.

After the puppy class, where a basis for good social behavior has been laid, the way is open to all further obedience training.

Some lucky children grow up with their schnauzers.

This fortunate child socializes with four schnauzers.

Protection Training

To finish off this list of suggestions, I must hoist a banner for protection-work training. Very often one hears, "A dog should only be confronted with this kind of work on condition that he is fully under control—that is, obedience trained." Sorry, but this is nonsense!

A Giant Schnauzer or even a Standard Schnauzer with whom one intends to compete in working trials should be introduced to an *elementary* form of protection work at the stage that, from a social point of view, is most suitable. So, at the end of the rank-order period and the beginning of the puberty period, the drive to catch a prey is ever increasing, and even more important, the young dog is now looking for a challenge to develop his defensive behavior. It is, thus, the ideal moment to reward him with the challenge he is looking for.

Protection training should be done with knowledge and correct technique. First of all, the handler should act as a pack leader and give full support to the young dog. The youngster will, therefore, be prepared to stand his ground because he is backed by the pack leader. Second, the decoy should always act in such a manner that the young dog finishes each conflict as a winner, never pushing the youngster into a defensive avoidance attitude. In that way, training will strengthen the young schnauzer's self-confidence and personality. At an adult age, a schnauzer progressively trained for protection work will stand by his man in all circumstances.

My conclusion is, if you want to train your schnauzer for working trials and make him a perfect all-rounder, then his tracking, adaptability, and protection-work abilities should be developed simultaneously from a young age.

First of all, they learned to play, to love, and to walk with their handlers.

At five months, these Schnauzers had learned to be well-behaved and to follow the example of their sire.

At seven months, they stole the show in the puppy class at Pietermaritzburg
Kennel Club Championship show.

Eight months — will they be good enough to do the job of a security dog?

The first confrontation with the strangely behaving human.

His first bite is a good one.

A good security dog isn't afraid of threatening sticks.

Above: Challenger's Cobia, C.D.F., owned by C.H. Brown. *Photo © C.H. Brown.*
Inset: Head study of a salt-and-pepper Standard with uncropped ears. Ch. Argenta's Eleonore, Int. Ch., Klubsieger, and Champion in Sweden. Owned and bred by B. and M. Niklasson (Sweden).

9

Cosmetic Surgery

During my conversation with Pam and Charles, I had experienced Pam as a practical and objective person. Her question—"Why do schnauzers have their ears and tails shortened while other breeds don't have to undergo this operation?"—again confirmed my opinion.

History and Traditions

It is said that the docking of tails and the cropping of ears is an old tradition based on practicality. The original rural and farm-dog breeds led a rather rough type of life. Fights resulting in lacerated ears were not unusual. Cart wheels and slamming doors could easily damage tails that were not fast enough to get out of the way. So, the thought was, perhaps, that early prevention was better than the later cumbersome cure. Maybe this sounds acceptable, but it does not explain why, for example, schnauzers, Rottweilers, Bouvier des Flandres, Dobermans, Boxers, and so forth are docked and why most of the shepherd breeds, which are also farm dogs, don't fall under the knife.

A number of countries on several continents condone the cropping of dog ears and also, more recently, the docking of tails. We must, therefore, have a closer look at these practices. Let us first try to find out where the docking and cropping tradition comes from and how, for the schnauzer, it evolved in his country of origin.

The old nineteenth-century literature is not always consistent in regard to docking and cropping. Reichenbach, in his 1834 book, shows a drawing of two undocked and uncropped predecessors of our modern schnauzer. Other authors mention that the tails and ears of these dogs were *usually* cropped. In those days, however, one did not look for beauty but rather for practicality, and the mutilation mostly took place, without real harm, during the vegetative period. We have seen that during the first days of life the pup's nervous system is still unfinished, and the response to painful stimuli occurs at the reflex (spinal cord) level rather than the conscious (cerebral) level.

Subsequent to von Schmiedeberg's publication of the first breed standard in 1884 with the statement "tails are docked" and "ears are cropped," 99 percent of all schnauzers born in Germany (up to 1 January 1987) have been cropped and continue to be docked at present (January 1994).

As the schnauzer had, by the time that the first breed standard was published, made his entry into the breed ring,

it became necessary to crop both ears symmetrically. In this way, ear cropping obtained an aesthetic status, and the result became fashion. If one wanted symmetrical and identically erect ears, one could no longer operate on tails and ears at the same time. Breeders continued to dock tails on the third day of life, the ears were too small to guarantee symmetrical cropping. On the other hand, experience taught that the best chance of obtaining nice upright and equally cropped ears was to have the whole business, including the healing process, finished before teething at four months. It was also felt that it was the breeder's responsibility to have the ears cropped and allow healing before the pups were delivered to their new homes. So, in Germany and in most other countries where ear cropping became the accepted practice, it became customary to crop during the sixth or seventh week so that the pups could leave at the age of twelve weeks, after their ears healed.

Dewclaws are rudimentary inner toes, which correspond to our thumbs or big toes, but have, for the majority of our urban dogs, lost their utility due to lack of movement on all kinds of surfaces. The nails do not wear down, and they can grow into long, sharp-pointed sickles that can tear off by hooking into each other or by catching on branches or other obstacles.

But here again, we encounter discrepancy and lack of logic in dogdom. Because if one accepts dewclaw removal as a safety measure, their removal should then be applied to, at least, all working breeds. In contradiction therewith, some breed standards require the presence of double dewclaws on the rear pasterns—for example, French Shepherd Dogs. On the other hand, there is also the fact that for those breeds whose standards call for cat feet, a little aesthetic assistance, which removes these claws, accentuates the required compact foot and clean-legged appearance.

As far as our schnauzers are concerned, it is the general custom in the United States and Great Britain to remove dewclaws. On the Continent and in FCI-affiliated countries in general, one usually removes the dewclaws from the hind legs only, and the operation is seldom performed on the front legs.

Procedures

For the majority of today's schnauzer breeders, the beginning of the vegetative period is particularly important because of tail docking and dewclaw removal. Let me first explain to you why, if these mutilations have to be done, the third or fourth day of life is best. There are three main reasons.

- Amputation of the tail on the third or fourth day does not provoke real trauma or stress
- The colostrum provides antibodies against infection
- There are now enough clotting factors in the blood to prevent excessive bleeding

We may conclude that tail docking is a nearly harmless and safe operation when carried out during the vegetative period. In spite of this, as adult and rational creatures, we should ask why the schnauzer standard prescribes that tails be docked at the third caudal vertebra whereas the majority of other dog breeds are not subjected to such artificial cosmetic alterations.

Now that we have agreed on the age for surgery and understand why it is done, we must ask how it should be done. First of all, I must tell you that in spite of breed standard's prescriptions—such as the tails must be docked at the second or third caudal vertebra—it is utopian to believe that the operator can determine this place by feeling the intervertebral spaces on a squirming pup. It is much more a question of having a feeling for proportions, of knowing that, if one amputates that far away from the little bottom, it will at a later stage visually correspond with the third caudal vertebral level.

In my opinion, the technique frequently used for sheep and also used by some dog breeders, by which one ties the little tail with a rubber ring so that the blood circulation is cut off and the residue dies, is a drawn-out procedure. No, tail docking is work for an experienced veterinarian who has the necessary equipment at his disposal and can operate in the required hygienic circumstances.

The operator needs an assistant to hold the puppy and to pull the skin of the tail in the direction of the body with his thumb and index finger before cutting with a scalpel or surgical scissors. Once the tail is docked, the skin slides back and covers the stump, which must be stitched with absorbable sutures. This closes the wound immediately and brings the skin neatly over the stump. It is also advisable to use an antiseptic spray or powder over the wound. The dewclaws are removed with the same precautions. In all cases, one makes sure that all bleeding has stopped and that the stumps look dry before the mother is allowed to join her docked offspring.

It is my experience that immediately after this operation, the puppies are more restless and noisy than usual. They give the impression of having lost their rudders and don't know in which direction to move. This upsets the mother, and she sometimes has the tendency to lick the little stumps excessively. Of course, this is not ideal, for the wounds have to stay dry to ensure quick healing. If the mother is so upset, let the pups satiate themselves while you prevent the mother from licking. Then, take the bitch away for a walk. In the meantime, the pups will fall asleep. When the mother comes back a while later, she will find her offspring have calmed down, and she will take them back peacefully, without the urge to lick.

To conclude, one may say that tail docking during the vegetative period is a virtually painless operation, which has mainly an aesthetic purpose, solves a breeding problem by bringing external equality in an artificial way, and—at the same time—solves the problem of possible injury. However, as we will see further, it deprives a schnauzer of one of his main means of communication.

In the old days, the ear-cropping techniques were not as proficient as they are now. Most of the time, the breeder or specialized "croppers" carried out this task without any type of anesthetic. Two particular techniques achieved popularity.

The first technique used a sharp blade that was specially forged in an S-shape in order to provide the required curve to the cropped ear. The puppy's ear was held against a chopping block, the blade adjusted on the right spot, and the superfluous area was amputated with a blow.

The second technique made use of specially manufactured pincers that were fitted over the ear until the required outline was obtained. The pincers were then tightened with screws. Next, the part of the ear that projected was cut along the border of the curved pincers with a scalpel.

The second method has been adopted by most veterinarians who, over the last decades, have taken over cropping operations from breeders and croppers. The vets at least do the job under slight narcosis, in hygienic circumstances, and with sterilized equipment. Due to the fact that they work under narcosis, some vets simply draw a line where the ear is to be cut and then amputate. Where the croppers left the ears to heal by themselves, the vets now stitch the wounds and bandage them.

To Dock and Crop or Not

Dewclaws. Although the little dewclaws of most of our domesticated dogs are no longer really functional and may present a source of potential injury, this problem can be solved by cutting the nail tips on a regular basis to prevent their growing too long. Amputation of the dewclaws serves mainly an aesthetic purpose.

Tails. It is important that I present my point of view for consideration. We all know that dogs are extremely socially oriented creatures, and this means communication. How could a pack function without communication? Of course, voice is important, but even more important is the faculty of communicating through body language. Here, the carrying, the wagging and moving of the tail in general, plays a leading part. I don't believe that a docked schnauzer really feels frustrated when he admires the waving feathers of an Irish Setter, but somewhere, human intervention, for whatever false reason, has created a paradoxical situation. Moreover, short-tailed canines cannot, like their "complete" counterparts, cover and protect their genitals.

In all honesty, we must admit that there is only a fashion factor at work. If it were for usefulness, then *all* dogs' tails would have to be docked. It is a matter of fact that a short-docked tail accentuates a cobby structure as well as a short coupling. Nearly all short-docked breeds such as the schnauzer have the following prescriptions in their standards: "the length of the body should be equal to the height at the withers." But this is only a minor part of the aesthetic argument. In my opinion, there is an additional reason: by docking, one resolves a difficult breeding problem. Do you really believe that, if one should suddenly leave a hundred schnauzer puppies undocked, the adults would all carry an identical tail in the same manner? Big mistake! You would never have seen such a huge variety of wagging attributes. It is my conviction that in the very near future all those people involved in schnauzer breeding will—just like their colleagues in Sweden, Norway, and Denmark are already doing—have to produce a tremendous effort of selective breeding to obtain Miniature, Standard, and Giant Schnauzers that carry a homogeneous, breed-typical tail. If the schnauzer breeders of the last century had tackled the tail problem by selective breeding instead of solving it with a stroke of the knife, our human brains would never have had a chance to get accustomed to the fashion of stumps.

Ears. First of all, I must state here that the cheap argument that cropped ears would be less susceptible to ear infections is totally invalid. If I dare to make such a statement, it is simply based on my experience. In 1976, I decided to stop all cropping of schnauzers born in my house. Since then, I have continuously owned about ten schnauzers. We have bred over 400 puppies. We never had a single vet bill for treatment of an ear infection, and seldom was an ear infection reported by owners of the puppies we bred. Ear infection is common in dogs with a too-narrow ear canal and, especially, in breeds with heavy, hanging ears. An uncropped schnauzer ear does not correspond to either condition. Moreover, it is too simplistic to compare the cropped ear of a schnauzer with the natural-standing ear of any other breed. The earflap of a cropped ear is not as mobile and efficient as the earflap of a natural-standing ear. A cropped ear will collect dirt while playing or allow water to penetrate while swimming more than a natural-standing ear or a natural-hanging ear.

In addition, pups who have been cropped at six weeks can hardly be put through the puppy personality test at the age of seven weeks. (Would you consent to undergo physical and mental tests with twenty stitches in the remains of your ears?)

There is a modern trend toward having all pups tattooed for identification. One of the methods is to apply the tattoo number in the ear, and cropping also creates problems in this regard.

If cropping has to be done, the operation should take place after the fear-imprinting period, namely ad the end of the socialization period (near the end of the twelfth week). It should exclusively be carried out by an experienced veterinarian who knows the art of stitching up wounds to accelerate the healing process.

I have already pointed out that in the precynologic days puppies' ears were sometimes mutilated when they were only a couple of days old. It was only when dog showing became a hobby that the need arose to present the animal with symmetrically erect ears. Therefore, the period of cropping had to be postponed to at least the age of six weeks. The fanciers of those days were not aware of imprinting periods and socialization, and they could not have cared less.

Let us forget about all the cruelty related to ear cropping that has taken place over the past hundred years and suppose that, at present, *all* ear cropping were carried out under narcosis by veterinary surgeons. As such, the operation itself is painless. But, the stitches, the bandages, the two-to-three week healing process that takes place during the periods of fear imprinting and socialization can be of no benefit to the puppy. I simply would like to ask you: "In your opinion, which puppies will benefit the most during their socialization period? Those who can romp together without limitations, or those who have a series of stitches on each side of their heads and can't play without experiencing continuous pain?"

Nobody can pretend that the cropping of a schnauzer's ears is strictly necessary. Nobody can deny that it is always more-or-less cruel and that it is always performed for man's weakness for fashion. The ever-returning argument that a cropped schnauzer is more beautiful is absolutely subjective and irrelevant.

As a schnauzer breeder with long-standing experience with natural ears, I can assure you that cropping the ears, again, solves a couple of breeding problems. First of all, there is the problem of the correct V-shaped and correctly carried natural ear. Besides, there is the situation that a natural ear must be properly high set as cropping cannot compensate for it. Moreover, there is no camouflage or compensation for faults of the skull or of cheekiness. In other words, while selecting for correct natural ears, one consequently and simultaneously cares for a better-structured head.

To conclude, I can only give you my own conviction, which is based on a long-standing love and deep respect for the schnauzer. I had no real difficulty understanding that any cosmetic surgical intervention applied to a schnauzer for the sole purpose of artificially enhancing so-called beauty conflicts with the ethical principles that characterize a civilized society. Our only excuse might be that we did not initiate the process but that we were victims of the fashion of a bygone era. Pity enough, it has been proven again and again that the modern dog fancier, despite modern knowledge, is not prepared to reverse the process. Only regulations enforced by national kennel organizations or, even better, governmental laws have proven to be successful.

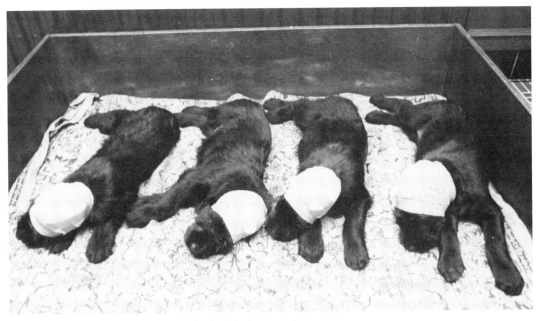

Stil sedated after the cropping operation, but back in the puppy box.

A miniature with cropped ears.

Below: To You, a miniature with natural ears, Ch. Travelmors (U.S.), bred by William Moore and owned by Pam Radford and Dorie Clark.

Pavo de la Steingasse Int. Ch. and champion in Mexico and America, a Standard with cropped ears owned by Margaret S. Smith (U.S.).

Elflein von Argenstein, a salt-and-pepper Giant with uncropped ears.

Argenta's Kimberly, at four months. Owned and bred by B. Niklasson, B. Andersson, and G. Garpas (Sweden).

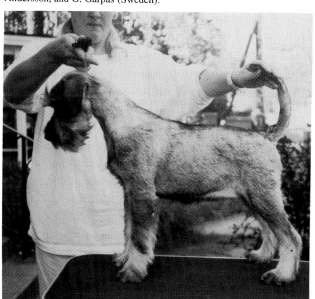

Mascar's Maegito, at seven months. Bred and owned by A. Radberg (Sweden).

Changing Values and New Laws

Based on the principle that whatever is created by God should not be mutilated by man, there have always been voices against tail docking and ear cropping fashionably practiced in some breeds.

Ear cropping was customary in Great Britain during the nineteenth century, and most of the fighting terrier breeds were mutilated in this way. The primitive techniques and inhuman methods connected with dog fighting must have contributed to the 1895 abolition of ear cropping by the Kennel Club (London). One must not forget that in those days dogdom was in the hands of the so-called higher classes, and none of their hounds or gundogs had ever been cropped. If poachers and villagers wanted to join the ranks of dog-show enthusiasts, they had to do so with terriers that could no longer be mutilated for low-class purposes. As such and in spite of the original opposition in the United Kingdom, very successful selection took place toward natural-standing or hanging ears. The Kennel Club was more lenient with regard to the docking of tails. Its relevant breed standards stipulating "tails customarily docked to . . ." left the choice to the fanciers who, as a general rule, have continued to dock. They have proven that they are in favor of this custom. They have difficulty visualizing the schnauzer with a natural tail, and they fanatically object against the introduction of any law prohibiting such cosmetic surgery. Most kennel clubs in countries sympathizing with the British Kennel Club soon enacted the same regulation.

It is amazing that, at the same time that cropping was banned in Great Britain, cropping gained popularity in most of the Continental countries. This can only be explained by the fact that the tradition of rural dog breeding and selection toward specific breeds was a long way behind. It was mainly between 1880 and 1920 that those types of dogs, which for many years had belonged to the rural population, made their way to the show ring, and the practice of ear cropping became the general rule. I base this statement on a study I made on the early development of the Bouvier des Flandres. While reading the judges' reports dated between 1900 and 1920, I could follow the process from half-erect ears, badly carried ears, over badly cropped ears to evenly cropped ears carried erect. While the British Kennel Club forced the fancier to obtain ear uniformity by selective breeding, the Continental national clubs left the door open for cropping. It is certain that cropping brought about uniformity faster, cropping techniques improved, and a fashion became established.

In spite of this, some Continental governments issued legislation by which, in regard to cruelty against animals, the cropping of dogs' ears became prohibited. Norway, Finland, Sweden, Denmark, and the Netherlands were the first to implement such laws. Switzerland followed later. In all other European countries, the practice of ear cropping continued to flourish. In the Netherlands, where cropping was prohibited by law, the fanciers simply took their pups to Germany or Belgium to be cropped. We know that, as far as schnauzers are concerned in their country of origin, compulsory cropping was imposed by the breed standard.

In 1963, the PSK became more lenient. The committee at its annual general meeting decided that cropped schnauzers should no longer be given preference over their uncropped counterparts. In other words, cropping was no longer compulsory, and the breed standards were adjusted accordingly. Two years later, in 1965, the PSK decided that the cropping of schnauzer puppy ears could only be done under anesthesia by a veterinary surgeon.

In 1972, the German government passed new legislation against cruelty toward animals. To the great relief of the majority of the German schnauzers fanciers, the prohibition of ear cropping was *not* enforced.

Over the past decades, the majority of the European countries have endeavored to form a joint government of independent states known as the European Community. At a 1986 meeting of the national delegates, proposals were submitted to introduce joint legislation with more extensive measures for the protection of pet animals.

On 13 November 1987, a meeting of the European Community in Strasbourg (France) put forth a bill that was signed by Belgium, Denmark, Germany, Greece, Italy, Luxemburg, the Netherlands, Norway, Portugal, Sweden, and Switzerland. The proposal of the *European Agreement for the Protection of Pet Animals* is summarized in the following paragraphs.

The preamble formulates the motivation on which principles the member states of the European Community have signed the joint agreement. Next to general consideration with regard to all animals, the preamble recognizes that man has the moral duty to respect all living creatures, and it emphasizes the special relationship that exists between man and his pets—

- In view of the importance of pets with regard to their contribution to the quality of life and their consequent value for society
- In view of the implication that the holding of a too large number of pets can have on the hygiene, health, and safety of man and other animals
- Considering that the holding of wild animals as pets should not be encouraged
- Being aware that pets are not always kept in conditions that are to the advantage of their health and welfare
- Stating that the attitude toward pets is often very divergent, sometimes because of lack of knowledge and consciousness
- Considering that a fundamental joint attitude with regard to the keeping and the practice and leading to responsible ownership of pets is not only a desirable but a real aim

The first chapter of the agreement defines pet animals, trade in pet animals, stray animals, appropriate authorities, and so forth. Chapter Two points out the principles related to the holding of pets, which is guided by the fundamental principle that nobody has the right to allow a pet to suffer or to create unnecessary pain. It explains the obvious conditions in which pets should be kept, and it gives instruction with regard to their breeding, acquisition, training, trade, commercial breeding, kennels, and pet shelters. It also deals with publicity, amusement, shows, and competitions in which pets are involved as well as the capture of stray animals, killing, and euthanasia.

Article 10 addresses surgical interventions and reads as follows:

1. Surgical interventions aimed at changing the exterior of a pet or for other noncurative purposes are prohibited and in particular
   a. The docking of the tail
   b. The cropping of the ears
   c. The section of vocal cords
   d. The removal of nails and teeth
2. Exception to these prohibitive regulations can only be accepted in the event that a veterinary surgeon states that a noncurative intervention is required for medical reason
   a. To the benefit of a particular animal
   b. To prevent procreation

The member states that have signed the agreement can accept it in its totality or, depending on local circumstances, apply exceptions to a particular clause or clauses.

On 1 April 1987, West Germany accepted the bill but excluded the clause prohibiting the docking of tails. The date to go into effect was 1 January 1988, and since then, it has been illegal to crop schnauzers' ears. After the unification of East and West Germany, the provisions became binding for all Germany beginning on 1 July 1989.

Sweden, Norway, and Finland and more recently (the second half of 1991) Denmark and the Netherlands implemented the European Community agreement, including the clause prohibiting tail docking, and Switzerland implemented the same rule in 1993.

This matter has been discussed for the first time at the 28 October 1989 International Schnauzer and Pinscher Union (ISPU) Congress in Germany. The congress has subsequently suggested that, in countries where tail docking is prohibited by law, the breeders should strive for a *saber tail*—a tail carried either upward or downward in a gently or slightly curved fashion.

At the congress held on 15–16 November 1991, the matter received even more attention. There were proposals to amend the breed standards accordingly. After discussion, it was felt that as long as Germany, as the country of origin, has not taken a final decision and that other countries are still waiting to take a final stand, no premature changes of the breed standards should be made.

At the moment (January 1994), it is a matter of fact that the last word has not been said. We may, however, accept that within the framework of Western European civilization the custom of cropping dogs' ears is on the way to extinction. In the event that, after the first trial period of five years, more countries apply the ban on tail docking, this fashion could also disappear. Whatever the final decisions, we may foresee that important changes will be made to the breed standards and that by the year 2000 the general appearance of the schnauzer, in many cases, will have changed dramatically.

Of course, we do not know if other countries will follow the European example and tighten up their legislation with regard to protection of pets. One could presume that in the event that Germany and the FCI change the schnauzer breed standards, other countries that are not FCI affiliates could consider the same changes. If this does not happen and, for example, docking and cropping continues on the North American scene, it will hardly be avoidable that this would result in a split of the breed. On the one hand, there would be the docked and cropped American schnauzer as opposed the European schnauzer with all his appendages. The contrast will be even more accentuated because of the American preference for a too long and, often, too soft coat.

Gipsy van't Wareheim, Ch. Belgium (Miniature). Owned by Y. and R. Coucke (Belgium).

Tamarack Miniature Schnauzer puppies. Bred by M. and B. Gale (South Africa).

10

Which Puppy Shall I Choose?

"Well, Pam and Charles, from what we have already explored, you will understand that choosing a puppy cannot be done in a minute or during a certain mood. Two criteria usually prevail when one has to choose a pup in a litter. First, are you looking for a puppy with show or breed-ring quality? Second—a more important and broader criteria— does the puppy fit you, your expectations, your family, and your surroundings? Here, the dog's exterior plays only a secondary role; character, temperament, and general behavior are more important."

From this point of view, it is very important to decide whether or not you should acquire a dog, then to determine the breed that suits you, and finally to select the pup carrying the most suitable potential to meet your expectations. It is of paramount importance that you confer with the breeder and explain in detail your requirements and how you intend to live with your dog.

With all respect, only an honest breeder with a thorough knowledge of dog and puppy behavior, who has watched the pups from the start, will be able to advise and assist in your choice. During recent decades, some dog fanciers have developed specific puppy tests with the idea of finding out who will suit who.

J. R. Toman, a well-known Dutch trainer of police dogs and author on this subject, insists that the future handler should first define, quite honestly, to which of the following character types he belongs:

Sanguinicus (temperamental)
Cholericus (short tempered)
Melancholicus (irresolute)
Phlegmaticus (indifferent)

Toman also classifies dogs into four character types:

Leader   = L
Docile   = D
Indifferent = I
Anxious   = A

In Toman's experience, the following character combinations give the best results:

Sanguinicus   + type L of both sexes + type D male
Cholericus   + type D of both sexes
Melancholicus   + type D female or type I male
Phlegmaticus   + type I of both sexes

An anxious type *(A)* may become a lovely pet, but from Toman's point of view as a trainer, this type of dog is unsuitable for any type of work. In my opinion, as far as schnauzers are concerned, an anxious or nervous type, even if it is a show winner, should never be used in a breeding program.

I truly believe that each serious breeder should subject all litters to some form of puppy test. By doing so, the breeder obtains two types of information. First, he is able to reach a conclusion about the general character quality of his breeding results; frequent occurrence of nervous pups is a warning to change parent combinations or even bloodlines. Second, the breeder is able to catalog the pups and individually match them with a particular type of buyer.

In 1975, William Campbell published *Behavior Problems in Dogs,* in which he describes a very interesting puppy test. The idea of puppy testing, especially since Campbell's findings, has gained enormous popularity among well-advised breeders.

Campbell's test has been extended and perfected, and in my opinion, the test elaborated by Wendy Volhard is essential and should be performed by all breeders before their puppies leave for new homes. An article describing the Volhard test is reprinted here.

Puppy Personality Profile

1. Excitability vs. Inhibitability: This trait is an inherited tendency which in the excitable dog makes him extremely responsive to external stimuli. Field trial retrievers are selected for this trait because they need to be constantly aware of the hunt, the fall of the bird, etc.

The inhibited dog shows more self control. This dog is more easily trained to react only upon certain cues. Campbell cites the Schutzhund German Shepherd as an example.

The balance between excitability and inhibitability is a poised, assured dog. The extreme of excitability would be a wild uncontrollable dog. The extreme of inhibitability would be the withdrawn, rigid and lethargic dog.

2. Active vs. Passive Defense Reflexes: This trait is the inherited tendency to react to stress by biting, freezing or running away. The dog with passive defense reflexes can be induced to bite only with difficulty or under extreme duress.

The field trial retriever has been selected for passive defense reflex so as to avoid killing wounded birds, etc. On the other hand, the Schutzhund Shepherd has been selected for active defense reflexes so he can easily be trained for protection. This is combined with his tendency towards inhibitability and allows the owner to train the dog to attack only in specific situations.

From Melissa Bartlett, "Puppy Personality Profile," *Pure-Bred Dogs,* March, 1979; reproduced by kind permission of the author.

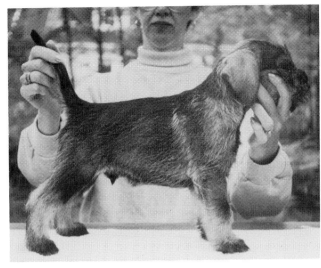

Argenta's Lavinia, at eleven months. Bred by B. Niklasson, B. Andersson, and G. Garpas (Sweden); owned by G. Bergsvist (Sweden).

Argenta's Kipling, at eight weeks.

Between eight and ten weeks, the breed connoisseur can make a fairly accurate evaluation of a puppy's potential show quality. This puppy has a nicely proportioned head, perfect topline, prominent forechest and chest reaching the elbows, slightly tucked-up underline, and strong legs as well as good, balanced angulation. The puppy already gives the impression of cobbiness, and above all, his coat is harsh and straight. All in all, he is a very attractive show prospect.

Which puppy shall I choose?

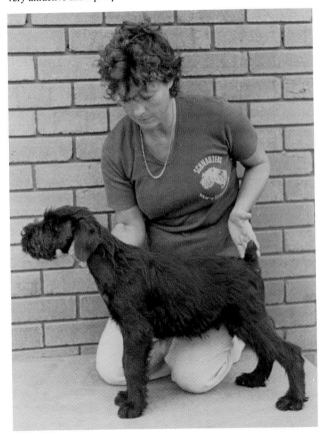

3. Dominant vs. Submissive: The dominant dog is the one which would grow up to be the pack-leader if he and the other puppies had been left to grow up on their own in the wild. He shows the behavioral tendency to dominate. This trait is expressed by biting, growling, mounting, direct eye contact, walking with head up, tail up, hackles up, etc. The dominant dog will have first pick of the food, places to sleep, etc. Dominance has been selected for in Fox Terriers, originally bred to drag foxes from their dens.

As Campbell points out, the dominant dog may challenge his human master and needs consistent, firm, calm handling. Lack of leadership on the owner's part with such a dog will result in the dog's assuming leadership. A dog's attempts to lead in today's hectic, complex society usually result in maladaptive responses such as overprotectiveness, nervousness, refusal to obey, and interfering with owner's interactions with other people.

Submissiveness is evident in the dog which accepts leadership. This is expressed in behavioral terms as nudging with the nose, pawing, tail down, ears down, lack of fighting, crouching and rolling over on the back, lack of eye contact, submitting to command. This dog can be influenced easily by the leader. This trait has been selected for in Spaniels who were originally bred to crouch while hunters shot or netted the birds.

The submissive dog generally responds to training and readily accepts a human leader. The extremely submissive dog on the other hand, which reacts to the slightest stress by crouching or tail-tucking may be difficult to train. A lot of encouragement and very gentle handling is needed to build confidence and to help it adapt to the stresses of living in the average household.

4. Independence vs. Social Attraction: The independent dog is not interested in human beings. He may be poorly socialized or simply a loner. This dog may work or hunt well on his own. This trait was selected for in the Basenji, for Example, a dog which originally hunted along with a bell around its neck; the humans followed the sound of the bell to the game.

The socially attracted dog shows an interest in people, enjoys being petted, follows human beings easily, and in general wants to be where they are. Poodles have been selected for this trait. They are turned into people and make good pets for this reason, which may explain why they have been number 1 in registrations for the last 18 years.

It is obvious that the combination of traits or tendencies with which a puppy is born will go into its temperament. The particular combination will result in a dog more suited for some things than others. For example, just because the dog has active defense reflexes doesn't mean he will be a good guard dog. If he is highly excitable and very independent, this dog may respond to any and all stimuli, be unresponsive to training, and also bite under the slightest stress.

In addition, Humphrey and Warner in their book *"Working Dogs"* suggest two other important inherited characteristics.

1. Sound sensitivity: The sound sensitive dog shows excessive fear, crouching, urinating, running away when confronted with a loud or sharp sound; the dog may over-react to gunshots, shouted commands, etc.

2. Touch sensitivity vs. insensitivity: The touch sensitive dog will be difficult to train with the standard training collar because the correction-snap sets off the dog's defense reflexes (biting, freezing or running away).

The touch insensitive dog shows little response to physical stimuli. A mighty yank of the training collar yields little, if any response. Touch insensitivity was selected for in the pit-fighting dogs in order for them to continue fighting despite severe wounds.

What is commonly called a "hard" dog is often a combination of dominance and touch insensitivity. This dog shows a strong tendency to lead, and will be difficult to train. When the owner attempts to assert himself through a corrective snap on the training collar, the dog doesn't respond because it cannot feel the collar. To get results, the owner will have to resort to more forceful methods of correction, or use a different stimulus.

Environment plays a tremendous part in developing a dog's potential. As Dr. Michael Fox puts it in "Understanding Your Dog";

"Genetic factors are transmitted by inheritance, but the traits themselves are modified by genetic and environmental factors. Training and early experience greatly influence these traits. . . ."

Clarence Pfaffenberger was able to put the critical stages of puppy development into practical application in the breeding program of Guide Dogs for the Blind. He used Scott and Fuller's research and supplemented it with specially developed puppy tests to pinpoint the potential guide dogs in a litter of approximately 8 weeks of age. Through planned breeding, careful attention to development, and puppy testing he raised the percentage of successful guide dogs in the breeding program from 9% to 90%.

An experiment of Clarence Pfaffenberger's, for example, demonstrates the importance of early socialization. After testing the population of 154 puppies who were all trained later for guide work he found: "of the puppies who had passed their tests and been placed in homes in the first week after the conclusion of the tests, ninety percent became guide dogs; those who were in the kennel more than one week and less than two weeks faired [sic] almost but not quite as well; those left in the kennel more than two weeks but less than three, showed only about 57% guide dogs; of those who were in the kennel more than three weeks after the tests, only 30% became guide dogs." ("The New Knowledge of Dog Behavior.") The break in socialization between testing and placing at this critical point (after 7–8 weeks) resulted in dogs who could not take the responsibility for a blind master, while their litter mates whose socialization had not been interrupted, succeeded at the task.

By using Campbell, Pfaffenberger and Working Dogs, the Volhards developed a system for testing puppies which would 1) indicate the dog's basic temperament traits and 2) indicate the dog with the most obedience potential.

All of Campbell's tests are included since these are indicators of how the pup will adapt to living with human beings. Most of the dogs in the U.S. today are first and foremost family companions, a fact which seems to have been largely ignored by breeders of show, field trial, and guard dogs.

There are three tests which are from Pfaffenberger to indicate the aptitude the puppy has for obedience work. (Pfaffenberger describes a number of other tests indicative of aptitude for guide work where it is critical that a dog be able to make intelligent decisions in response to unexpected situations.) If he is guiding a blind master, his master's life may depend upon it. This ability is not a matter of life and death in the obedience ring, although exhibitors sometimes seem to think so. One test is from Working Dogs, where in 1934, a test was suggested for touch sensitivity in the German Shepherd. A slightly modified version is included in the Volhard tests.

The Results is [sic] called the Puppy Aptitude Test (PAT), since it indicates which pup has the most aptitude for the desired task or purpose. The test is administered in a standard fashion to minimize human error. Conditions under which testing takes place are as follows:

1) Ideally, puppies are tested in the 7th week, preferably the 49th day. At 6 weeks or earlier the puppy's neurological connections are not fully developed. (If the test is conducted between 8-10 weeks, the puppy is in the fear imprint stage and special care must be taken not to frighten it.)

2) Puppies are tested individually, away from dam and litter mates, in an area new to them and relatively free from distractions. It could be a porch, garage, living room, yard or whatever. Puppies should be tested before a meal when they are awake and lively and not on a day when they have been wormed or given their puppy shots.

3) The sequence of the tests is the same for all pups and is designed to alternate a slightly stressful test with a neutral or pleasant one.

4) There is less chance for human error, or the puppies being influenced by a familiar person, if the tests are administered by someone other than the owner of the litter. A friend of the owner, or the prospective buyer can easily learn to give the test.

5) I found it helpful to arrange the tests in a concise chart form following the order in which they are given. In addition, since I found it difficult to use Campbell's scoring code, I simply gave each response a number. While testing numerous puppies, the Volhards found that a number of puppies showed responses not on Campbell's test. These

observations are included in the test with an apostrophe in order to differentiate them from Campbell's original tests. The Pfaffenberger tests were also given a number so that all scores can be compared and a chart was devised for checking a puppy's total performance at a glance.

6) Also included in the Obedience Aptitude Tests is a section on structure. Over 60 breeds conform to what is called "conventional body type," that is 45 degree shoulder layback and 90 degree angulation front and rear. The greater the deviation from this norm, the less efficiently the dog will be able to perform obedience exercises. Other impediments to efficiency are HD, cowhocks, eastie-westie feet, crossing in front or rear when gaiting. A simple guide to follow for puppies at this age (7–8 weeks) is "what you see is what you get" notwithstanding the all-too-familiar assurance "don't worry, he'll grow out of it." Be particularly wary of the statement, "he's not much of a conformation dog but he'll do fine in obedience." This could mean the dog is perhaps mismarked or has light eyes but is structurally sound. However, often it means that the dog has a serious structural fault. This dog will be unable to take the strenuousness of training and competing in the obedience ring. If you feel that evaluating structure accurately is above your head, seek competent help.

7) Last but not least, the prospective puppy testor [sic] must have a chance to observe the parents of the litter, preferably both parents but at least the dam. If the sire and/or dam have characteristics which are not desirable there exists a good chance some, if not all, of the puppies will have inherited these undesirable traits.

The safest and easiest thing to do when faced with parent dogs of undesirable temperament is simply to look for another litter of pups whose sire and dam more closely conform to your ideals. If you must have a pup from this litter pay particular attention to the test scores of the litter and do not select a pup which shows any tendency towards undesirable traits.

Interpretation of Scores

—**Mostly 1's:** This dog is extremely dominant and has aggressive tendencies. He is quick to bite and is generally considered not good with children and elderly. When combined with a 1 or 2 in touch sensitivity, will be a difficult dog to train. Not a dog for the inexperienced handler; takes a competent trainer to establish leadership.

—**Mostly 2's:** This dog is dominant and can be provoked to bite. Responds well to firm, consistent, fair handling in an adult household, and is likely to be a loyal pet once it respects its human leader. Often has bouncy, outgoing temperament; may be too active for elderly, and too dominant for small children.

—**Mostly 3's:** This dog accepts humans as leaders

The following is a concise chart explaining each test and the scoring, a sample score sheet and an interpretation of the scores:

TEST	PURPOSE	SCORE	
SOCIAL ATTRACTION: Place puppy in test area. From a few feet away the testor coaxes the pup to her/him by clapping hands gently and kneeling down. Testor must coax in a direction away from the point where it entered the testing area.	Degree of social attraction, confidence or dependence.	Came readily, tail up, jumped, bit at hands.	1
		Came readily, tail up, pawed, licked at hands.	2
		*Came readily, tail up.	3
		Came readily, tail down.	4
		Came hesitantly, tail down.	5
		Didn't come at all.	6
FOLLOWING: Stand up and walk away from the pup in a normal manner. Make sure the pup sees you walk away.	Degree of following attraction. Not following indicates independence.	Followed readily, tail up, got underfoot, bit at feet.	1
		Followed readily, tail up, got underfoot.	2
		*Followed readily, tail up.	3
		Followed readily, tail down.	4
		Followed hesitantly, tail down.	5
		No follow or went away.	6
RESTRAINT: Crouch down and gently roll the pup on his back and hold it with one hand for a full 30 seconds.	Degree of dominant or submissive tendency. How it accepts stress when socially/physically dominated.	Struggled fiercely, flailed, bit.	1
		Struggled fiercely, flailed.	2
		*Settled, struggled, settled with some eye contact.	3
		Struggled then settled.	4
		No struggle.	5
		*No struggle, straining to avoid eye contact.	6
SOCIAL DOMINANCE: Let pup stand up and gently stroke him from the head to back while you crouch beside him. Continue stroking until a recognizable behavior is established.	Degree of acceptance of social dominance. Pup may try to dominate by jumping and nipping or is independent and walks away.	Jumped, pawed, bit, growled.	1
		Jumped, pawed.	2
		*Cuddles up to testor and tries to lick face.	3
		Squirmed, licked at hands.	4
		Rolled over, licked at hands.	5
		Went away and stayed away.	6
ELEVATION DOMINANCE: Bend over and cradle the pup under its belly, fingers interlaced, palms up and elevate it just off the ground. Hold it there for 30 seconds.	Degree of accepting dominance while in position of no control.	Struggled fiercely, bit, growled.	1
		Struggled fiercely.	2
		*No struggle, relaxed.	3
		Struggled, settled, licked.	4
		No struggle, licked at hands.	5
		*No struggle, froze.	6
RETRIEVING: Crouch beside pup and attract his attention with crumpled up paper ball. When the pup shows interest and is watching, toss the object 4-6 feet in front of pup.	**OBEDIENCE APTITUDE** Degree of willingness to work with a human. High correlation between ability to retrieve and successful guide dogs, obedience dogs, field trial dogs.	Chases object, picks up object, and runs away.	1
		Chases object, stands over object, does not return.	2
		Chases object and returns with object to testor.	3
		Chases object and returns without object to testor.	4
		Starts to chase object, loses interest.	5
		Does not chase object.	6
TOUCH SENSITIVITY: Take puppy's webbing of one front foot and press between finger and thumb lightly then more firmly till you get a response, while you count slowly to 10. Stop as soon as puppy pulls away, or shows discomfort.	Degree of sensitivity to touch.	8-10 counts before response.	1
		6-7 counts before response.	2
		5-6 counts before response.	3
		2-4 counts before response.	4
		1-2 counts before response.	5
SOUND SENSITIVITY: Place pup in the center of area, testor or assistant makes a sharp noise a few feet from the puppy. A large metal spoon struck sharply on a metal pan twice works well.	Degree of sensitivity to sound. (Also can be a rudimentary test for deafness.)	Listens, locates sound, walks toward it barking.	1
		Listens, locates sound, barks.	2
		Listens, locates sound, shows curiosity, and walks toward sound.	3
		Listens, locates the sound.	4
		Cringes, backs off, hides.	5
		Ignores sound, shows no curiosity.	6
SIGHT SENSITIVITY: Place pup in center of room. Tie a string around a large towel and jerk it across the floor a few feet away from puppy.	Degree of intelligent response to strange object.	Looks, attacks and bites.	1
		Looks, barks and tail-up.	2
		Looks curiously, attempts to investigate.	3
		Looks, barks, tail-tuck.	4
		Runs away, hides.	5
STRUCTURE: The puppy is gently set in a natural stance and evaluated for structure in the following categories: Straight front Front angulation Straight rear Croup angulation Shoulder layback Rear angulation (See diagram to right)	Degree of structural soundness. Good structure is necessary.	The puppy is correct in structure.	good
		The puppy has a light fault or deviation.	fair
		The puppy has an extreme fault or deviation.	poor

Straight front   Straight rear   Shoulder layback   Front angulation   Croup angulation   Rear angulatic

easily. Is best prospect for the average owner, adapts well to new situations and is generally good with children and elderly, although may be inclined to be active. Makes a good obedience prospect and usually has common sense approach to *[sic]* live.

—**Mostly 4's:** This dog is submissive and will adapt to most households. May be slightly less outgoing and active than a dog scoring mostly 3's. Gets along well with children generally and trains well.

—**Mostly 5's:** This dog is extremely submissive and needs special handling to build confidence and bring him out of his shell. Does not adapt well to change and confusion and needs a very regular, structured environment. Usually safe around children and bites only when severely stressed. Not a good choice for a beginner since it frightens easily, and takes a long time to get used to new experiences.

—**Mostly 6's:** This dog is independent. He is not affectionate and may dislike petting and cuddling. It is difficult to establish a relationship with him whether for working or for pet. Not recommended for children who may force attention on him; he is not a beginner's dog.

A) When combined with 1's, especially in restraint; the independent dog is likely to bite under stress.

B) When combined with 5's the independent dog is likely to hide from people, or freeze when approached by a stranger.

No clear pattern: (several 1's, 2's and 5's). This dog may not be feeling well. Perhaps just ate or was recently wormed. Wait two days and retest. If the test still shows wide variations (lots of 1's and 5's) he is probably unpredictable and unlikely to be a good pet or obedience dog.

TIPS

3 in social attraction and social dominance:
The socially attracted dog is more easily taught to come and is more cuddly and friendly. Its interest in people can be a useful tool in training, despite other scores.

1 in restraint and 1 in touch sensitivity:
The dominant aggressive dog, insensitive to touch will be a handful to train and extremely difficult for anyone other than an exceptionally competent handler.

5 in stability:
This is likely to be a "spookey" dog which is never desirable. It requires a great deal of extra work to get a spooky dog adapted to new situations and they generally can't be depended upon in a crisis.

5 in touch and sound sensitivity:
May also be very "spooky" and needs delicate handling to prevent the dog from becoming frightened.

In conclusion, I would like to say that I am grateful for having had an opportunity to observe Puppy Aptitude Testing and I mean to present this article much in the same manner as the Volhards presented it to me, not a gospel but as one way of matching the right dog with the right owner.

With the soaring number of unwanted pets. I feel it is important to be able to select a pet which is likely to fit the owner's needs and adapt to complexities of modern life. It is important for the prospective buyer to have a tool to recognize what he is seeing.

Most people would never dream of buying a car because "it was the nicest color" but many people will buy a puppy because it "has the best markings." I shudder to think what most parents would say if their daughter told them she would marry the first man to walk up to her on the street, but they would think nothing of it if she picked a puppy because it was the first out of the whelping box. This puppy may be the right choice, then again, it may not, depending on what other traits make up its temperament. Hopefully, the PAT will help the prospective buyer make a more educated choice.

The PAT can also be tailored to needs of the breeder. In the case of the Volhards, the aptitude tests were developed to show obedience potential. It would be easy enough to test for aptitude in other areas such as field trial work, scent hound work, sheep herding, (see Fox, 1972) and so forth. Testing puppies is certainly not a new idea—Fortunate Fields in 1934 describes puppy tests for the working G.S.D.

The breeder would use the information in the PAT not only to help determine which pup is most suited for which home but also to determine what temperament to select for. An example might be a breeding of an extremely sensitive but very socially attracted bitch with a medium sensitive but independent stud hoping for medium sensitive puppies which accepted leadership and liked people. However, this combination could produce extremely sensitive independent puppies, exactly the opposite of the desired result. The breeder could, by testing the puppies determine which characteristics each puppy had inherited and then breed only from puppies possessing the desired combination.

In the final analysis, owning and training a dog can and should be a joy. Much of this goal is achieved through hard work, but is infinitely easier by starting out with the right dog. Whether the PAT is used by a breeder, buyer, or trainer, I hope it will help contribute to a successful experience in dog ownership.

Puppy Kennel

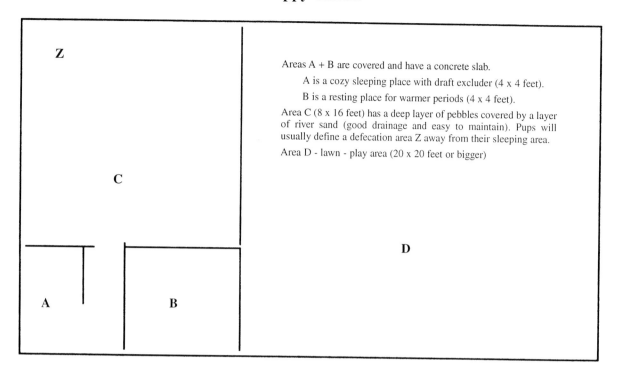

Areas A + B are covered and have a concrete slab.

    A is a cozy sleeping place with draft excluder (4 x 4 feet).

    B is a resting place for warmer periods (4 x 4 feet).

Area C (8 x 16 feet) has a deep layer of pebbles covered by a layer of river sand (good drainage and easy to maintain). Pups will usually define a defecation area Z away from their sleeping area.

Area D - lawn - play area (20 x 20 feet or bigger)

Edith Gallant and some of her Giant Schnauzers.

Introduce children to the new puppy by having them sit quietly on the floor or ground beside the pup. Teach them to support the puppy carefully with both arms when picking him up. Never leave young children with a young puppy unattended.

11

The Big Day—Your Schnauzer Puppy Arrives

The fact that Pam and Charles had decided to acquire a schnauzer left me with no other option but to inform them about some basic preparations and principles one should consider before the puppy arrives.

Are You Duly Prepared?

Although it is essential to be mentally well prepared, from a practical point of view, one must also be physically prepared. A dog is a pack animal whose way of life is largely defined by acquired habits. Once a habit is entrenched, it is terribly difficult, at a later stage, to modify it. In particular, the "imprints" experienced during youth are virtually indelible. Therefore, one must make sure that the habits that develop during the first weeks of the puppy's stay in its new environment correspond with the way of live that you will expect and tolerate later. This means that the new owner and his whole family must make up their minds beforehand as to what will be permitted and what will be forbidden to the new dog. If, in your opinion, the young schnauzer is allowed to jump on the sofa and sleep on your daughter's bed, that is your business. One should, however, never apply the following reasoning: "Ah! The puppy is so sweet, let him sleep on the bed. We will put him in the kennel when he is older." Big mistake! My best advice is that the whole family discuss and agree upon laws and regulations before your schnauzer arrives. These rules must be adhered to from the first minute the puppy enters into your life.

Every future dog owner should decide beforehand about the following: the resting place in the house, the feeding and drinking area, and the territory.

The Resting Place
This should be a spot out of any draft where the dog's basket or cushion will have a permanent place. It is important that this corner is out of the way of all normal human traffic in the house, but at the same time, the dog must be able to observe his other (human) pack fellows. Generally, "Doggy" is sent to this place when the family is eating, he is in the way, he comes in the house with wet paws, and so forth.

In general, a young dog that is sleeping in his particular resting place must be left alone. This youngster needs rest, and children or adults interfering with or teasing a young dog while resting should be reprimanded.

My advice regarding the purchase of bedding is an oval basket in hard plastic or fiberglass (cannot be chewed) large enough for the full-grown schnauzer.

In the basket, you can lay a triple-folded blanket or cushion that can easily be washed. Ordinary cushions are easily ripped apart. Foam-rubber cushions absorb the moisture from the dog's coat as well as from the air, often resulting in a damp bed.

Feeding and Drinking Area
The best buy is a set of two stainless steel dishes suited to the size of your schnauzer, fitting in a stand so that they cannot be overturned and, by adjusting their height, will allow the dog to eat without spreading his legs. This set should be placed in a spot where the schnauzer will not be disturbed and where it is easy to clean under and around the stand.

As a general rule, a dog who is eating should be left alone. Children or adults who tease a dog at this time should be punished. It is your responsibility to use authority at that moment, otherwise the punishment will be inflicted by the dog himself sooner or later.

By law of nature, forged in the pack over thousands of years, the group eats together, but the threshold to open active aggression is exceeded when jealousy around the prey (food) occurs. So, if you want to be a pack partner and you ignore such an elementary law or interfere with your partner's part of the prey, you must be prepared for the consequences.

The Territory
It is of paramount importance that a young schnauzer, with the help of his handler (pack leader) explores and defines his territory. By law of nature, a territory should be progressively explored and respected. A schnauzer who learns the boundaries of his territory will not become a wanderer. At the same time, he will develop that natural sense of responsibility to watch and warn of intruders in the territory and even to guard and protect it if necessary. If your property is properly fenced, this will easily be considered the boundary. However, if this fence if not puppy proof and the youngster finds the opportunity to explore neighboring grounds, he will consider them a logical extension of the territory, particularly when in his rank-order period he discovers companions and bonds with them.

It is very important to teach your pup how far he can go and make it clear to him that your gate, even when open, represents the limit. Chasing after running children, bicycles, and motorcycles must be nipped in the bud. When such habits related to the drive to catch prey develop at a young age, you will never eradicate them, and you dog will take advantage of any occasion to break the rules of the boundaries and chase fleeing prey. You should rather teach your schnauzer to react only when strangers enter the property (his territory). You will find that his reaction is strongest in the center or heart of the territory—that is, the location of the sleeping area. A youngster, when strongly confronted at the boundary of his territory will normally avoid direct conflict. If the opponent continues his threat and comes forward, the youngster will back off in the direction of his sleeping place. During the retreat, his courage will grow proportionally, and the avoiding attitude will shade into an aggressive attitude. It is important as a dog owner to be aware of such natural laws.

If a young schnauzer, while developing his sense of guarding property, is supported by his pack leader, the threshold of protective reaction will become closer and closer to the territory boundary.

Another law of nature states that a stranger who performs the necessary submission and greeting ritual to the pack leader can be accepted in the pack as a guest. Again, a dog handler should be aware of this and play the game. In this way, visitors will, after the greeting ceremony, be accepted and treated with respect. I truly believe that it is not only much easier to educate a young dog but also much more enriching when one understands the dog's natural drives, customs, and laws that must be obeyed. For the greeting ritual, a dog greets the pack superior by a submissive mouth-nose nudging. Thus, it is completely natural that your young schnauzer, wishing to greet you respectfully as the senior pack member, tries to reach your face, and because you have decided to walk on your hindquarters, the dog must jump up against you. So, if you don't want, at a later stage, to possess a full-grown schnauzer who, each time you come home, plants his wet front paws on the door of your Mercedes and shoves his nose against the window in a desperate attempt to reach your nose, make sure you modify the greeting ritual to human standards. Therefore, when your puppy wishes to greet you, bend forward and bring both hands to his nose level. With one hand, stroke the head to prevent jumping while allowing the other hand to be nose nudged. Although the puppy definitely prefers to kiss your mouth, he will sooner or later accept your hand as a substitute.

To conclude:
- A ten- to twelve-week-old puppy should, together with the pack leader, *start* to explore and progressively define his territory
- At the same time, a defecation area—away from the lair and easy to find—should be demarcated
- Don't forget the greeting ritual and give the puppy the necessary support at the first signs of showing territorial protectiveness

Too many youngsters are told to shut up while developing their early sense of territorial consciousness. A schnauzer is a watchdog; a Giant Schnauzer is a guard and defense dog. If you cannot take a little motivated barking, look for a Basenji.

What to Feed Your Schnauzer

I believe it's worthless to go into all the different types of diets. On this subject, there are enough books and articles in dog magazines. Anyway, a conscientious breeder will give you all the necessary advice.

In my opinion, it is necessary that each schnauzer owner should understand that his precious pet is, by nature, just like his wild brethren, mainly a carnivore. Humans usually can't understand and consider it a vice that their darling dares to prefer dirty tripe to a tender rump steak. There is nothing vicious, only logic, in this. A dog's digestive system is not suitable for breaking down the connective tissue of vegetation, though he needs nutritive ingredients found in plants. In the wild, a canine's only resort is to kill a herbivore, open its belly, tear out the stomach, open the wall, discard the superfluous grass, and devour the meaty lining with alveoli full or predigested herbs. When satiated by this first course, canines tear off some red meat and, finally, chew the bone. Altogether, this comprises a perfectly balanced meal. So, if one day you want to spoil your schnauzer and alternate the well-balanced and carefully composed commercial dog chunks (which are flavored and colored to appeal to owners), please give him a full dish of dirty (unwashed) tripe and an uncleaned bone. A soft calf's knee will do wonders for your pup. A hard marrowbone will be a treat for your adult schnauzer.
- Don't try to humanize your so adorable and cuddlesome Miniature; sweets are just too terrible for his teeth
- Feed your schnauzer adequate and balanced meals at fixed times and a fixed place
- Make sure he always has *fresh* water available

Elementary Care

For hundreds of centuries, the wolf survived without any form of inoculation or veterinary help whatsoever. The secret of this is logical, natural selection. Only the weak succumb, and the strong survive and procreate. Although this law is still applicable, we can't fully apply it when domestic dogs live with evolved humans. The simple reason is that, because of this close coexistence, we have to adhere to some hygienic regulations.

Schnauzers are a sound breed. Beside some routine visits, you very seldom have to take a schnauzer to a vet. Hereditary disorders such as congenital eye cataract in Miniatures or hip dysplasia in Giants, which have arisen during recent decades, have been kept under control by conscientious breeders. So, when purchasing a puppy from a reliable kennel, there is less chance that you will be confronted with such evils. However, some elementary health care has to be considered.

First of all, an inoculation scheme generally applicable to all breeds should be adhered to. Your puppy will have received his first inoculations at the age of five or six weeks. The breeder's veterinarian records the vaccinations into an individual record that accompanies the pup. As one can't define exactly how long the maternal antibodies remain effective, the first vaccines could be partially or totally destroyed by these antibodies. Therefore, the vaccinations must be repeated at the age of twelve or thirteen weeks.

The vaccinations provide an ideal opportunity for first contact with your vet. He will update the vaccination record and inform you about future inoculations. On the first visit, ask the vet to do a routine checkup. His verdict will usually confirm your trust in the breeder and the breed. If, however, some parasites are found, the vet will recommend the treatment. The area where one lives and the season influences your dog's sensitivity to parasites. A schnauzer enjoying the rainy season in subtropical Africa is more susceptible to parasites than his brother gamboling in the Canadian winter snow. Depending on the circumstances, you will have to adapt the parasite-control scheme. The African schnauzer will have to be dipped weekly and wormed every two months, whereas the Canadian schnauzer might not need any dipping and only annual worming.

Housebreaking and Basic Education

It is important that, from the moment your puppy arrives, you should try to condition him to use a suitable defecation area. This technique is again based on natural laws. From his fourth week—as soon as he starts to leave the lair, a cub will not soil the immediately surrounding area. The other cubs soon follow the first (potential pack leader) and do their business in a corner away from their sleeping and playing area. Exactly the same happens with our domestic dogs, provided that the breeder gives them the opportunity to behave in this natural way.

For example, breeder X rears his Giant Schnauzer pups in a beautiful kennel with a comfortable sleeping place. The 7-by-14 foot concrete run is fenced off with an expensive welded mesh. The kennel is cleaned twice a day with high-pressure water and disinfected regularly. This situation looks very professional, and no costs have been spared. However, a 7-by-14 foot run is not big enough for eight pups to determine a defecation area and a play area. In addition, they are imprinted to relieve themselves exclusively on a hard (concrete) surface because they have no other choice. So, do not be surprised when a nine-week-old pup, leaving this golden cage to join your family, prefers the stone floor of your veranda or the kitchen floor for his droppings over a remote sandy corner in the garden.

Breeder Y designed his puppy kennel as shown in the drawing. From past experience, I have observed that pups, from four weeks of age, never soil area A or B. At the age of six weeks, they identify area Z as the defecation area. They move around in area C, but their real games take place in area D.

A pup from breeder Y, because of being *imprinted* to defecate on sand or occasionally on grass, will continue this habit in his new home, on condition that the new owners give an opportunity to do so. Therefore, one may put forward the following argument: avoid at all costs your pup's developing the obnoxious habit of soiling your home.

If, as an attentive owner, you turn your pup outside each time he stretches himself after a nap, finishes his meal, or is observed drinking a lot, praise your darling as soon as he "spends his penny" where you want, and you will have a housebroken pup in a minimum of time. If, instead of this, when leaving for work in the morning, you lock the pup up in the house expecting him to control himself until you return at five o'clock, you are completely unrealistic because a pup has to relieve himself at least ten times a day. If, on top of this, at your return, you are upset and rub the pup's nose in the dirt, you prove you really understand nothing about dogs. *You* left the playful pup locked up without any chance to relieve himself in a suitable place. Besides, as he was alone (no socially oriented creature likes this), he probably pulled down your tablecloth or tore your fluttering curtains into pieces.

Of course, a Miniature or Standard Schnauzer can prosper in a flat or small house without a garden, provided that the owner takes him out frequently, or when leaving the pup alone, the owner conditions the pup to use a layer of newspaper—the top sheet should still carry the scent of previous use.

If properly applied, the doggy bylaws made before the pup's arrival provides the best and most practical elementary training. A young dog that has learned to abide by the house rules will be a very easygoing chap when taken to training classes at a later stage.

Besides, I would like to advise all new schnauzer owners to take educational profit from all normal situations. For example, if the puppy spontaneously runs toward you, then for goodness sake, use the command "come!" and praise the pup on arrival. If the little one, on his own, goes down on his bum, stroke his head and tail and tell him to "sit!" Very soon, he will associate the word with the action and sit on command. Before the age of six months, at least ten words—such as no, come, sit, heel, and go—can be taught without undue effort. This simply depends on your aptitude as the pack leader.

The most natural educational resource is your happy and praising voice, which can change to a heavy, negative "no!" in a way that imitates the growl of the pack leader. If the puppy does not respond to this warning growl and commits a flagrant breach of the rules, the pack leader should grab the offender by the scruff of the neck and give him a good shaking. This type of punishment may be applied only when the pup is caught red-handed. The use of a check (choke) chain in later training is based on the same principle. It is a direct communication line from the handler to his pupil, and it achieves exactly the same results as the equivalent reprimand in nature.

Canine behaviorists have proven that a six-month-old wolf receives enough elementary training to function in the hunting pack. Our domestic dogs possess the same potential and are able, when properly instructed, to behave correctly at the age of six to seven months. All they then need is further perfection and experience in life.

How to ALPHAbetize Yourself
(How to Help Your Dog Regard You as Leader)

If your dog is rather pushy and out of control, lacks respect for your point of view and doesn't mind letting you know about it, he or she could be showing signs of the ALPHA SYNDROME!

The Alpha Syndrome is at the root of many behavior problems. IN MOST CASES, WE ARE NOT REALLY DEALING WITH A PROBLEM DOG, BUT A PROBLEM ENVIRONMENT OR PROBLEM RELATIONSHIP BETWEEN DOG AND OWNER. Dogs, just like their ancestor, the wolf, need a leader. If the dog is not provided with appropriate guidance, if in the dog's opinion, you are not a worthy leader, your dog may try to take over and call the shots. In other words, your dog may be running for higher office.

From Terry Ryan, "How to ALPHAbetize Yourself"; reproduced by kind permission of the author.

The ALPHAbetizing plan will make an improvement on how your dog views the social hierarchy in your pack. This plan involves changing daily interactions with your dog. It does not resort to punishment and very few actual TRAINING exercises are used.

Implement as many of the concepts as you possibly can. Stay with it for several weeks. Your dog did not climb to the top of the totem pole overnight, therefore it may take a little time to change your pal's mind about things. As your dog becomes rehabilitated, you may gradually phase out these corrective measures.

The following notes will help you remember the principle features of each ALPHAbetizing concept. . . .

Good luck and remember—dog ownership is not a democracy. Be firm, be patient, be consistent, but be ALPHA.

A leader must first get the follower's attention. Encourage eye contact several times a day: Call your dog's name, help the dog make eye contact with you by tracing a line with your hand between your dog's face and yours. You can make your hand more interesting by holding a toy or other inducement. Even a one second glance should be reinforced with praise or a reward. You are setting up communication channels and a bond between you and your dog.

A leader is dependable. Scheduled (rather than free choice) meals aid in house training problems and puts your dog in a position of dependence on you for food. (More than one meal a day will relieve hunter "stress.") Food is a primary reinforcer. Use it to your best advantage.

Leaders eat first. If your meals coincide with the dog's scheduled meals, make it a point to feed the dog AFTER you have eaten. Dogs are nonverbal communicators. This is a statement. Remember the National Geographic specials! Which wolf eats first?

Earning praise and treats. Stop all food treats and petting for your dog during this rehabilitation period EXCEPT what is "earned" by obeying a command. Examples: If your dog comes to you for attention, tell the dog to "sit" before petting. A brief heeling session can precede a treat. Don't worry, this is only a temporary measure until your dog's behavior improves!

Leaders go first. Don't allow your dog to charge in and out of "territory" before you. At the door of your home, vehicle, or at a fence gate, put your dog on a stay, go through the fence first, then call the dog in or out.

The leader controls the territory. A follower yields to the leader. For instance: If your dog is lying down in a hallway and you wish to pass, MAKE YOUR DOG MOVE, don't step over or around.

Leaders mean what they say. When giving your dog a command, don't beg or scream, speak in low, firm tones. And remember, no matter how simple the command, give it only once and make sure to help your dog comply.

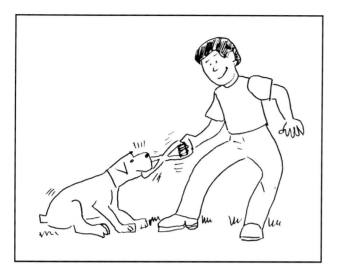

Leaders are winners. "Control the games, control the dog."

Ordinarily tug-of-war games are inappropriate for a pushy dog. It may escalate assertiveness and when you let go, your dog considers it a "win." An important message can be conveyed, however, if you play by these rules: Keep the game brief so your dog won't become overly excited. Be sure to WIN (have your dog release the toy to you) and while your dog is watching, put the toy away for the day, out of your dog's reach.

Life with your dog is not a democracy. But please be a kind and gentle dictator! I'd like to think of it as a partnership, with you making the important decisions! To help explain this to your dog, for now, you get the bed! Your dog may sleep in your bedroom at night, but until the behavior problems resolve, not on your bed. Sleeping together in the bed makes you seem like a littermate, an equal. Besides, there have been MANY alpha confrontations regarding possession of resting areas!

Talk to your veterinarian. About neutering or spaying your dog. Frequently this procedure has a positive impact on behavior problems and your veterinarian will explain numerous other benefits as well.

A thorough exam is important to determine if your dog's misbehavior is caused by a physical problem.

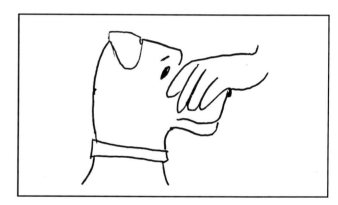

Muzzle control is a naturally dominant gesture. Put your hand over the top of your dog's muzzle and gently hold it there for a few seconds. This can be a regular part of your petting and attention.

Belly up is a natural acceptance posture. Once a day invite your dog over for a free belly rub. Show your pet how enjoyable this gesture of submission can be.

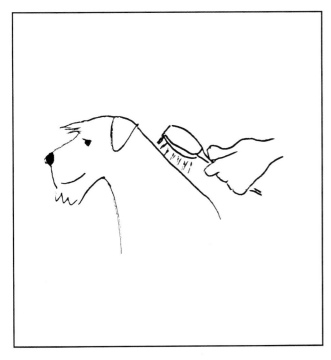

A follower allows gentle handling. Have regular grooming sessions with your dog. With positive reinforcement, gradually include "sensitive" spots, if any. Your goal is to have your dog relax and allow you to brush (or at least pet) the belly area.

Down is a subordinate position. Have your dog hold one 30-minute down-stay per day. Enforce it! This can be done while you eat a meal or read the paper, but be sure you are in a position to help your dog stay down.

"Train, don't complain." Give your dog about twenty minutes of obedience training a day. Break it up into two or three sessions. You do not have to be a member of an organized obedience class for this, but the guidance of a qualified instructor and the group experience for the dog are valuable. Give a command, help your dog comply, praise for a job well done.

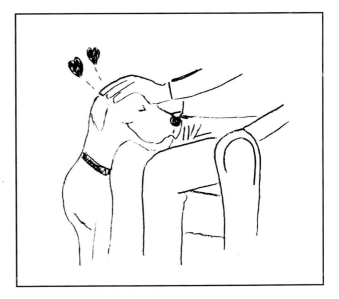

Alpha owners are fun. Do some things you know your dog will enjoy, but you should remain "in charge" of these activities. For example: If your dog likes to retrieve, tell your pal to COME, help with compliance if necessary, and as a reward, play fetch. Help your dog release the object immediately on command. When play is over, praise and as the dog watches, put the object away.

Leaders are fair, kind, consistent. Be firm, not harsh. Don't work with your dog if you lose your patience, but stay with it! The concept of an alpha owner will become clear to your dog with consistent repetition.

Argenta's Kimberley. Bred and owned by B. Niklasson, B. Andersson, and G. Garpas (Sweden).

Amethyst, Mabelle, and Vivian v. Napoleonstock (Standard) with their breeder, M. Loh (Germany).

Lady with Miniatures.

These are not shaggy seals but swimming
Giant Schnauzers.

A pack of schnauzers after a swim in the
sea. From left to right: Bella (the leader),
Cora, Enak, and Bles.

Ch. Malenda Masterblend at Risepark (Miniature). Owned by Messrs. Newman and Day (Great Britain).

12

The Schnauzer's Coat and How to Care for It

Roots and Genes

To begin exploration of the subject of the schnauzer's coat, we must look at its description in the some breed standards.

1. R. von Schmiedeberg, who in 1884 elaborated the wirehaired pinscher's first breed standard, makes the following statement: "His coat is as wiry as possible. On the snout are moustaches, whiskers, and bushy eyebrows."

2. The breed particularities drawn up in 1907 by Dr. Zurhellen's Bavarian Schnauzer Club stipulate that the schnauzer's coat is dense, hard, and wiry; on the back—when viewed against the course of the hair—rather upward standing, neither short nor lying flat. Shorter on the ears, forehead, legs, and feet.

3. The present-day German standard gives the following description: The coat is wirehaired. It should be harsh and dense. The coat consists of a dense undercoat and a harsh topcoat, which should be short. The topcoat should be wiry, never shaggy nor wavy. The hair at the head and legs is also harsh; on the forehead and ears, it is shorter. The hallmarks of the schnauzer are the harsh and bushy eyebrows which slightly overshadow the eyes.

From these descriptions, it is evident that the purebred schnauzer was conceived with a wirehaired coat and that this prescription still stands. We may ask where such a coat comes from. We have seen that for many hundreds of years the smooth-haired pinscher and the wirehaired pinscher happily lived together in the southern parts of Germany. These dogs had the same origins and morphology. They were interbred, and one could find smooth-haired and wire-haired puppies or variations in the same litter.

At present, nobody can establish where the wirehair hailed from. Reichenbach, in 1834, wrote that, in his opinion, the existence of the wirehaired type of pinscher must find its origin in a cross of a curly type of dog with a smooth-haired breed. We know, indeed, that a cross between a dominant smooth hair and a dominant curly hair can give some wirehaired pups. Nobody knows if, when, and how such an infusion happened.

What we know is that—even a hundred years after the smooth-haired pinscher and the wirehaired pinschers split into two different breeds and from that moment the two coat types have been strictly separated in breeding—the schnauzer's wirehaired coat is not dominant in all its genes. In other words, it is not genetically fixed. The genes responsible to the correct coat are complex. Even if for breeding purposes, we exclusively used sires and dams with the correct coat phenotype, it does not mean that the combination of their genes will result in a correct undercoat and topcoat for all of their pups. Because of the genetic complexity, it is virtually impossible to establish if a particular sire or dam is genetically sound for the correct type of coat. Our only chance in this complicated process is to exclusively use parents who at least *display* the correct coat—that is, the correct phenotype—which will improve the odds of success.

I am convinced that, in the old days of the wirehaired pinscher, this principle was applied for the particular reason that a long and woolly haired offspring was undesirable because such a dog was not practical for the type of life he was destined for. An occasional cross with a smooth-haired pinscher did not seem to give problems in this regard. I believe that it rather gave a boost for a correct wirehaired texture.

Texture of the Schnauzer's Coat

From the breed standards, we learn that the schnauzer's coat is composed of a soft, short, dense undercoat covered by a wiry topcoat.

First, a look at the texture and function of the undercoat. It consists of a thick and close-to-the-skin layer of soft hair, which has the obvious function of keeping the skin warm and is an essential part of the schnauzer's insulating system. This undercoat should, ideally, cover the whole body. One can only see and evaluate the presence and quality of the undercoat by touching through the topcoat. I know by experience that a schnauzer with a too long, shaggy, or wavy topcoat often lacks the necessary undercoat. As such, his coat is not only incorrect because of the excessive topcoat but also because of the absence of undercoat.

The schnauzer's topcoat is straight and wiry and does not lie smoothly on the body. In other words, when you look at the coat, it give the impression of harshness and stands *slightly* away from the body. When touched, the coat feels straight, and there is a slight resistance when you try to bend it between your fingers. Only then can the coat be qualified as wiry.

Why is this so important? Not merely because the topcoat is described as such in the breed standard but, above all, because it provides the schnauzer with an ideal and practical outfit, protecting him in all weather conditions and requiring minimal grooming. The straight topcoat that does not lie tight on the body is supported by the oil produced by sebaceous glands, making an ideal insulator against hot-and-cold air, rain, snow, dirt, and injury.

A long, wavy topcoat without an undercoat may be a suitable coat for a hairdresser or dog groomer who wants to

This puppy has a correct straight wirehaired coat.

These four-month-old Giant Schnauzers with promising conformation have different parents, and all of the parents have correct wirehaired coats.

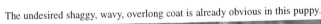

The undesired shaggy, wavy, overlong coat is already obvious in this puppy.

create glamour or to camouflage conformation faults, but it is totally useless for the schnauzer himself and impractical for the average owner.

When dealing with coat texture, it is obvious that one should also mention its ideal length. The wirehaired coat is stripped twice a year—growing steadily between strippings—and no specific measurements can be given. What we can establish is the *maximum* length of the ideal topcoat just before it reaches the stage where it dies and needs to be stripped. Of course, we must different between the Miniature, Standard, and Giant Schnauzer, and the figures remain approximate. In my experience, the maximum length that a Miniature Schnauzer's coat may reach is about 4 to 5 cm (1½ to 2 in). The Standard's coat may grow slightly longer to about 5 to 6 cm (2 to 2¼ in), and the Giant's coat (depending on the size of the individual dog) may obtain a maximum length of 6 to 7.5 cm (2¼ to 3 in). Schnauzer coats that grow beyond these limits are no longer straight and wiry but develop undesired shaggy or wavy structure.

While on this subject, I must stand up for the breed and warn the potential fancier against those breeders who disregard the correct schnauzer coat. The basic concern about a schnauzer's coat starts with the breeder. There are fanciers who strive for a too long coat on which they can spend hours of tailoring so that, after being profusely sprayed with lacquer, it can impress a nonspecialist judge. Persons who have made this into their hobby cultivate the coat of their dreams by any means. Consequently, they deny their schnauzer the fundamental right to be a *schnauzer*. They rear their Miniature Schnauzers in small pens and their Standard and Giant Schnauzers in confined areas. Such show dogs are not allowed to romp around, to play, to be active—in other words, to develop their physical and mental capacities in a normal, schnauzer-like way. The only purpose reserved for them is to grow fur that—after the necessary, specialized, cumbersome, and time-consuming manipulation—must serve to boost their owner's ego. Of course, such dogs are also used for breeding. I can only assure the potential fancier that a real schnauzer with a correct schnauzer coat is a much more practical asset. If you opt for glamor, bear in mind that such external charm only lasts for a short while after the dog is picked off the grooming table. A schnauzer with a correct wirehaired coat will, even after a walk in the rain followed by a routine brushing, look neat and attractive. I am not taking a stand against dog shows and grooming schnauzers for dog shows. I am simply warning against any kind of exaggeration by which the breed hallmarks are altered.

Coat Color

The nineteenth-century smooth-haired and wirehaired pinschers—in other words, the ancestors of modern pinschers and schnauzers—occurred in a wide range of colors.

Their coats varied from flaxen over red and brown to gray in all its combinations; some were solid black, others black and tan or with other shades. The split into smooth-haired pinschers and wirehaired schnauzers followed by a century of selective breeding and amended breed standards resulted in clear prescriptions. The black and tan, together with the related brown colors, were reserved for the pinschers, whereas the range of gray shades and black were allocated to the schnauzers.

As it stands, the breed description, applicable in the breed's country of origin, for the Standard Schnauzer and the Giant Schnauzer makes provision for two colors—solid black and salt and pepper. As for the Miniature Schnauzer, the range has been extended with black and silver and, more recently, with pure white.

Let us have a look at the description of each of these colors.

The breeding aim for the *salt-and-pepper* color is a medium shade, evenly distributed and intensely pigmented, with a gray undercoat. Admissible shades range from iron-gray to silver-gray. Every shade has a dark facial mask to emphasize the expression, and the color of the mask harmonizes with the shade of the body color. White markings on the head, chest, and legs are undesirable.

The particular gray shade is obtained by the fact that each individual hair is black-and-white banded in a specific way. The fact that the breed standard makes provision that the intensely pigmented shade must be evenly distributed over the whole body entails that one should find only banded hairs and that, ideally, no pure white hairs should be present.

Solid black does not need detailed explanation. The topcoat and undercoat are both black. However, I would like to comment that for young dogs it might happen that one finds some dispersed white hairs; also a tiny white spot on the chest can occur, but this should disappear after the third stripping. It might happen that a brown tinge appears through the black. This can be temporary and due to a poor and dull condition of the coat, though certain lines are sensitive to it.

For the *black-and-silver* Miniature Schnauzer, the breeding aim is a black topcoat with a black undercoat, with white markings above each eye, on the throat, the cheeks, front part of the chest, the forelegs, the pasterns, the paws, the inside of the hindquarters, and under the tail. The forehead, neck, and outside of the ears should be black.

The *white* Miniature Schnauzer has a pure white topcoat and undercoat. In Germany, this variety has been selectively bred for over the past thirty years and under the usual strict control of the PSK. Although the variety is already listed in the FCI registry for purebred dogs, it has not yet (as of January 1993) been awarded with champion challenge certificates at international shows. It is, however, foreseeable that this will be granted in the near future.

It is important to mention here that in the schnauzer's country of origin and in countries abiding by the German breed standard, breeding between varieties is not practiced, as a general rule. This has proven to be a valuable help in obtaining the salt-and-pepper shades that are evenly colored from top to bottom. It has also improved the black-and-silver Miniature Schnauzers in the way that the black remains black and does not fade into bluish-gray at a later age. Also, the fact that the German breed standard does not make provision for long leg furnishings has helped to keep the correct coat structure and intense salt-and-pepper pigmentation over the entire body.

Later, when we compare the details of breed standards in different countries, it will become clear that the above principles and prescriptions are not observed consistently in all countries. I feel that I should give preference to the directives as laid down by the parent club in the breed's country of origin, where a team of breed specialty judges headed by their senior judge ensures that the breed standard is interpreted in its correct context. As such, fashion and preferences of uninformed fanciers have only a minor voice.

Basic Coat Care

It is now time to explain how a correct wirehaired schnauzer coat should be cared for. I believe that here I should give priority to the routine grooming of 95 percent of all schnauzers that just share a happy life with a family without sustaining the pressure of a show career. All grooming is, in principle, aimed at maintaining cleanliness and health.

To understand how we can achieve this in the most simple way, we must, before all, be aware that the schnauzer's wirehaired coat grows in a cycle. Each cycle takes an average of six months, during which the coat grows to its full length and reaches a peak of normal ripeness. At that stage, unlike most other coat types, the schnauzer's coat does not start shedding to continue such a process over a prolonged period. It has the particularity that at that moment it can be plucked or stripped. The ripe topcoat is removed by hand in a couple of hours' time, instead of the classical shedding process, which lasts several weeks and leaves old hair everywhere. If left in the rough, the schnauzer will try to rub his skin against a tree trunk, a wall, or any suitable surface and, as such, remove the dead coat in patches.

Two or three weeks after the topcoat has been stripped and the new stubble come through, it is time to give the same treatment to the undercoat. This means that the coat is plucked in two sessions. First the topcoat, and once this starts growing again, the undercoat is removed. All pores are now free of the old hair, and the renovation process can start without any hindrance.

Although the above described stripping method gives the required results, it must be stressed that it can only be applied to schnauzers with a correct coat structure. In addition, the fanciers who master the art of hand stripping are rare. Therefore, many schnauzer coats are simply clipped. Even when taken to a grooming parlor, clipping is often a general rule, either because hand stripping is too time consuming and expensive or because the professional has not mastered the art. If you really care for your schnauzer's coat, try to strip it yourself, or find a professional who can deal with wirehaired coats.

Routine Grooming and Maintenance

When you decide to acquire a schnauzer, you can't ignore the minor daily job of routine maintenance grooming. Although a correct wirehaired coat will not easily snarl, the longer hairs of the eyebrows, the whiskers, and some occasional longer hairs on the legs can tousle up. Besides, one can't avoid the fact that the coat collects some dirt. A daily routine brushing and combing is, therefore, absolutely required.

The equipment for routine care is a slicker brush and a metal medium-toothed comb. Grooming is facilitated by placing the dog on a raised surface. This does not have to be an expensive grooming table. An old table with a piece of ridged rubber to prevent slipping will do the trick.

From the moment your puppy arrives, make it a habit to give him a daily brushing from top to bottom and to comb the food particles out of his beard and whiskers. Don't allow *any* struggle. Grooming is not only essential for the dog's health but also vital for your position as a pack leader for the schnauzer to learn to accept that this must be done.

Although the brushing must be thorough, there is no reason that it should be painful. Consequently, your dog should not resist. If he does so, be firm. Grab him by the neck or by the whiskers and, together with the command "no!" give him a gentle shake and continue grooming. Don't feel sorry or pamper him, or he will struggle to be rewarded by pampering. Above all, don't give in, or he will struggle, growl, or bite because he has learned that when he does so, he can win this battle. In other words, he becomes the pack leader or alpha wolf, the one in control of the situation.

Once you have sorted out the dominance issue, you will discover that your skill improves by the day and that your schnauzer has learned to appreciate these sessions. It is also advisable to always have an old towel at a fixed place to wipe your schnauzer's beard after he has quenched his thirst; otherwise, he will wipe his whiskers against your trousers or sofa—some even favor Persian carpets.

If you stick to the maintenance routine for the first 6–7 months until your schnauzer is ready for his first stripping, you deserve my congratulations. Meanwhile, you should have decided if your darling is going to have that first stripping with a groomer conversant with the procedure, if it will be done with an acquaintance who is prepared to teach you, or if you are going to dare undertaking the task based on the instructions in this chapter.

If you don't learn to strip your schnauzer, you must take him to a groomer who knows how to do it correctly. However, I would *strongly* advise that you learn this skill. It not only saves a considerable amount of money but also improves the relationship with your dog. A canine relationship is based on communication, and the value of a stripping session, which lasts several hours, cannot be underestimated.

Once your first stripping has been completed, return to your routine daily grooming as before. However, I would suggest that once a week you use the serrated side of the stripping knife to rake through the coat to remove all loose and dusty underwool, fine dirt, and even parasites will be removed.

You will be surprised by how successfully you can maintain the condition of a schnauzer's coat by adding this simple and less time-consuming step. If your schnauzer has the correct coat texture, this step can often extend the period between strippings to eight or ten months. I have seen some schnauzers who ended up with one summer stripping a year.

A schnauzer whose coat is maintained this way seldom needs a bath except, for example, when he rolls in some objectionable substance. When a bath is necessary, use a shampoo designed for canine coats. All other soaps or detergents risk the removal of natural oils that protect the coat. My schnauzers bathe very seldom but have a swim in a river or a nearby lake at least every second week. I realize that my dogs are privileged to live where there is no real winter. I can assure you, however, that a schnauzer with a correct coat is not afraid to swim in very cold water and that, after a good shake, he will dry very quickly.

External parasite supervision and control is easy. During the daily brushing sessions and definitely during the weekly fine-combing sessions, you will observe the odd tick or flea and remove most of them. In that way you will reduce the tick-dipping sessions that are all noxious to a certain extent.

Stripping the Coat

Stripping requires an investment in the following equipment: stripping knife, straight-bladed scissors, hand (or motor-driven) clipper blades. If you have decided to look after your schnauzer's coat, you must also be equipped to trim the tip of his nails from time to time, so you must also buy a parrot-nosed nail clipper. Once you have gone through these costs, I can only encourage you by stressing that thousands before you have undertaken this task. Some have failed and spent their money for nothing, but many have succeeded, to the benefit of their schnauzer and themselves. The outcome depends on the strength of your desire to gain some dexterity.

For the first endeavor, wait until the coat is really ripe so that it can be easily plucked. On a free Saturday afternoon, place your schnauzer on his accustomed grooming table. Start stripping from the top of the neck downward. Grasp

tufts of the hair between thumb and index finger and give a quick, short pull in the direction of hair growth.

Most people prefer to use a stripping knife. The tufts of hair are then grasped between the thumb and the edge of the knife and plucked out, never cut.

At your first attempt, you will not be able to finish the stripping of the complete coat in one session, even if your subject is a Miniature Schnauzer. If you finish the neck, the shoulders, and the back on the first day, you can carry on with the rest of the body later. (I will explain further how to proceed in stages.) If the undercoat were removed simultaneously, the subject would be completely naked and left with unprotected skin for a couple of weeks. Therefore, it is of common practice that these two layers are stripped with an interval.

A couple of weeks after you have completed the stripping of the topcoat and when you can feel the new stubbles pricking through, it is time to reserve the same treatment to the undercoat. Again, there should be no cutting. The fine and overripe hairs are plucked out.

With the barber-type scissors, trim the too-long hairs of the beard and eyebrows as well as some possible long hair on the legs or chest. Use your clippers to trim the hair on the ears, some parts of the head, under the tail, and so forth.

Strip and Clip It Yourself

For schnauzers headed for a show career or for pet owners who like perfection, the grooming of their schnauzer will, of course, maintain the original goal of promoting cleanliness and health; however, emphasis is placed on enhancing the schnauzer's attractive appearance. As I pointed out before, the schnauzers' rustic quality should never be sacrificed in favor of glamour or fashion. When intending such procedures, one should consider giving ample attention to your subject's conformation or to the way his physical structure conforms to the breed standard.

Assuming that your schnauzer's breeder produced him from good wirehaired strains, it will not be difficult to obtain a wiry, harsh, and tight coat. On average, it will take about eight weeks for a coat to grow to acceptable show condition. This is not an absolute rule, and you will have to learn from experience how much time your schnauzer's coat needs to reach peak condition. I have already mentioned that in order to be successfully stripped the schnauzer's coat must be blown; in other words, it must have grown out so that it is dead and stands out from the body, asking to be plucked. If necessary, the schnauzer can be left for a couple of weeks in this rough condition, depending on the date he has to be ready to start the show season.

Stripping the Topcoat
1. Body, front, and rear legs. (Diagram 1) If your schnauzer has learned to stand on a grooming table, you

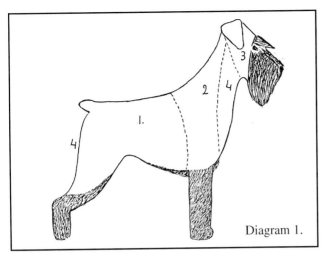

Diagram 1.

dog and take very small amounts of hair by scratching with your forefinger and thumb. Try to avoid the use of a stripping knife or take care not to pinch or cut the skin.

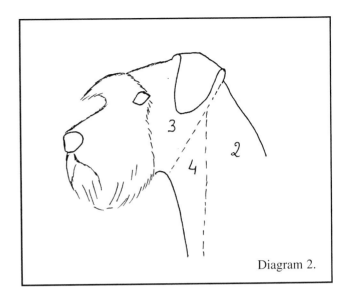

Diagram 2.

will not need a retaining post and loop to keep him under control, though groomers dealing with strange dogs need such aids. (See Diagram 1.)

If you are right handed, start by standing on the dog's right side, slightly to the rear. Place your left hand behind the dog's neck and start stripping the coat with your right hand, beginning behind the shoulder and working toward the tail.

Hold the stripping knife in your hand so that its blade lies against the index finger. Ruff a small amount of the coat with your thumb, which remains under the displaced hair, and bring the stripping knife in contact with the hair and your thumb by gently clenching your hand. Trap the hair between the blade and thumb, and pull it out with a firm, plucking motion in the direction of its growth. Do not cut the hair by twisting your wrist too briskly. Only strip the body and the rear legs during this session.

As a beginner, test to see that you are not cutting but properly stripping the coat. This can be done by stroking a stripped area against the grain. If you feel sharp stubbles, you are not doing a good job. The area should only be covered by a downy undercoat, the dead topcoat having been removed by the roots.

When you complete a stripping session, have a look at the skin. If it looks pink or irritated, use some baby oil or coat oil to soothe the irritated area.

2. Neck and shoulders. (Diagram 1.) About two weeks after the first session, apply the same technique to the coat of the neck and shoulders. Wait another week to strip the remaining areas under Step 3 and Step 4. This method of staggered stripping is not to make it easier for you but simply because of the way hair growth varies on different parts of the body. By stripping it in stages, you will obtain a uniform coat at show time. Of course, if you are not interested in showing, you can strip the entire topcoat on the same day or week.

3. Head and ears. (Diagram 2.) The head and ears are very sensitive areas to strip, and the plucking is done between the thumb and forefingers. Stand in front of the

4. Front and tail. (Diagram 1 and 3.) Strip the front and tail as shown. These are the last parts and should be done about two weeks before show time.

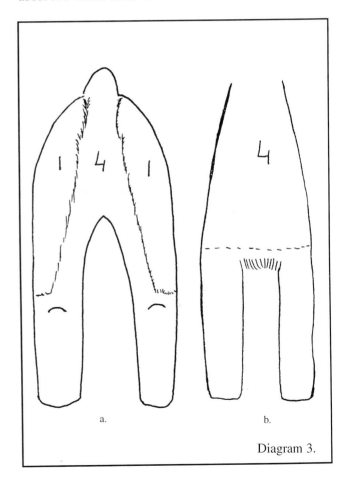

a.   b.

Diagram 3.

Stripping the Undercoat

After the topcoat has been completely stripped, there is little to do for a couple of weeks—except routine brushing.

When the new coat begins to appear, time has come to strip the undercoat in the same sequences and the same way as the topcoat. Of course, one has to avoid plucking the new hair along with it.

Clipping

This is the final touch, to be done one week before show time. (Diagram 1 and 2)

1. Head. Comb the hair on the face forward from a line just above the eyebrows to the corners of the mouth. Place a short cutting blade on your clipper, and clip the head from above the eyebrows to the base of the skull, then from the outer corner of the eyes to the base of the ear, and from the corners of the mouth to a *V* at the throat.

2. Ears. Clip the front and the back with a short cutting blade.

3. Neck and forechest. (Diagram 1 and 3.) Clip from the throat down the front of the neck and forechest to a point level with the prosternum (foremost part of the breastbone). This give a clean, straight line.

4. Tail. For docked tails, clip from the base of the tail to the tip on the underside. The upper side of the tail must be stripped.

Undocked tails must be stripped.

5. Inside of upper thighs and underbelly. (Diagram 1.) Using a short cutting blade, hold the clipper diagonally across the inner corner of the leg, and clip downward to the hock. Then, clip the stomach up to the navel. On males, trim the excess hair on the penile sheath, always clipping downward.

6. Eyebrows. (Diagram 4a and 4b.) Shaping a schnauzer's head, especially the eyebrows and beard, will do a great deal to the correct expression. Comb the eyebrows directly forward, using a long stroke to include the beard. Trim the outer edges of the eyebrows so that they are level with the side of the head. Then, cut them diagonally from the outer edge to the center with a single stroke.

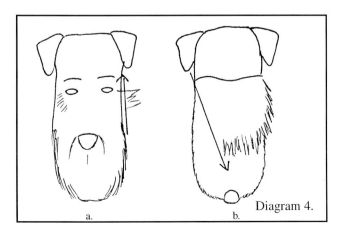

Diagram 4.

7. Beard. (Diagram 5.) Comb the beard forward and grasp both the beard and the muzzle; then, cut with the straight-edged scissors along a line extending from the corner of the mouth to the corner of the eyebrows. Remove all excess hair that cannot be held.

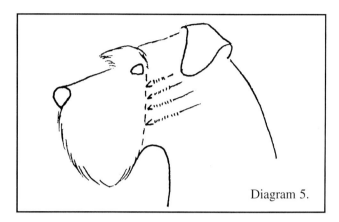

Diagram 5.

8. Front legs. (Diagram 6a.) If necessary, comb the leg hair so that it stands out from the legs. Looking down from above the dog and with the scissors pointing straight, carefully trim to achieve the appearance of a column. Viewing from the front, trim the furnishings so that they do not extend outward from the elbows. Viewing from the side, trim the leg hair in a straight line from the point of the elbow down to the table's surface. Trim the hair on the feet in a full circle so they appear round, not pointed.

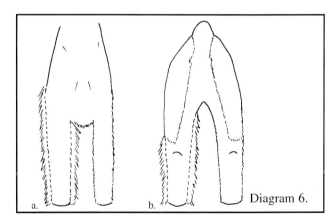

Diagram 6.

9. Hind legs. (Diagram 6b.) If necessary, comb the leg hair so that it stands out from the legs. Trim the hair from both the inside and the outside of the leg to leave a clearly defined line and to give the rear quarters a clean, archlike appearance. The hocks should be round and straight to correspond with the front legs as much as possible. The feet should look round and compact.

10. Under chest. (Diagram 1.) Trim the hair so that it does not extend beyond the elbows. Gently taper upward and back, past the last rib.

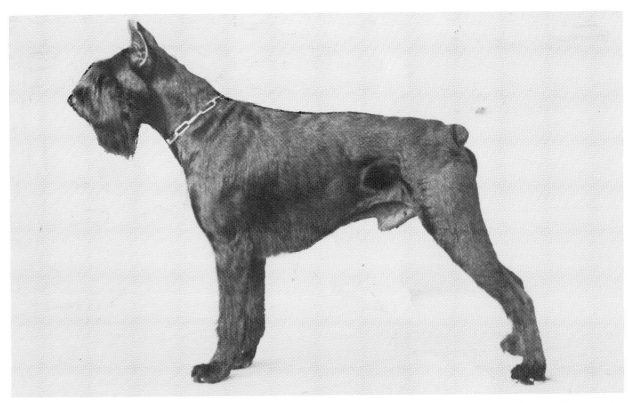

Ch. Gabo v. Krayenrain—*Bundessieger, Klubsieger PSK,* and champion in Germany and Switzerland (Giant). Bred by E. Somaini (Germany).

13

The International Schnauzer

I felt that Pam and Charles as interested fanciers should understand the function, structure, and relationships between organizations that have a profound influence on their schnauzers.

The Pinscher-Schnauzer Klub 1895 e.V. (PSK)

The Pinscher-Schnauzer Klub (PSK) is the international parent breed club in Germany. Earlier, I explained how Josef Berta founded the club in 1895 and how it received its present name in 1922. The PSK, despite setbacks suffered during the First and Second World Wars, has grown steadily into a strong and sound organization that looks after all pinscher and schnauzer breeds with authority.

The PSK, as sole representative of the pinscher and schnauzer breeds in Germany, is affiliated with the Verband für das Deutsche Hundewesen (VDH)—or, more simply, the German Kennel Club—which is affiliated with the Fédération Cynologique Internationale (FCI). As such, the PSK if fully in charge of and responsible for the well-being of all schnauzers (Giant, Standard, and Miniature) and pinschers (Miniature, German, and Affenpinscher). The PSK registers all pinscher and schnauzer litters and writes up their official pedigrees, which are certified by the VDH and the FCI.

In 1992, the PSK had over 15,000 members, of which 600 reside outside Germany. The German members belong to one of the 188 regional pinscher and schnauzer clubs (*Ortsgruppe*). These independent regional clubs are, according to their location, affiliated with one of the sixteen provincial organizations (*Landesgruppe*). Delegates of the regional clubs discuss matters at the provincial level, and delegates of the provincial organizations deal with matters at the national (PSK) level.

Breed shows, Protection Dog (Schutzhund), and International Working trials (*Internationale Prüfungsordnung* or IPO), breed surveys, traffic-tested companion dog stakes, agility, cross country, four-event matches, and so forth are organized through the regional and provincial clubs. Each year, one of the provincial clubs, duly charged by the PSK, organizes the annual breed specialty show (*Jahressiegerauslese*) and another club the annual Schutzhund title event (*Bundesleistungssiegerprüfung*), which is reserved to the twenty Giant Schnauzers that qualify in the selection stakes.

Within the framework of the PSK committee, specific members are appointed as senior breed warden (*Hauptzuchtwart*), judges' headman (*Richterobmann*), junior handling and general agility and training sport (*Jugendhandlung und Breitensport*), and sports trustee (*Sportbeauftragter*).

The *chief breed warden* supervises and coordinates the work of the breed wardens. Hip dysplasia matters are also his responsibility. For Giant Schnauzers, Standard Schnauzers, and German Pinschers, only sires and dams that have been graded HD-0 or HD-1 may be used for breeding purposes.

Each breed warden visits the breeders in his assigned region and reports in detail on all litters born. The breed warden visits each litter twice—once immediately after birth and a second time to tattoo each puppy—and travel costs are paid by the breeder. No litter can be registered without a specific report completed in quadruplicate by the breed warden: Two copies go to the PSK with the application for registration (one goes to the chief breed warden, the other goes to the provincial breed warden); a third copy is kept by the acting breed warden; the fourth copy is given to the breeder. The document contains full information on the sire and dam. It reports how the birth took place (complications or not), and it gives multiple details about the puppies. Moreover, the warden reports where the pups were born (house, kennel), the type of conditions in which they are kept and reared, the mother's state, how the mother and pups react to a stranger, whether the breeders has other dogs, and so forth. Based on a minimum of five such positive reports and under the condition that the pups are reared in a social family environment, the "seal for selected kennel" (*Zwingergutesiegel*) can be awarded to the breeder.

Instructions and recommendations for breeders and breed wardens are published in the PSK's monthly journal.

The *judges' headman* calls an annual meeting for *all* PSK recognized specialist judges. Specific problems related to the different breeds and their judging are discussed. Recommendations for uniform judging standards are agreed upon. It should be noted that in Germany, the pinschers and schnauzers are judged only by PSK judges, and the credentials of foreign judges must be approved by the PSK.

The *sports trustee* represents the PSK at the meetings of the German Dog-Sport Association (*Deutscher Hundesport Verband, e.V.* or DHV) and the Working Commission of Purebred Dog Clubs and Working Dog Associations (*Arbeitsgemeinschaft der Rassehundezuchtvereine und Gebrauchshundeverbände* or AZG). He coordinates, within the framework of the PSK, all dog-sport related activities and has a monthly column in the PSK magazine.

By differentiating the types of pedigrees issued, the PSK encourages breeders to use parents that have succeeded in the traffic-tested companion dog stake, the breed survey

(Ankörung), Schutzhund, or IPO tests and have achieved recognition at breed shows. Depending on the qualifications of the parents, a pedigree may have one of three additional notations.

1. Körzucht (selected breeding). Giant Schnauzers, Standard Schnauzers, and German Pinschers eligible for this rating must meet the following conditions:
   a. Two ratings of "excellent" or "very good" awarded by two different judges after the minimum age for breeding (eighteen months for Giant Schnauzers, fifteen months for Standard Schnauzers and German Pinschers)
   b. Hip X-ray rating of HD-0 or HD-1
   c. Qualified in the breed survey (Ankörung)

Miniature Schnauzers, Miniature Pinschers, and Affenpinschers eligible for this rating must meet the following conditions:
   a. As above, but the minimum age is 12 months
   b. (No hip X-ray examination for HD is required)
   c. Succeed in the traffic-tested companion dog stake (BH)

2. Leistungszucht (selected for advanced training). Only for Giant Schnauzers, Standard Schnauzers, and German Pinschers.
   a. As above
   b. As above
   c. Qualified for Schutzhund or IPO Grade I (see Chapter 15)

3. Kör-und Leistungszucht. Qualified for both 1 and 2.

The club publishes an annual studbook (Zuchtbuch), a substantial book featuring all registered litters. It also includes a complete list of pinschers and schnauzers awarded championship status during the year.

The studbook describes recognized titles and awards.

International Champion. This title, awarded by the FCI, requires three challenge certificates (CACIBs or *Certificat d'Aptitude au Championnat International de Beauté*) awarded at FCI approved international shows. These awards must be won in three different countries and under three different judges. One CACIB must be obtained in the owner's country of permanent residence or in the breed's country of origin. For breeds that are "submitted to working tests," only two CACIBs are required, but in addition, the dog must qualify for a Schutzhund or IPO Grade I.

Jahressieger (Jsg), Jahresjugendsieger (Jjsg), and Jahresseniorensieger (Jssg). These titles (always followed by the year) are awarded to schnauzers and pinschers at the PSKs annual specialty show (*Jahressiegerauslese*) for the best-of-breed dog and bitch (*Jsg*), best junior dog and bitch (*Jjsg*), and best veteran dog and bitch (*Jssg*).

Deutscher Schönheits Champion. This German championship title is awarded by the VDH to all pinschers and schnauzers that have won the challenge certificate at their own *Landesgruppe* specialty show plus five CACs (*Certificat d'Aptitude au Championnat*) at any German show. The rating of "excellent" in the open class or "very good" in the junior class at the PSK's annual specialty show also counts as the equivalent of one CAC. The same applies to a qualification at the schutzhund title event (*Bundesleistungssiegerprüfung*). At least one year must lapse between obtaining the first and the last CAC, and the CACs must be awarded by at least three different judges. A hip rating of HD-0 or HD-1 is also required for Giant Schnauzers, Standard Schnauzers, and German Pinschers.

Klubsieger PSK (Kbsg). The title of club champion is awarded to all pinschers and schnauzers obtaining three CACs (only from open class, over fifteen months) under at least two different judges, one of which is a PSK judge. At least one year must lapse between obtaining the first and the last CAC. A hip rating of HD-0 or HD-1 is also required for Giant Schnauzers, Standard Schnauzers, and German Pinschers.

VDH Champion. This title is awarded by the German Kennel Club (VDH) to all breeds. In German shows with CACIB status, the VDH puts, in addition, special VDH awards at stake. Four of these VDH awards must be won to obtain the title of VDH champion. One or two of the CACs may also be won at VDH-recognized specialty shows, which are awarded to a dog or bitch winning first place in open class, working dog class (entrants qualified for Schutzhund or IPO), or champion class and graded "excellent."

Bundessieger (Bsg) and *Bundesjugendsieger (Bjsg).* These titles (always followed by the year) are awarded to all breeds at the VDH annual national championship show (*Bundessiegerauslese*) for the best-of-breed dog and bitch (*Bsg*) and the best junior dog and bitch (*Bjsg*).

ISPU-Sieger (ISPUsg) and *ISPU-Jugendsieger (ISPUjsg).* These titles (always followed by the year) are awarded to pinschers and schnauzers at the International Schnauzer-Pinscher Union (ISPU) annual specialty show for the best-of-breed dog and bitch (*ISPUsg*) and the best junior dog and bitch (*ISPUjsg*).

Europasieger. The *Europasieger* and *Europasiegerin* titles were awarded to the best-of-breed and best-of-opposite-sex winners at the annual German *Europasieger-zuchtschau*. Under pressure from the FCI, which argued that European champion was misleading for a title awarded at a specific German show, this title is no longer awarded.

Weltsieger. The *Weltsieger* (World Champion) and *Weltsiegerin* titles are awarded to the best-of-breed and best-of-opposite-sex winners at the annual World Championship show sponsored by the FCI and hosted by an appointed FCI member club.

Missy

Previous page: Ch. Skansen's HZS Sacha v. Diamond. Owned by Sylvia Hammerstrom. Top-winning Giant bitch in the United States, with six all-breed Best-in-show wins as of 1991.

Top Left: Ch. Otti van't Wareheim (Giant). Bred and owned by J. and E. Gallant (Republic of South Africa).
Top Right: Ch. Keay's I'm a Jetsetter—champion in the United States, Canada, and Bermuda (Giant) Bred and owned by N. and J. Keay (Canada).
Middle Left: Stablemaster's Superman, ISPUsg 1995 (Giant). Bred by Faberge-Frances (Finland) and owned by Casali-Cortegiani (Italy).
Middle Right: Ch. Ike v.d. Lederhecke (Germany).
Bottom: Ch. Skansen's Gentleman Thief, No. 1 Stud dog with 80 champion offsping as of 1991.

Top: Snob v. Bartenwetzer (Giant), a qualified search-and-rescue dog, at work with the army in Switzerland.. Bred by W. Schicker (Germany).

Left: Six of the top-winning ladies in Sweden, champions all. Owned by Boel and Mikael Niklasson (Sweden).

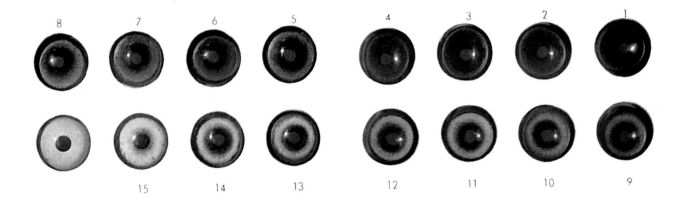

Top: Eye colors: 1, 2, 3, and 4 are desirable, 5 and 6 are still acceptable, 7 and 8 are no longer acceptable, 9 and 10 are undesirable,, 11 and 12 are absolutely undesirable, 13 and 14 are rejected

Left: White Miniature from Germany.

Bottom: Miniature Schnauzer puppies at "van't Groeningheheem." Y. and R. Coucke (Belgium).

Miniature Schnauzersat "van't Groeningheheem." Y. and R. Coucke (Belgium).

Int. Ch. and Ch. in Belgium, France, Germany, the Netherlands Regal Cora posing on a dolmen in wintry Denmark. Bred by A. Kirsten and owned by J. and E. Gallant.

Top: Bella van Invictus (Giant), bred by C. Aerts (Holland) and owned by J. and E. Gallant, shown with her best friend Philippe.
Middle Left: Ch. Negus-Volker van Hilbelinkhof—Int. Ch., Jahressieger, Europasieger, Weltseiger, and champion in Spain, Portugal, France, Monaco, and Germany (Standard). Bred by H. J. Lutjenkossink (Netherlands) and owned by M. and A. Gil de Biedma (Spain).
Middle Right: Pepsy de Ludolphi and Mascar's Morella (Standards).
Bottom Left: Ch. Lisser de Ludolphi—Int. Ch., VDH-sieger, Klubsieger PSK, Europasieger, and champion in Italy, France, Germany, Austria, Switzerland, and Yugoslavia (Standard). Bred by D. Gustin (Belgium) and owned by F. Meneghello (Italy)
Bottom Right: Ch. Peajay's Charlie Waters. Owned by Elaine Walton.

Top: Brickmark Sacha (Miniature). Bred and owned by M. Brick (New Zealand).
Middle Left: Ch. Malya Ushi and Feldmar Snow Crystal at Malya—both Int. Champions and champions in Italy (Miniatures). Owned by A. Torregianai (Italy).
Middle Right: Ch. Penlan Peter Gunn—Salt and Pepper, cropped ears, whelped 1973. Very influential sire with 73 Champions; top winner.
Bottom: Ch. Blythewood Storm Damage. Owned by Joan Huber. One of the top winners in 1991 and 1992.

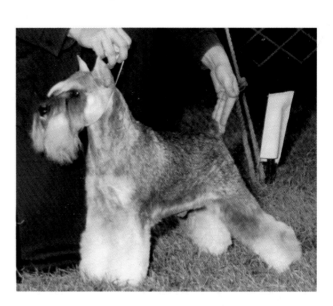

Top: Ch. Heidi's Christmas Bell (U.S.) bred and owned by Joan and Jeff Hodges, is a BIS winning bitch (Miniature).
Middle Left: Ch. Remi v. d. Gehrder Pumpe—Int. Ch., VDH-Sieger, Bundes-jugendsieger, Bundessieger, Europa-jugendsieger, Lubsieger PSK, and champion in Germany, Luxemburg and the Netherlands (Miniature). Owned by H. Gortemaker (Netherlands).

Middle Right: Ch. Feldmar Night Reveler (Miniature). Bred by M. Feld (U.S.) and owned by M. Brick (New Zealand)
Bottom: Ch. Malenda Masterblend at Risepark (Miniature). Owned by Messrs. Newman and Day (England).

Germany

Tyras v.d. Lederhecke (Giant) at seven months. Bred and owned by W. Buschel (Germany).

Ch. River v. Napoleonstock—*Jahresjugendsieger, Klubsieger PSK, VDHsg, Bundessieger,* and champion in Germany (Standard). Bred and owned by M. Loh (Germany).

Amethyst, Mabelle, and Vivian v. Napoleonstock (Standard) with their breeder, M. Loh (Germany).

Dosty v. d. Goliathhöhe (Standard). Bred and owned by H. Weisz (Germany).

Belinda v. d. Goliathhöhe (Standard). Bred and owned by H. Weisz (Germany).

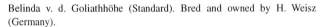

Bonni v. Westerwiesen and Ante v. Westerweisen (Miniatures). Bred and owned by J. Krage (Germany).

Belgium

Ch. Cortes de Ludolphi—Int. Ch., *Klubsieger PSK, Jahressieger, Weltsieger.* Winner Amsterdam, and champion in Belgium, France, Germany, and the Netherlands (Standard). Bred by Mrs. D. Gustin (Belgium).

Ch. Iber Chapiro—Int. Ch. (Standard). Bred by A. Degroot; owned by W. Pelsmaekers (Belgium).

Italy

Malya Togo—Jahressieger (Giant). Bred by M. Pozzi; owned by A. Torregiani (Italy).

Ch. Scedir Ares—Int. Ch., Bundessieger, VDHsg, Klubsieger PSK, and champion in Italy, France, Finland, Switzerland, Germany, Austria, Denmark, Yugoslavia, Luxemburg, and the Netherlands (Miniature). Bred by F. Ferrari; owned by A. Torregiani (Italy).

Performance. The annual studbook also gives a complete breakdown of all *performances* achieved by any pinscher or schnauzer during the previous year. The following Schutzhund and IPO tests are listed: Grade I, II, and III; *Fährtenhund* (FH, tracking dog); *Ausdauerungsprüfung* (AD, endurance test); *Diensthund* (DH, service dog); *Rettungshund* (RH, rescue dog); *Wachhund* (WH, guard dog); and *Begleithund* (BH, traffic-tested companion dog). In addition to the dog's names are statistics of all passes and failures.

Thereafter follows a list of all dogs entered for the *Ankörung* (breed survey), and finally, the enumeration of all hip dysplasia examinations done during the year.

While working on the manuscript for this book, I visited the PSK office on several occasions. I can only state that it is a strong and effective organization. Due to its structure and efficiency, our breeds are in responsible hands. It is difficult for me to understand how some national kennel clubs or schnauzer clubs in other parts of the world can make decisions, even with regard to the breed's standard, without consulting the international parent breed club. I feel that every schnauzer specialty club in the world should endeavor to promote the authentic schnauzer and refuse to concede to local demands or trends, as these are often based on a lack of knowledge.

To contact the PSK, address correspondence to Pinscher-Schnauzer Klub, 1895 e.V., Barmer Strasse 80, 5630 Remscheid 11, Germany.

The International Schnauzer-Pinscher Union (ISPU)

There had always been good contact between the German PSK and schnauzer and pinscher clubs in other countries. In 1977, the idea arose to create an organization where schnauzer and pinscher club delegates from different countries could meet to exchange opinions. Invitations were extended, and the inaugural meeting took place on the 19 March 1977, in Gütersloh, Germany in association with the annual meeting for specialist breed judges.

Sweden, France, Belgium, Switzerland, Poland, Norway, the Netherlands, Denmark, Austria, Finland, and Yugoslavia sent delegates to the first meeting of the International Schnauzer-Pinscher Union (ISPU).

Heinz Höller, as chairman of the PSK, was appointed chairman of the ISPU, and Marianne Frestadius (Sweden) was elected as the vice chairman. The main goal of the organization was a collective effort to foster and further improve the schnauzer and pinscher breeds. It was also decided that future changes to the breed standards should be discussed at an ISPU meeting.

Italy and Israel joined the ranks at the second ISPU meeting in Berlin on 12–13 August 1978. A better description of the natural noncropped ear was formulated. Judges

sheets were made available in the languages of all affiliated countries. The recognition of the white Miniature Schnauzer as a variety was discussed as well as problems about the breeding of the salt-and-pepper Giants and black-and-silver Miniatures.

The third ISPU meeting took place on 22 May 1981 at the world championship show in Dortmund, with a new delegate from Spain and an observer from Great Britain. Professor Schleger (Austria) was a most-appreciated guest lecturer speaking about hereditary problems. Other themes were cropping prohibition, quarantine regulations, artificial insemination, and joint ISPU breed shows.

In 1984, another ISPU meeting was held. It was unanimously decided that preference should be given to the European Continental coat type for schnauzers. Other topics on the agenda included noncropped ears and hip dysplasia.

On 28–29 March 1987, another ISPU meeting was held in Dortmund. Some of the most important items were the following:

1. Although ear cropping has now been forbidden in West Germany and Dr. Räber (Switzerland) insists on omitting the description of the cropped ear from the standard, it was felt that for the time being the description should remain unchanged.

2. The drawings from Mrs. Esser illustrating the different schnauzer and pinscher breeds with uncropped ears were discussed and accepted as models for letterheads and medals.

3. Dr. Reinhardt gave a very comprehensive talk about the increasing occurrence of small tumors on the toes of black schnauzers.

4. Peter Burtzik gave a clear survey of hip dysplasia examinations, results, and progress. He continued with a lecture on the schnauzer's and pinscher's temperament and character.

5. Dr Räber's talk about breeding for colors was extremely interesting. Consequently, a proposal was formulated for the attention of the FCI to better control and forbid dyeing of certain breeds and varieties.

After the sudden passing away of Heinz Höller in December 1987, the vice chairman Peter Burtzik ran the PSK until Theo Hünecke was elected chairman at the 1988 AGM meeting. The ISPU meeting of 28–29 October 1989 was led by Theo Hünecke.

It had become a tradition that guest speakers address the meeting on subjects of special interest. At the 1989 meeting, Prof. Harting explained the evaluation of hip dysplasia and made a comparative study of different evaluation criteria in different countries. Dr. Keil (chief breed warden) warned against diseases that have been diagnosed in our breeds and seem to be hereditary; in particular, cases of epilepsy and diabetes. Eye diseases such as congenital juvenile cataract and progressive retinal atrophy have been reported from the

The Netherlands

Ch. Celesta van Sephesyl—Int. Ch. and champion in the Netherlands (Miniature). Bred and owned by E. Wieldraayer (Netherlands).

Quintus Inki van de Vanenblikhoeve at nine months (Standard). Bred and owned by H. Bruintjes-Schaap (Netherlands).

Björn van de Schipbeek and Questie Voinaika (Standards) at the famous winner's show in Amsterdam. Owned by J. Beeftink.

Ch. Coson's Emily (Standard). Bred and owned by Mr. Kessel (Netherlands).

Ch. Erik Basko van het Bakerveld—*Weltsieger* and champion in the Netherlands (Standard). Bred by G. A. Onstenk; owned by J. van Dorp (Netherlands).

Ch. Uriëlle van de Goudakkers—Int. Ch. and champion in Belgium, Germany, and the Netherlands (Standard). Bred by W. Wielheesen; owned by J. Beeftink (Netherlands).

The Netherlands

Ch. Igor Donnie van de Vanenblikhoeve—*Bundessieger* and champion in the Netherlands (Standard). Bred and owned by H. Bruintjes-Schaap (Netherlands).

Ch. Ajoeri van de Reeënhorst (Giant). Bred by Mrs. de Haan; owned by J. Liet (Netherlands).

Ch. Layke van de Ooskant—*Bundessieger* and champion in Luxemburg (Miniature). Bred and owned by H. Bosgoed (Netherlands).

Ch. Hweeko Rivale Wakefield—Int. Ch., *ISPU-Sieger, Europasieger, Jahressieger,* and champion in Belgium, Finland, Luxembourg, and Monaco (Standard). Bred by Dr. T. L. Tan; owned by Neil P. Kelly (Netherlands).

Switzerland

Schnauzi's Sambo at the age of six months. Bred and owned by F. Steiger (Switzerland).

Ch. Schnauzi's Noblesse. Bred and owned by F. Steiger (Switzerland).

United States but have not, as yet, been diagnosed in Continental lines. Dr. Alfrink spoke about movement and gait.

A specific item discussed by the meeting was the problem of dyeing coats. It was agreed that judges should be allowed to take samples of suspected coats for analysis. It was also agreed that a ISPU show would be organized every second year. Dr. Peper, the VDH president, was at the meeting and promised that CACs would be made available for this show.

Of all the ISPU meetings since the inaugural in 1977, the one on 15–16 November 1991 was undoubtedly the most significant. First of all, I must mention that after the death of Heinz Höller in December 1987, the PSK, and consequently, the ISPU experienced some changes in the committee. It was not easy to compensate for the loss of Heinz Höller's national and international relationships and the experience and leadership developed over seventeen years as chairman of the PSK.

At its annual general meeting in May 1991, the PSK again appointed a new presidium with Kurt Spiecker as chairman. Mr. Spiecker thereby also became the new president of ISPU. The agenda he prepared for the meeting included all actualities with relation to schnauzers and pinschers. Mr. Spiecker distinguished himself as a most constructive chairman, handling each item of the agenda with precision and accuracy.

At the election for the rest of the ISPU Committee, the following delegates were elected: Mme. Seltz (France), Mme. Rossier (Switzerland), Mr. Van Melis (Netherlands), and Mrs. Höller—Secretary-Treasurer (Germany).

The president opened the meeting with the announcement that the FCI had recognized the White Miniature Schnauzer as a breed. However, as this variety is still in a developmental stage, no CACIB would be awarded at any FCI licensed show for the time being.

While on the subject of the Miniature Schnauzer, the problem of a complete (forty-two teeth) scissors bite as required by the standard was discussed. The delegates decided that for the small breeds within the ISPU ranks (that is, Miniature Schnauzer, Miniature Pinscher, and Affenpinscher) one should definitely continue to strive for complete dentition; however, a maximum of two missing first premolars may be considered as acceptable for a rating of "excellent."

The next very important and controversial item on the agenda was the coat of the Miniature Schnauzer and the American approach to it. It was pointed out that, in fact, the problem of the American Miniature Schnauzer was more complex than just the coat difference. If one compares the new standard proposed by the American Miniature Schnauzer Club with the FCI standard, there are some fundamental differences in describing the breed.

To begin with, there is the American statement that the Miniature Schnauzer is a terrier type. This categorically contradicts the FCI standard. Directly linked with this terrier-like concept is the American description of the head, forechest, and topline with the position of the tail. The head, as pictured by the American standard, favors the length and tapering seen in many terrier breeds. By omitting the clause that the prosternum must clearly extend beyond the shoulder blades and upper forearms, the Americans leave the door open to an under-developed forechest, again enhancing the terrier look. Whereas the Germans describe the topline with a *slightly rounded* croup and a high-set tail (carried at two o'clock), the Americans require a totally straight topline with a tail carried erect and docked so short that it can no longer be established if the dog has an over-erected hare tail. Furthermore, the Americans emphasize the sloping topline and, therefore, breed for overangulated hindquarters so that they can present their Miniatures with the hind feet set far back to enhance the sloping effect.

In addition to these differences of type, there is a major deviation in describing the coat and color. For many years, the breeding goal of the Germans has been to obtain an intensely pigmented salt-and-pepper color *evenly distributed over the whole body, including the legs.* They ask for a darker facial mask but do away with *all white* fading described in the American standard.

More importantly, the *texture* of all color varieties is at stake. In the opinion of the Germans, a schnauzer is wire-haired from top to bottom. Such coat has to be kept clean and groomed for function, never for fashion. The American show Miniature Schnauzer is bred, raised, and groomed purely for fashion. The Americans strive for extreme furnishings, which may be of any texture except silky.

At the meeting, Dr. H. Räber, an author and schnauzer authority from Switzerland, felt that the divergence of the American from the Continental Miniature Schnauzer had become so extreme that the time had come to distinguish between two different breeds. During the discussion that followed and based on a practical demonstration by Mrs. Jordal (Denmark) with a salt-and-pepper Miniature Schnauzer that is not only an American champion but also has won many European championship titles, the following evidence came forth:

- In the United States, the Miniature Schnauzer is the most popular breed in the terrier group
- For the past fifteen years, American Miniature Schnauzers have often been successfully introduced in Continental lines
- The European public has shown interest in the more elegant "Americanized" Miniature Schnauzer
- Splitting the Miniature Schnauzer into two breeds would create enormous administrative problems, the formation of new clubs, and so forth

From the above points, delegates reached the logical final decision to follow the middle road policies.

Sweden

Ch. Argenta's Augustine—Int. Ch., *Klubsieger PSK,* and champion in Sweden, Finland, and Norway. Bred and owned by B. Niklasson, B. Andersson, and G. Garpas (Sweden).

Ch. Argenta's Griffith—*Klubsieger PSK* and champion in Sweden and Norway. Bred by B. Niklasson, B. Andersson, and G. Garpas; owned by S. Bergqvist (Sweden).

Argenta's Kimberley and Argenta's Kasimir at four months. Bred by B. Niklasson, B. Andersson, and G. Garpas (Sweden).

Ch. Mascar's Müllra. Bred by A. Radberg (Sweden).

Ch. Mascar's Maessak—Int. Ch. and champion in Sweden and Norway. Bred by A. Radberg (Sweden).

Ch. Mascar's Meinecka—Int. Ch. and champion in Sweden and Norway. Bred by A. Radberg; owned by H. Gelderman (Sweden).

- Improve the Continental Miniature Schnauzer where necessary by using good American imports
- Allow *no* tolerance where the wirehaired quality of the coat is concerned or for the correct pigmentation of the salt-and-pepper color, which must be evenly distributed over the whole body and legs
- Concede that for a companion dog like the Miniature Schnauzer, some tolerance should be allowed to this grooming-oriented breed and accept that the hair on the legs of the Miniature Schnauzer should not be longer than the hair on the body and should have the same structure

This was agreed by the delegates, and Mr. Spiecker confirmed that the judges should be instructed accordingly and that the allowance for longer hair on the legs of the Miniature Schnauzer did *not* apply to the Standard or Giant Schnauzers, as this would be detrimental to their functions as a utilitarian or working dog.

Still on the subject of the Miniature Schnauzer, Mr. Jordal, chairman of the Danish Miniature Schnauzer Club explained that his club had endeavored to collect as much information as possible on congenital juvenile cataract and progressive retinal atrophy. All information had been placed into a data bank, and he invited all members present to forward all results of examinations to the Danish club so that as much information as possible could be collated.

When Mr. Spiecker opened the discussion about tail docking, the tension in the assembly rose markedly. Currently, the governments of Norway, Finland, and Sweden have prohibited the docking of tails by law, beginning 1 January 1991; Denmark and the Netherlands are implementing the same law, beginning in 1992. Since 1987, the matter has been discussed at the level of the government of the European Community, and it is likely that other member countries are going to implement the same legislation.

The delegates expressed general concern about the proposed laws. Dr. Räber pointed out that our purebred dogs should be considered a cultural heritage. Changes implemented by law should be considered only after consent by directly involved parties. As a veterinary surgeon, Dr. Räber expressed skepticism that the docking of dog's tails should be prohibited while at the same time allowing the docking of lamb's tails and dehorning of calves. Lambs and calves are precocious—that is, they have a fully developed nervous system at birth and experience pain during the often rudimentary surgery.

The delegates concluded:
1. That the ISPU would send a well-motivated letter to the European Community through the correct channels, pointing out this discrepancy.
2. That, at present, the German breed standards for schnauzers and pinschers should not be altered to include a description of the undocked tail because:

- One has, as yet, no idea of how the average undocked tail should look; however, the Scandinavian dogs will, within the next few years, provide us with far more insight on the future conformation of the typical schnauzer tail
- It is also very likely that the tail of the Miniature Schnauzer will differ from the natural appendage of the Giant and Standard and will, therefore, require a different description

Thus, it was decided to adopt a wait-and-see policy, and breeders in countries where docking is prohibited were again advised to select for saber tails.

Mr. Mauerhofer (Switzerland) suggested that, in addition to the annual ISPU breed show, an ISPU International Working Trial (IPO) should be organized for Giant Schnauzers.

Before the meeting closed, it was further decided that the ISPU should meet every second year.

At a special general meeting held on 25 September 1993, a new PSK committee was elected. Among its tasks will be to prepare and organize all activities and festivities planned for the PSK Centenary in 1995.

Arnold Dierkes, the newly elected president, took the chair for the 1993 ISPU meeting, which was held on 23–24 of October. He proved to be an effective leader.

Mrs. Annmarie Thomassen from Sweden, as a voice for the Nordic Kennel Club was elected into the committee.

Applications for ISPU membership were received from clubs in Russia and the Czechoslovakian Republic. Further contact would be made with the Czech club for making payment of subscription in Deutsche Marks. The Russian application could not be accepted as the Russian clubs are not unified in a national dog club that is a member of the FCI.

The American Working Schnauzer Federation (AWSF) had also submitted its application. It was noted that the AWSF is a member of the American Working Dog Federation, which has undertaken steps to become a member of the FCI. Subject to the American Working Dog Federation becoming an FCI member, the AWSF would automatically be accepted as an ISPU member. In the meantime, it will be considered as a guest, allowed to take part in ISPU activities but without voting rights at the meetings.

The organization of the future ISPU shows was allocated as follows: 1994, Austria; 1995, Germany (Centenary); 1996, Sweden and Norway (subject to the quarantine regulations being lifted); 1997, Switzerland.

The dyeing of Miniature Schnauzer coats was also debated. The meeting unanimously agreed that this evil should be combatted. The German Kennel Club regulations make provision for a judge to use his discretion. If he suspects a dog of being dyed, he can refuse to place it. However, the ISPU is not empowered to generalize this rule. Each representative should approach its national kennel club with the request to issue a similar ruling.

It was brought to the attention of the meeting that in France the tendency has arisen to replace the term *poivre et sel* (pepper and salt) with *sable charbonné marqué de sable* (sable charcoal marked with sable). It was felt that this was incorrect and that the term *poivre et sel* should stand.

Addresses of the ISPU affiliated clubs may be obtained from the PSK head office.

Verband für das Deutsche Hundewesen, e.V. (VDH)

The VDH or German Kennel Club is the national all-breed kennel organization. Its offices are at Hoher Wall, 20 Dortmund 1.

The history of the VDH goes back to 1863 when, for the first time in Germany, a dog show was organized in Hamburg. It was, however, only in 1878 that a formal orga-nization—*Vereins zur Veredlung der Rassehunde* (Associa-tion for the Improvement of Purebred Dogs) was formed. In the same period, several specialty breed clubs were estab-lished.

In 1906, under the urging of Baron von Gingins, German dogdom was restructured as the *Kartell der Stammbuch-führende Specialklubs für Jagd- und Nutzhunde* (Cartel for Pedigree Issuing Breed Specialty Clubs for Hunting and Utilitarian Dogs). In this way, the most important clubs joined forces. Although the specialty clubs continued to draw up and issue their own pedigrees and annual stud-books, they did so under the supervision and coverage of the national organization, which also assumed responsi-bility for the supervision and coordination of different dog shows.

In 1910, it established contact with the Austrian, Swiss, and Belgian national dog organizations and, in 1911, took part in the inaugural meeting of the FCI.

The First World War caused a setback, but the organiza-tion recovered and, after a few years, again controlled breed specialty clubs, working dog organizations, and shows in general.

In 1933, the new National Socialist government imposed its ideas and forced a reorganization of German dogdom. On 1 October 1933, the *Reichsverbandes für das Deutsche Hundewesen* (Governmental Association for German Dogdom), under the leadership appointed by the party, came into operation. Nevertheless, the FCI, at its 1934 gen-eral meeting in Monte Carlo, elected H. Glockner (the German chairman) as chairman of the FCI. Germany was also asked to organize the forthcoming cynological world congress and world dog show, which took place in Frankfurt on 26–28 April 1935. More than 3,300 dogs rep-resenting fourteen nations were entered, and over 60,000 spectators visited the show. This set new standards in the FCI ranks.

The National Socialist government, however, increas-ingly exercised its authority and completely disturbed the normal function of German dogdom. On declaration of World War II, 16,000 working dogs were requisitioned, and 20 percent of these were selected as service dogs for the troops. Germany withdrew from the FCI. SS Reichsführer Himmler appointed one of his men as director of dog mat-ters. The war totally disrupted German dogsport as a hobby. In 1943, the head office of the national club was destroyed by bombs.

After the war and division into East and West Germany, with the help of some dog-loving members of the British occupation forces in 1945, West German dog fanciers tried and slowly succeeded to resurrect their hobby. Otto Borner was the driving figure behind this movement, and as secre-tary of a new West German dog organization, he published the first edition of its new magazine *Unser Rassehund*[1] in 1948.

At the 1949 general meeting, the 60,000 members were represented by a committee that unanimously decided to name their new organization *Verband für das Deutsche Hundewesen, e.V.* (VDH) and to apply for renewed affilia-tion with the FCI. In the years that followed, West German dogdom recovered steadily from the setbacks of the war.

At the 1955 FCI annual general meeting in Luxemburg, the West German chairman W. Dewitz was elected chair-man of the FCI. Consequently, the cynological world con-gress and world dog show were organized, with great success in 1956 in Dortmund.

By 1958, the VDH membership had grown to 150,000, and by 1964, this had increased to 210,000. More and more German judges were invited to judge in other countries.

In 1973, the FCI world congress was again held in Dortmund. Thirty-seven countries took part, with an entry of more than 5,000 dogs.

The German National Kennel Club celebrated its seventy-fifth anniversary in 1981. Dr. Bandel had been elected chairman of the FCI, and the world show and con-gress were again held in Dortmund. With nearly 9,000 entries, a new world record was set.

By the beginning of 1990, the VDH had grown to about 150 specialty clubs, representing nearly 700,000 members.

Then, something happened that nobody believed pos-sible—the Berlin Wall came down, and East and West Germany were reunited. The West German specialty clubs and the working and hunting dog associations opened their doors to East Germans. The amalgamation has taken place, and the VDH now represents the whole of German dogdom.

For the dog fancier anywhere in the world intending to import a dog from Germany, it is important to know that pedigrees can be issued by the breed specialty club (e. g., the PSK). It is necessary that, when a German dog is ex-ported, a set procedure is followed to give that pedigree international status. The German exporter of a schnauzer must send the pedigree to the PSK and indicate the name and address of the consignee. The PSK endorses the pedigree with the address of the new owner, and the VDH adds a letter stating that the PSK is the recognized holder of the breed's studbook and that the pedigree is recognized by foreign countries.

Most German pedigrees are very detailed and give extended information on the sire, dam, and other ancestors. Abbreviations referring to details are usually explained on the back of the pedigree.

In 1991, under the chairmanship of U. Fischer, the VDH again organized the FCI world event.

The VDH is undoubtedly the strongest FCI member. It also has an enormous cynological impact all over the world because of the international popularity of many of its national breeds.

Fédération Cynologique Internationale (FCI)

On 22 October 1911, representatives of the national dog organizations of Austria, Belgium, France, Germany, and the Netherlands decided to join forces to form an international federation with the specific aim of linking their efforts to foster the well-being of purebred dogs.

The First World War terminated this initiative, but it was revived in 1921 by a joint action of the Belgian Société Royale Saint Hubert and the French Société Canine Centralé. Other countries followed, and since 1932, international cynological congresses were organized, the first one held in Florence, Italy.

The FCI, whose registry office is presently in Thuin, Belgium, acquired legal status by the Belgian law of 25 October 1919, relating to international associations with philanthropic, religious, scientific, artistic, and educational aims.

The following are the goals of the FCI: to encourage and promote breeding and use of purebred dogs whose health and physical features meet the standard set for each respective breed and are capable of working, hunting, and accomplishing functions in accordance with the specific characteristics of the breed; to protect the use, keeping, and breeding of dogs in the member countries; to support free exchange of dogs and cynological information between member countries; and to initiate the organization of dog shows and working tests. The FCI shall, in particular, by issuing special regulations, take care of the following:

1. The mutual recognition of studbooks and pedigrees
2. The mutual recognition of kennel names and the establishment of an international register of kennel names and judges
3. The promotion of scientific research, which is of fundamental importance in cynology, and the free exchange of scientific information and breed standards as established by the countries of origin or countries of patronage of the respective breeds, which must be recognized by other countries as far as they are not in contradiction with national laws
4. The standardization—to all possible extent—of the national regulations by issuing regulations for international breed championships shows and working championships and by keeping a list of the breeds qualified to take part in such championships, seeking to maintain the high standard of judges appointed for international breed shows and working trials, supporting certain member countries if necessary in conjunction with other national organizations by providing professional information and necessary cynological experts
5. Defining—after prior approval of the representative of the breed's country of origin or country of patronage—and publishing the characteristics of each breed, and in any case, the standard of a new breed or any change in an existing standard will not be internationally acknowledged, however, unless the FCI's commission of breed standards and in cases of a new breed also the scientific commission have examined them and stated their opinion on the subject concerned
6. The mutual recognition of the penalties and procedures established by member countries

The FCI recognizes and accepts membership of only *one* national dog organization representing its country. There are *federated* and *associated* members. Associated members cannot be represented on the FCI general committee or on any of the FCI commissions. They may attend and take part in general assemblies but may not vote.

At the end of 1992, the list of FCI members was as follows:

Europe
- *Federated members:* Austria, Belgium, Denmark, Finland, France, Germany, Luxemburg, Hungary, Italy, Monaco, the Netherlands, Norway, Poland, Portugal, Spain, Sweden, Switzerland
- *Associated members:* Bulgaria, Croatia, Cyprus, Czechoslovakian Republic, Estonia, Greece, Iceland, Ireland, Rumania, San Marino, Slavonic Republic, Slovenia

Latin America
- *Federated members:* Argentina, Brazil, Chile, Colombia, Dominican Republic, Ecuador, Mexico, Panama, Paraguay, Peru, Puerto Rico, Uraguay, Venezuela
- *Associated members:* Bermuda, Bolivia, Costa Rica, Cuba, Guatemala, Honduras, San Salvador

Asia
- *Federated members:* Korea, Israel, Japan, Philippines, Taiwan, Thailand
- *Associated members:* Bahrain, Hong Kong, India, Indonesia, Malaysia, Singapore, Sri Lanka

Africa
- *Federated members:* Morocco, South Africa

Spain

Ch. Garse van de Havenstad (Giant). Bred by C. de Meulenaer; owned by J. Sanchez (Spain).

Ch. Elmo v. d. Hohen Ward—best in show in Madrid, winner of the trophy of the king of Spain (Giant). Bred by B. Binjash; owned by J. Sanchez (Spain).

Ch. Pele de Pichera—*Europasieger, Bundessieger,* and champion in Spain. V. Barat and V. Giner (Spain).

Ch. Domino Manso Pelegri at Kanix (Standard). Bred by M. and A. Gil de Biedma (Spain); owned by K. and S. Wilberg.

South Africa

Ch. Pyrra van't Wareheim, APT (Giant). Bred and owned by J. and E. Gallant (Republic of South Africa).

Ch. Bastian van't Wareheim, APT, IPO III (Giant). Bred and owned by J. and E. Gallant (Republic of South Africa).

- *Associated members:* Madagascar, Zimbabwe
Australia
- *Federated members:* Australia
- *Associated members:* New Zealand

Since the 1991 changes in the Eastern Block, countries such as Russia have applied for membership. It must be noted that based on the FCI constitution only one national dog club per country can be accepted. Some of these countries will have to sort out their internal dog affairs and unify their clubs before FCI membership can be obtained. Addresses of affiliated members can be obtained from FCI, 13 Place Albert I, B-6530 Thuin, Belgium.

The management of the FCI is organized by a general assembly, a general committee, an executive committee, and commissions—legal commission, scientific commission, and the commission for breed standards. It is understandable that the scientific commission, which is composed of academics and scientists, coordinates the scientific cynological research within the FCI ranks. This commission will also tackle specific problems and advise or instruct accordingly.

The commission for breed standards is also composed of highly qualified cynologists. Any amendment to a breed standard or any new breed standard must be submitted to this committee for final perusal, discussion, and approval before it becomes binding in the member countries.

Beside the compulsory commissions, others have been set up; for example, the commission for working dogs, which has elaborated the rules and regulations for international working trials. Others are related to activities specific to certain groups or breeds; for example, pointers, spaniels, retrievers, terriers, sighthounds, sled dogs, and sheepdogs. There are also commissions dealing with agility and obedience as well as shows and judges.

The FCI encourages kennel clubs in affiliated countries to give their breed shows as well as working and hunting trials an international status. If the conditions are met, the FCI will place CACIBs and CACITs at the disposal of the clubs. This means that under such conditions, a dog that qualifies in an international breed show may, in addition to the national CAC, be awarded an international CACIB. The same applies to CACITs for international working and field trials.

Based on the required number of CACIBs and CACITs obtained in different countries under different judges and over a certain period of time, the FCI will award the title of International Champion for breed, working, or field trials.

The Kennel Club (London)

The 1873 foundation of the Kennel Club (KC) in London, the first national dog organization, ushered in a new era. The British invented the modern dog sport. In those days, they already had many purebred breeds, and they needed a registry and governing body. The British

Empire was in full expansion, and in the following decades, British subjects in the most remote parts of the world established kennel clubs, inspired by the KC's example.

It is obvious that, under the circumstances, the KC felt no need to join an umbrella organization such as the FCI, which they had not invented and did not need. British cynology, strengthened by its geographic isolation and the introduction of quarantine, grew into a stronghold on its own. Consequently, in the Western world, the approach to dogs and related matters, somehow, diverged in two directions. On the one hand, the KC, with influx in the English-speaking world, and on the other hand, the Continental European way, which promoted its opinions through the FCI.

From the beginning, the British approach was very businesslike. They invented breeding kennels, boarding kennels, kennel maids, grooming parlors, vets for pets, and so forth. In the following century and compared to the number of imports, the United Kingdom exported an astonishing number of dogs.

Where the FCI continued to promote the original working ability by submitting all traditional working breeds to an elementary working test specifically related to each breed before international championship titles could be awarded, the British did not really believe in breeding dogs that, at the same time, could win in the show ring and at the same time perform in working or field trials.

The approach to obedience and working and field-trial training in the KC area of influence and in the Continental European context is based on different techniques and directed toward different goals. In the United Kingdom, these normal canine activities are not, in principle, promoted for purebred show dogs. They are to a large extent considered as an outlet for purebred dogs that are not necessarily competing in the show ring and for crossbreds. In other words, very few show dogs participate in obedience classes or working trials because the mental and physical qualities required for this are not considered of primary importance by the show-dog fancier.

The tradition of selecting and training modern purebred guard dogs is a Continental heritage. What I'm trying to point out is that in the schnauzer's country of origin a dedicated breeder endeavors to obtain the seal of selected breeder for beauty and the purpose of advanced training *(Kör-und Leistungszucht)*. Even if, therefore, he has to work his Standard or Giant Schnauzer to obtain a pass in the breed survey and a qualification in SchH I or IPO 1. In the eyes of the KC, Schutzhund does not deserve recognition, and such tests are not officially available under KC regulations.

Under KC regulations, the dog breeds are divided into sporting and nonsporting and classified in six groups: hounds, gundogs, terriers, toys, working, and utility. The utility group has traditionally been reserved for those breeds that don't find an obvious place in one of the other groups.

Denmark

Ch. Klondaike's Diplomat (Miniature). Bred by B. and N. Jordal (Denmark).

Israel

Ch. Daisy Bar Hod, SchH I (Giant). Owned by A. Trafikant (Israel).

New Zealand

Brickmark Louie (Miniature). Bred and owned by M. Brick (New Zealand).

Brickmark Black Jack (Miniature). Bred and owned by M. Brick (New Zealand).

United Kingdom

Ch. Risepark Chase the Ribbons. Bred by P. Newman; owned by Messrs. Newman and Day (Great Britain).

Ch. Risepark The Leading Lady., Bred and owned by P. Newman (Great Britain).

Ch. Malenda Masterblend at Risepark. Bred by Glenys Allen and owned by Messrs. Newman and Day (Great Britain).

Ch. Risepark Here Comes Charlie. Owned by Messrs. Newman and Day (Great Britain).

For many years, the Schnauzer Club of Great Britain has successfully cared for the well-being of all schnauzers, which were all shown in the utility group. The club kept contact with the Continent, and in spite of quarantine regulations, several good schnauzers were imported. The British breeders, undoubtedly, contributed to the selection of a good, natural uncropped ear, and they developed outstanding grooming skills.

In 1980, Clifford Derwent and other Giant Schnauzer fanciers undertook the transfer of their breed from the utility to the working group, and they established a separate Giant Schnauzer Club. It seems that, since this separation, the breed's quality and popularity in the United Kingdom have improved.

As an outsider, I can only guess what will happen if, through the influence of the European Community and the opening of the tunnel under the Channel, British quarantine regulations are altered, allowing schnauzers from both sides of the Channel to be shown together. I realize that many conservatives may shiver or be shocked by such presumptions. It is my belief, however, that by the year 2000 Picadilly's Dreamer and Baldur v. Strohblumental (possibly both with natural tails) will compete against each other in Birmingham and Dortmund.

The North American Scene

The purebred dog tradition in North America was inaugurated in 1885 by the foundation of the American Kennel Club (AKC). Very much in line with what I wrote about the KC, the AKC has, even more, honored the point of view that there is no business like show dog business. The Americans have perfected the system and techniques of professional handling.

There is no other country where show dogs and people owning and showing them have attained such status. The whole tradition is so big that the majority of fanciers believe that the rest of the world is miles behind and of no importance. Showing dogs has become a big affair where, in many cases, fashion prevails. The show dog has attained the status of an object to be exhibited. This attitude is often at the expense of canine individuality. Such dogs are bred, raised, and conditioned exclusively for the show ring. Moreover, breed standards are often revised on the basis of the trend set by show dogs. The 1991 revision of the American Miniature Schnauzer Club definitely indicates that direction.

This emphasis on show dogs is, presumably, the reason that, next to the AKC, there are so many dissident dog organizations in the United States, virtually all of them related to the working abilities of gundogs, hounds, and guard dogs.

Like the KC, the AKC and the Canadian Kennel Club (CKC) have no reciprocal agreements with the FCI or other kennel organizations. There exits a gentleman's agreement by which pedigrees are recognized and judges exchanged.

The North American show dog fraternity is so massive and powerful that it has created its own independent style. Breed specialty clubs for foreign breeds are often unaware of what is going on in their breed's country of origin. After all, they may argue, the demand of the American public is a greater imperative. As an outsider, I believe that the demand of the American public, the potential schnauzer buyer, is based on the schnauzers that are winning in the show ring because these dogs and their titles speak to the public's imagination. It is, therefore, the responsibility of the schnauzer specialty clubs to promote the type of schnauzer that is most practical and useful for the public, even if this is not fully in line with the glamour preferred by the judges who give their very own interpretation to the breed standard.

As chairman of a schnauzer club in another part of the world, it is my experience that the only effective way to reverse a trend is for the national breed clubs to send educational material and express their wishes to judges. To really promote and protect a breed, it is essential that these recommendations are based on the directives and trends as fostered by the breed authorities in its country of origin.

During 1991, the Working Schnauzer Federation was established in the United States. This body promotes Schutzhund training and competition for schnauzers. The content of *Schnauzer Browser,* their quarterly magazine, clearly indicates their success. There is a good possibility that an American team will be competing in Germany in the 1993 ISPU-IPO World Championship.

In 1992, the Giant Schnauzer Club of America undertook the revision of the breed standard with the goal of combating exaggerations of size, coat, and color. They realized that, over the past few decades, an "American type" has been developing. They are aware that this kind of Giant diverges too much from the German ideal. They are also aware that the trend is likely to continue unless breeders, handlers, and judges pay closer attention to the standard.

Unless Americans take drastic steps, American schnauzers will diverge more and more from their brothers. This would be a big pity because American schnauzers have so many fine qualities.

I felt that by now I had provided Pam and Charles with quite some information on schnauzers. Before leaving them, I promised to send them an illustrated breed standard together with more details on performance tests and training in general.

---

[1] *Our Purebred Dogs.*

A head study of Ch. Boris v. d. Schipbeek, a salt-and-pepper Standard with uncropped ears. Bred by J. Beeftink (Netherlands).

14

A Comparative Study of Three Breed Standards— PSK, KC, and AKC

Introduction

This chapter presents an illustrated and comparative study of three breed standards—PSK, KC, and AKC. The novice schnauzer owner could well think that this is thoroughly misleading and promptly ask the following questions.

- Aren't schnauzers the same in all countries?
- Why are there different descriptions of the breed?

Let me explain. It should be clear that the schnauzer is a German breed and that the original standard was drawn up in Germany. This happened before the schnauzer was exported to other countries and became well-known in other parts or the world. The original breed standard was amended from time to time to reflect the evolution of the breed. Such breed descriptions or changes are compiled by breed connoisseurs within the bosom of the breed's specialty club in the country of origin.

The previous revision to the schnauzer standard was in 1973. A new proposal was formulated and tabled for approval at the 1995 AGM of the PSK. Once such a proposal for amendments has been discussed at the PSK committee level, the document is referred to the VDH, the national dog organization. After approval, the VDH forwards it to the FCI commission for breed standards for final perusal and decision. Once approved by the FCI, the breed standard or changes are published in the language of the country of origin and translated into French, German, Spanish, and English. From that moment, the standard is binding in all FCI federated member countries. Associated countries and nonmember countries with independent national dog organizations such as the KC, AKC, and the CKC can, of course, use their own discretion in such matters.

I strongly suspect that in the old days, when the first schnauzers were exported from Germany, the FCI system of making English translations of the breed standard available was not available. As such, the kennel clubs in Great Britain and North America had to provide their own translations. Such translations can be verbally and grammatically correct, they can even contain improvements, but if one does not have direct ties with the specialists in the breed's parent club, it is difficult to capture the real spirit in which the breed particulars must be interpreted. Besides, if one embraces the attitude that imported breeds have to be reduced to common standards, it is logical that the new descriptive details of the imported breed will differ from those of its homeland, and because of this different types of schnauzers will slowly develop. Local fashion and a lack of specialist judges guided by the parent breed club encourages this trend.

At this stage, I may state that the FCI breed standard for schnauzers is used by all FCI federated countries and most of the associated ones. The American version is used in the United States, and the Canadians have a slightly different wording. The KC version is, of course, used in the United Kingdom, and I assume, similar wording is used in New Zealand and Australia. In South Africa, the KC standard is used for Miniatures and Standards, but due to a request by the specialty club, the FCI standard is used for the Giant Schnauzer.

During 1992 the American club has proposed some important changes to the AKC standard for the Miniature Schnauzer. The American Giant Schnauzer Club has decided to adopt a policy whereby judges and fanciers should be reminded of the specific prescriptions as far as coat and size of the Giant Schnauzer are concerned. This emphasizes that although a good American description of the breed exists, judging does not always take place in accordance with this standard.

In view of their centenary activities and in line with the recommendations by the FCI the PSK has reworked and restructured complete new standards for pinschers and schnauzers.

The new standards were finalized on the 16th of June 1995. They have been sent to the V.D.H. for approval and reference to the Commission for Breed Standards of the F.C.I. It is possible that this Commission still recommends that a few minor changes are made or that one or another description is better defined.

After translation in English (already completed), French, and Spanish, they will become effective and binding in all F.C.I. federated countries.

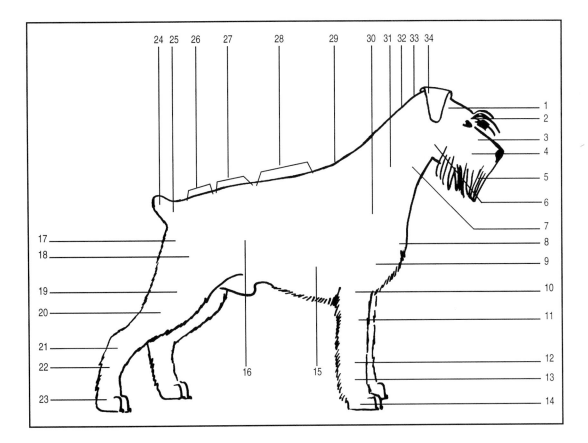

Figure 14-1.
Topographical
anatomy.

1. Skull
2. Stop
3. Foreface
4. Muzzle
5. Chin
6. Cheek
7. Throat
8. Prosternum
9. Upper Arm
10. Elbow
11. Forearm
12. Wrist
13. Forepastern
14. Forefoot
15. Rib cage
    (Chest, Brisket)
16. Flank
17. Buttocks
18. Upper Thigh
19. Stifle Joint
20. Lower Thigh
21. Hock Joint
22. Rear Pastern
23. Hind Foot
24. Tail
25. Set on of Tail
26. Croup
    (Rump)
27. Loin
28. Back
29. Withers
30. Shoulder
31. Neck
32. Crest
33. Nape
34. Ear

Figure 14-2.   Skeletal
anatomy.

1. Skull
2. Mandible
3. Shoulder Joint
4. Prosternum
5. Humerus
6. Ulna & Radius
7. Carpus
8. Metacarpus
9. Phalanges
10. Sternum
    (Breastbone)
11. Chest
12. Femur
13. Stifle Joint
14. Tibia & Fibula
15. Hock Joint
    (Tarsals)
16. Metatarsals
17. Phalanges
18. Hip Joint
19. Pelvis
20. Coccygeal
    Vertebrae
    (Tail)
21. Sacrum
22. Lumbar Vertebrae
23. Thoracic Vertebrae
24. Scapula (Shoulder
    Blade)
25. Cervical Vertebrae

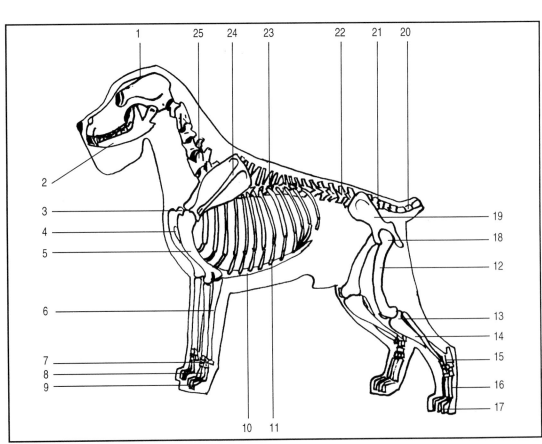

Heading of the 1995 P.S.K. Breed Standards for Schnauzers

FCI-Standard Nr.: 181

Name of the breed:
Riesenschnauzer
Giant Schnauzer

Translation:
Johan Gallant / Walter Schicker
6 Sept. 1995.

Country of origin: Germany

Date of publication of the original standard: 16.06.1995.

Utilization:
Protection- and companion dog.

FCI classification:
Group 2 / Section 1: Pinschers and Schnauzers

With working test.

Short historical overview:
In the southern German regions where he generated, he was originally used as a cattle driver. Around the turn of the century some determined breeders recognized his outstanding working abilities and his valuable character and temperament. His official registration commences in 1913 and already in 1925 he obtains the *official* recognition and classification as a "Working Dog Breed".

FCI-Standard Nr.: 182

Name of the breed:
Schnauzer
Standard Schnauzer

Translation:
J. Gallant & W. Schicker
6 September 1995.

Country of origin: Germany

Date of publication of the original standard: 16.06.1995.

Utilization:
Watch- and companion dog.

FCI classification:
Group 2 / Section 1: Pinschers and Schnauzers

No working test.

Short historical overview:
Because of his affinity with horses he was originally used in southern Germany as a stable dog. He received popularly the name "Rattler" (rat catcher) because of his outstanding ability to kill rats. In 1895, at the establishment of the first German speciality club for the breed, he was still registered as "wire-haired Pinscher".

FCI-Standard Nr.: 183

Name of the breed:
Zwergschnauzer
Miniature Schnauzer

Translation:
J. Gallant & W. Schicker
6 September 1995.

Country of origin: Germany

Date of publication of the original standard: 16.06.1995.

Utilization:
Companion dog.

FCI classification:
Group 2 / Section 1: Pinschers and Schnauzers

No working test.

Short historical overview:
Around the turn of the century, a smaller type of Schnauzer, which in those days was still referred to as "Miniature Wire-haired Pinscher", made his way from the Frankfurt/M region. From the panoply of different shapes, sizes and types, the jumble of wiry, wooly, and silky coat structures, it proved to be a difficult task to create a smaller dog which in exterior and character would correspond with his taller brother—the Standard Schnauzer.

Comparative Study of Three Breed Standards

Pinscher-Schnauzer Klub (PSK) * Kennel Club London (K.C.) * American Kennel Club (A.K.C.)

I am providing a comparative study of the PSK, KC and AKC standards. This is not intended as a critical study but as an objective comparison of the German version with the opinions in other parts of the world. It is my personal belief that *for any dog breed in the world,* its breed standard as elaborated by the parent club in its country of origin should be considered as the lighthouse.

Miniature Schnauzer Standards

This section emphasizes and illustrates the essential points of the PSK standard and indicates where deviations have occurred in the KC and AKC standards. It also stresses the areas in which fashion or local trend has encouraged deviation. When reading through these standards, I got the impression that the German version is intended to describe the ideal every day schnauzer, while the AKC standard describes the Miniature exclusively for the purpose of the show ring.

Table 14-1. (Miniature Schnauzer)

PSK (Germany)	KC (London)	AKC (United States)
GENERAL APPEARANCE Small, strong rather thickset than slim, wirehaired, the smaller version of the Standard Schnauzer without dwarflike (toyish) appearance **PROPORTIONS** Square-built; nearly square in proportion of body length to height at withers. The length of the head (from tip of nose to occiput) is in proportion to the length of the back (from withers to set on of tail) in ratio of 1 : 2.	**GENERAL APPEARANCE** Sturdily built, robust, sinewy, nearly square (length of body equal to height at shoulders). Expression keen and attitude alert. Correct conformation is of more importance than colour or other purely beauty points.	**GENERAL APPEARANCE** The Miniature Schnauzer is a robust, active dog of terrier type, resembling his larger cousin the Standard Schnauzer in general appearance, and of an alert, active disposition. Faults: Type; toyishness, ranginess or coarseness.

Comment (Table 14-1). There is a good approach from all parties. However, the Germans don't agree that the Miniature is of terrier type. It is my belief that the divergencies between the American Miniature Schnauzer and the European counterpart, which will come to light in our further study, all find their origin in this incorrect classification.

Table 14-2. (Miniature Schnauzer)

PSK (Germany)	KC (London)	AKC (United States)
BEHAVIOR AND CHARACTER His traits correspond with the ones of the Standard Schnauzer and are enhanced by the temperament and the mannerism of the miniature dog. Cleverness, undauntedness, endurance and alertness make the Miniature Schnauzer a pleasant pet as well as a watch- and companion dog which can easily be kept in a smaller house (apartment or flat).	**CHARACTERISTICS** Well balanced, smart, stylish and adaptable. **TEMPERAMENT** Alert, reliable, and intelligent. Primarily a companion dog.	**TEMPERAMENT** The typical Miniature Schnauzer is alert and spirited, yet obedient to command. He is friendly, intelligent and willing to please. He should never be over-aggressive or timid. Faults: Temperament: shyness or viciousness.

Comment (Table 14-2). In principle, all parties have the same point of view. It is, however, essential that I digress on the trait of endurance as pointed out in the PSK standard. In their opinion, the Miniature Schnauzer, although a smaller dog, has great physical capacity. He can fit in an apartment but at the same time, he can romp for hours in all weather conditions. In Germany, many Miniatures compete in all kinds of dog sports, and it is not unusual to see them qualifying in the endurance test, which consists of a 10 km (6½ mi) run next to a bicycle.

Bite and Position of Teeth

(a) A correct scissors bite with the outer surfaces of the lower incisors engaging with the inner surfaces of the upper incisors when the mouth is closed.

(b) An incorrect pincer (even) bite in which the cutting surfaces of the upper and lower incisors meet edge to edge.

The narrowing of the head starts from the eyes toward a blunt nose. The distance from the top of the skull to the eyes is equal to the distance from the eyes to the tip of the muzzle.   (a) Top view.   (b) Side view.

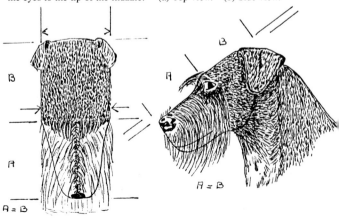

Table 14-3. (Miniature Schnauzer)

PSK (Germany)	KC (London)	AKC (United States)

HEAD

SKULL: The skull is strong and elongated, without pronounced occiput. The head is in harmony with the substance of the dog. The forehead is flat and unwrinkled and runs parallel to the ridge of the nose.

STOP: The stop is markedly emphasized by the eyebrows.

FOREFACE:
NOSE: The tip of the nose is full and black. The ridge is straight.
MUZZLE: Ends in a moderately blunt wedge.
LIPS: Tight and black.
JAWS/TEETH: Strong and rounded. A full complement of strong, pure white teeth meeting in a scissors bite. There should be 42 teeth.
JAW MUSCLES: The masseters are strongly developed; however the cheeks should not be protruding to disturb the rectangular shape of the head (with beard).
EYES: Of medium size, oval, directed forward, dark and lively. The eyelids are tight.
EARS: Folded ears, V-shaped, set high and carried symmetrically with the innersides touching the head, turned forward in the direction of the temples with the parallel folds not surfacing the upper-line of the skull. (In countries where as yet no ban on cropping exists, cropped ears must be carried symmetrically in an upright poise.)

HEAD AND SKULL

Head strong and of good length, narrowing from ears to eyes and then gradually forward toward end of nose. Upper part of the head (occiput to the base of forehead) moderately broad between the ears. Flat, creaseless forehead; well muscled but not too strongly developed cheeks. Medium stop to accentuate prominent eyebrows. Powerful muzzle ending in a moderately blunt line, with bristly, stubby moustache and chin whiskers. Ridge of nose straight and running almost parallel to extension of forehead. Nose black with wide nostrils. Lips tight but not overlapping.
MOUTH: Jaws strong with perfect, regular and complete scissors bite, i.e. the upper teeth closely overlapping the lower teeth and set square to the jaws.
EYES: Medium sized, dark, oval, set forward, with arched bushy eyebrows.
EARS: Neat, V-shaped, set high and dropping forward to the temple.

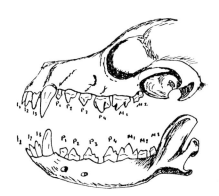

HEAD

Strong and rectangular, its width diminishing slightly from ears to eyes, and again to the tip of the nose. The forehead is unwrinkled. The top skull is flat and fairly long. The foreface is parallel to the top skull, with a slight stop; and it is at least as long as the top skull. The muzzle is strong, in proportion to the skull; it ends in a moderately blunt manner, with thick whiskers which accentuate the rectangular shape of the head.
Faults: Head: coarse and cheeky.

TEETH

The teeth meet in a scissors bite. That is, the upper front teeth overlap the lower front teeth in such a manner that the inner surface of the upper incisors barely touch the outer surface of the lower incisors when the mouth is closed.
Faults: Bite. Undershot or overshot jaw. Level bite.

EYES

Small, dark brown and deep-set. They are oval in appearance and keen in expression.
Faults: Eyes: light and or large and prominent in appearance.forward, dark and lively.

EARS

When cropped, the ears are identical in shape and length, with pointed tips. They are in balance with the head and not exaggerated in length. They are set high on the skull and carried perpendicularly at the inner edges, with as little bell as possible along the outer edges.
When uncropped, the ears are small and V-shaped, folding close to skull.

Comment (Table 14-3). The PSK standard mentions that the skull is elongated—that is, not square but slightly rectangular, definitely not trapezoidal. However, the muzzle ends in a moderately blunt wedge. This means that the narrowing of the head starts from the eyes toward a blunt nose, *not* from the ears to the eyes and then again to the nose as is common in many terrier heads. This is not the ideal and should, therefore, not be described as such.

The PSK standard insists on a full complement of forty-two teeth meeting in a scissors bite. Incorrect and incomplete bites are hereditary and as little deviation as possible should be tolerated.

The correct proportion of muzzle to skull is 1 : 1. To specify that the foreface is *at least* as long as the skull allows proportions of 1.2 : 1. This may be typical of a terrier head but not for a schnauzer head.

The comment that the eyelid should be tight draws attention to the possibility that it may be loose, indicating ectropion (loose lower eyelid). I believe that both—ectropion and entropion (turned-in lower eyelid)—are hereditary problems, creating discomfort, and both should be taken into account in any judge's decision making.

Table 14-4. (Miniature Schnauzer)

PSK (Germany)	KC (London)	AKC (United States)
NECK • Profile: The muscular nape is curved upward. The neck blends harmoniously into the withers. • Form: Powerfully fitted, yet refined, nobly crested, in proportion to the substance of the dog. • Skin: Unwrinkled and fitting tightly to the throat (dry neck).	**NECK** Moderately long, strong and slightly arched; skin close to throat; neck set cleanly on shoulders.	**NECK** Strong and well arched, blending into the shoulders, and with the skin fitting tightly at the throat.

Comment (Table 14-4). One of the main features that gives the Miniature Schnauzer an expression of nobility is a strong, well-muscled but, at the same time, elegantly crested neck that blends into the shoulders with a flowing line—that is, not set in a clear angle.

The Miniature Schnauzer's head must be carried proudly, in a natural way. It is artificial if, in the show ring, a handler pulls a Miniature's head and neck upward and forward to obtain a crested neck, and the ideal picture of the neck's line running parallel to the line from stifle to hock.

Table 14-5. (Miniature Schnauzer)

PSK (Germany)	KC (London)	AKC (United States)
BODY • Topline: Slightly sloping from withers to croup. • Withers: High and clearly defined. • Back: Short and firm. • Loin: The distance from the end of the ribcage to the pelvis is short, giving the impression of a short-coupled dog. • Croup: Slightly rounded, flowing over into the set on of tail. • Chest: Moderately broad, ribs well sprung, in cross-section oval, brisket deep and reaching just below the elbows. The forechest is, through the prosternum clearly extending beyond the shoulder joints, markedly pronounced. • Underline and belly: The under-chest raises slightly towards the loin. The belly is moderately drawn up. • Tail: Docked to 3 joints. Harmoniously continuing the slope of the croup and carried slightly raised. (In countries where tail docking is prohibited by law, it can be left in its natural state).	**BODY** Chest moderately broad, deep with visible, strong breastbone reaching at least to height of elbows, rising slightly backward to loins. Back strong and straight, slightly higher at shoulder than at hindquarters, with short, well developed loins. Ribs well sprung. Length of body equal to height from top of withers to ground. **TAIL** Set on and carried high, customarily docked to three joints.	**BODY** Short and deep, with the brisket extending at least to the elbows. Ribs are well sprung and deep, extending well back to a short loin. The underbody does not present a tucked-up appearance at the flank. The backline is straight; it declines slightly from the withers to the base of the tail. The withers form the highest point of the body. The overall length from chest to buttocks appear the equal the height at the withers. Faults: Chest too broad or shallow in brisket. Hollow or roach back. **TAIL** Set high and carried erect. It is docked only long enough to be clearly visible over the backline of the body when the dog is in proper length of coat. Fault: Tail set too low.

Comment (Table 14-5). Three very important details need to be clarified.

1. It is not enough that a schnauzer has a deep chest extending beyond the elbows. It is also essential that he displays a moderately broad chest with a *forechest* that is formed by the most forward part of the sternum clearly extending beyond the line formed by the shoulder blades and the upper arms. Such a forechest, together with correct angulation of the forequarters, is an absolute for the well-constructed schnauzer. It differentiates the schnauzer from the terrier, and this detail should never be omitted from any schnauzer breed standard.

2. The PSK standard requires a slightly rounded croup, which must be viewed as a cardinal sin by the straight-back advocates.

Malya Togo—*Jahressieger* (Giant) and Ch. Malya Poptor—Int. Ch., *Klubsieger* Italy, and champion in Italy (Miniature). Bred and owned by Milia Pozzi (Italy). All schnauzers have the same basic proportions, no matter what their size.

It is anatomically and physiologically extremely important that the spinal column is not composed of straight segments. Besides containing the spinal cord, the spine functions as a flexible chassis to which the whole motive system is linked. It is extremely important that the spine, over its entire length, maintains its normal anatomical curves to fulfill its function of flexible shock absorber and spring.

The angle of the croup is defined by the position of the sacrum, to which the caudal vertebrae (tail) are linked. The lay of the croup is determined by the way in which the dog wants to express his mood by holding or moving his tail in a certain manner. A lively schnauzer, when in a situation requiring alertness will instinctively tighten the muscles running over the sacrum to the tail, raise the tail, and level the croup. To please the judge, a level croup may be achieved by making your schnauzer stand alertly.

3. The PSK standard requires that the docked tail is set high and carried slightly raised. An over-erect or hare's tail (which American's refer to as a *gay* tail) is considered a fault. This means that the base of the tail begins at the end of the sacrum and that the stump is carried at one or two o'clock.

This requirement is linked to and can be explained by the normal anatomical spinal curves. Moreover, we must bear in mind the tendency in some countries toward non-docked tails, which in schnauzers, should be of the saber type that is carried either upward or downward in a gently or slightly curved fashion. The saber tail is an extension of the slightly raised stump. Schnauzers that have been bred for flat croups and over-erect tail carriage will produce offspring with curled tails.

Table 14-6. (Miniature Schnauzer)

PSK (Germany)	KC (London)	AKC (United States)
FOREQUARTERS • General: The forelegs are constructed as strong supports, they are straight viewed from all sides and stand moderately wide (neither too narrow nor too wide). • Shoulders: The shoulder-blade is long, well angulated, lying close and flat. The shoulder is well muscled. • Upper arms: Long, well angulated, and strongly muscled. • Elbows: Close to body. • Forearms: The length of the forearms must correspond with the length of the upper-arms. Viewed from all sides they must be straight. • Wrists: These joints may not be broadened. • Pasterns: Firm, vertical when viewed from the front and slightly angulated to the ground when seen from the side. • Forefeet: Short and round. They have tightly closed, well arched toes (cat's paws), with dark nails, and hard, tough pads.	**FOREQUARTERS** Shoulders flat and well laid. Forelegs straight when viewed from any angle. Muscles smooth and lithe rather than prominent; bone strong, straight and carried well down to feet; elbows close to the body and pointing directly backwards.	**FOREQUARTERS** Forelegs are straight and parallel when viewed from all sides. They have strong pasterns and good bone. They are separated by a fairly deep brisket which precludes a pinched front. The elbows are close, and the ribs spread gradually from the first rib so as to allow space for the elbows to move close to the body. Faults: Loose elbows. **SHOULDERS** The sloping shoulders are strongly muscled, yet flat and clean. They are well laid back so that from the side the tips of the shoulder blades are in a nearly vertical line above the elbow. The tips of the blades are placed closely together. They slope forward and downward at an angulation which permits the maximum forward extension of the forelegs without binding or effort. Both the shoulder blades and the upper arm are long permitting depth of the chest at the brisket.

Comment (Table 14-6). The angles of the forequarters and hindquarters are important and must be in harmony with each other to allow the schnauzer to move in a free and effortless way. For a compact and square-built dog such as the schnauzer, it is important that his kinetic system is joined in such a manner that, when trotting, the forward-moving hind paw reaches a place level with the one where the opposite front paw touched down. Therefore, the ideal angulation of the forequarters consists of the shoulder blades sloping forward at an angle of nearly 45 degrees toward an imaginary horizontal line and the upper arms sloping back at a similar angle. Such balanced angulation will allow the required reach of the forequarters.

It is also essential that the front pasterns are slightly angled—about 10 degrees—at the carpal joint (wrist) to give the necessary kick.

Ch. Timmy van de Drie Harten—Int. Ch., *Klubsieger,* and champion in Germany, Luxemburg, and the Netherlands (Miniature). Owned by M. Rulkens (Netherlands).

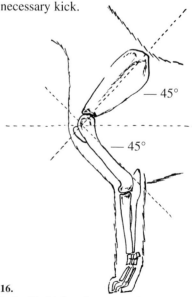

Figure 14-16.
Ideally, both shoulder blade and upper arm lay on an angle of about 45 to 50 degrees—well laid back. The forepastern has an angle of about 10 degrees.

Table 14-7. (Miniature Schnauzer)

PSK (Germany)	KC (London)	AKC (United States)
HINDQUARTERS • General: Seen from the side they are slanting, viewed from behind parallel. • Upper thighs: Long, in harmony with the substance of the dog, directed forward, broad and strongly muscled. • Knee: Clearly angulated, is situated straight between the upper and under thigh, without pointing inward nor outward. • Under thighs: Long and strong, length in correct proportion to the whole build of the hindquarters. • Hock joint: Angulation well pronounced. • Rear pasterns: Longer than the front pasterns, yet not too long, not disturbing the harmony. • Hind feet: As forefeet, only longer. No rear dewclaws.	**HINDQUARTERS** Thighs slanting and flat but strongly muscled. Hind legs (upper and lower thighs) at first vertical to the stifle; from stifle to hock in line with the extension of the upper neck line; from hock vertical to ground. **FEET** Short, round, cat-like, compact with closely arched toes, dark nails, firm black pads, feet pointing forwards.	**HINDQUARTERS** The hindquarters have strong-muscled slanting thighs, they are well bent at the stifles. There is sufficient angulation so that, in stance, the hocks extend beyond the tail. The hindquarters never appear overbuilt or higher than the shoulders. The rear pasterns are short and, in stance, perpendicular to the ground and when viewed from the rear are parallel to each other. Faults: Sickle hocks, cow hocks, open hocks or bowed hindquarters. **FEET** Short and round (cat feet) with thick, black pads. The toes are arched and compact.

Comment (Table 14-7). After the explanation of the angulation of the forequarters, I must simply add that, to be in harmony with the front, the upper thigh (femur) lies at a straight angle toward the slightly sloping pelvis. This implies that in a normal stance the upper thigh is slightly directed forward, and *not* vertical to the ground or stretched backward. Ideally, we find an angle of 120 degrees at the stifle (knee joint) and 140 degrees at the hock, which will place the rear pastern in a line vertical to the ground.

Figure 14-18.
The ideal angulation of the hindquarters is 120 degrees at the stifle joint and 140 degrees at the hock.

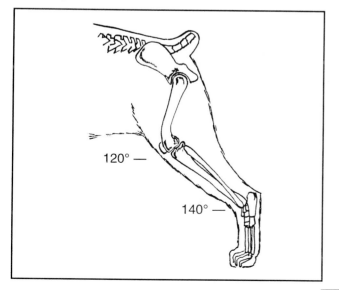

Ch. Feldmar Pistol Pete (Miniature). Bred and owned by M. Feld (United States).

Table 14-8. (Miniature Schnauzer)

PSK (Germany)	KC (London)	AKC (United States)
GAIT	**GAIT/MOVEMENT**	**MOVEMENT**

GAIT

Dogs move in 3 different ways: walk, trot and gallop. When on lead the dog will normally walk, although the most frequent movement is the trot. Gallop is possible. Walk and trot have to be performed in diagonal sequence. Typical for the trot is an ample ground covering, free and smooth movement, with powerful drive from the rear and good reach in the front. Viewed from the rear or the front the legs move in straight lines.

Comment (Table 14-8). The AKC standard gives a perfect and complete description of the trot. The fact that the PSK standard also mentions walk and gallop indicates that it is not merely designed for the show ring. It is essential that the trot is performed in diagonal sequence (left front leg moves forward together with right rear leg and vice versa)—that is, no pacing gait. It is also worthwhile to stress that the forward-moving hind paw should reach the place where the front paw has just been. A dog with a good drive from the rear will, when observed from behind, show the soles from the paw that is stretched backward.

GAIT/MOVEMENT

Free, balanced and vigourous, with good reach in forequarters and good driving power in hindquarters. Topline remains level in action.

MOVEMENT

The trot is the gait at which movement is judged. When approaching, the forelegs, with elbows close to the body, move straight forward, neither too close nor too far apart. Going away, the hind legs are straight and travel in the same planes as the forelegs.

Note: It is generally accepted that when a full trot is achieved, the rear legs continue to move in the same planes as the forelegs, but a very slight inward inclination will occur, it begins at the point of the shoulder in front and at the hip joint at the rear. Viewed from front or rear, the legs are straight from these points to the pads. The degree of inward inclination is almost imperceptible in a Miniature Schnauzer that has correct movement. It does not justify moving close, toeing in, crossing, or moving out at the elbows.

Viewed from the side, the forelegs have good reach, while the hind legs have strong drive, with good pick up of hocks. The feet turn neither inward nor outward.

Faults: Single tracking, side gaiting, paddling in front, or hackney action. Weak rear action.

Figure 14-19.
Movement—as speed increases, the feet gradually converge toward the center line.
(a) When approaching, the forelegs move straight from the shoulders, with the elbows close to the body.
(b) Going away, the hind legs more straight from the hips.

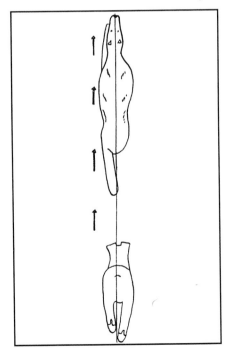
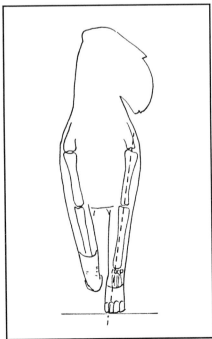
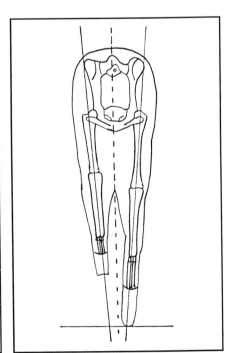

Ch. Sonshea Scarlett Streamers of Risepark. Owned by Messrs. Newman and Day Brookside (Great Britain). →

Ch. Felix van't Wareheim (Miniature). Bred by J. and E. Gallant; owned by P. Briggs (Republic of South Africa).

Table 14-9. (Miniature Schnauzer)

PSK (Germany)	KC (London)	AKC (United States)
SKIN Tight fitting over the whole body (dry skin). The black dogs have a medium grey skin, the pepper and salt has a lighter pigmentation, in black and silver medium grey and in white as dark as possible. **COAT** TEXTURE The coat is wirehaired. It should be wiry and close. It consists of a thick undercoat and a hard flat-lying topcoat, which under no circumstances should be too short. The topcoat is wiry, never shaggy or wavy. The hair at the head and the legs is also harsh; on the forehead and the ears slightly shorter. The typical hallmarks are a not too soft beard and the bushy eyebrows which slightly overshadow the eyes. COLOR a. Solid black with black undercoat b. Pepper and salt c. Black and silver d. Pure white with white undercoat The breeding aim for the pepper and salt color is a medium shade, with an evenly distributed and intensely pigmented "peppering," and a grey undercoat. Admissible are the shades ranging from dark iron-grey to silver-grey. All shades must have a dark mask which harmoniously fits the particular shade and emphasizes the expression. Lighter markings on the head, chest and legs are undesirable. The breeding aim for the black and silver Miniature Schnauzer is a black topcoat with a black undercoat; with white markings above the eyes, on the throat, on the cheeks, on the front part of the chest—two separate triangles, on the front pasterns, on the paws, on the inside of the hindquarters and under the tail. Forehead, neck and outside of the ears should, like the topcoat, be black.	**COAT** Harsh, wiry and short enough for smartness, dense undercoat. Clean on neck and shoulders, ears and skull. Harsh hair on legs. Furnishings fairly thick but not silky. **COLOR** All pepper and salt colours in even proportions, or pure black, or black and silver. That is, solid black with silver markings on eyebrows, muzzle, chest and brisket and on the forelegs below the point of the elbow, on inside of hind legs below the stifle joint, on vent and under tail.	**COAT** Double, with hard, wiry, outer coat and close undercoat. The head, neck, ears, chest, tail and body coat must be plucked. When in show condition the body coat should be of sufficient length to determine texture. Close covering on neck, ears and skull. Furnishings are fairly thick but not silky. Faults: Coat too soft or too smooth and slick in appearance. **COLOR** The recognized colors are salt and pepper, black and silver and solid black. All colors have uniform skin pigmentation, i.e. no white or pink skin patches shall appear anywhere on the dog. Salt and pepper. The typical salt and pepper color of the topcoat results from the combination of black and white banded hairs and solid black and white unbanded hairs, with the banded hairs predominating. Acceptable are all shades of salt and pepper from light to dark mixtures with tan shading permissible in the banded or unbanded hair of the topcoat. In salt and pepper dogs, the salt and pepper mixture fades out to light gray or silver white in the eyebrows, whiskers, cheeks, underthroat, inside the ears, across chest, under tail, leg furnishings, and inside hind legs. It may or may not also fade out on the underbody. However, if so, the lighter underbody hair is not to rise higher on the sides of the body than the front elbows. Black and silver. The black and silver generally follows the same pattern as the salt and pepper. The entire salt and pepper section must be black. The black color in the topcoat of the black and silver is a true rich color with black undercoat. The stripped portion is free from any fading or brown tinge and the underbody should be dark.

Table 14-9. (Miniature Schnauzer) *continued*

Sambo vom Rhedaer Tor and Jockel vom Rhedaer Tor (Miniatures). Bred and owned by Max Barth (Germany).

Black. Black is the only solid color allowed. Ideally the black color in the topcoat is a true rich glossy solid color with the undercoat being less intense, a soft matting shade of black. This is natural and should not be penalized in any way. The stripped portion is free from any fading or brown tinge. The scissored and clippered areas have lighter shades of black. A small white spot on the chest is permitted as is an occasional single white hair elsewhere on the body.

Disqualifications: Color solid white or white striping, patching or spotting on the colored areas of the dog, except for a small white spot on the chest of the black. The body coat color in salt and pepper and black and silver dogs fades out to light gray or silver white under the throat and across the chest. Between them there exists a natural body coat color. Any irregular or connecting blaze or white mark in this section is considered a white patch on the body which is also a disqualification.

Comment (Table 14-9). As far as coat and color are concerned, we have reached a point of conflict. The fact is that the PSK standard is governed by a team of specialist judges who know the breed in all its detail and have compiled a description that is not only utterly correct but also must, at the same time, protect the breed in its essential quality as a practical dog not to be manipulated by fashion.

The deviations in the AKC standard indicate that they have all been inspired by the American dog-show system.

For the edification of the average Miniature Schnauzer fancier, I wish to emphasize that in German terms the correct and most practical schnauzer coat is wirehaired from top to bottom, and there are no fluffy furnishings on the legs. The coat is stripped from top to bottom twice a year. The salt-and-pepper Miniature Schnauzer is salt-and-pepper from top to bottom; if not, the white furnishings on the legs will be soft and require more care. If your aim is a practical Miniature Schnauzer, remember this point.

Ch. Remi V. D. Gehrder Pumpe—Int. Ch., *VDH-Sieger, Bundesjugendsieger, Bundessieger, Europajugendsieger, Klubsieger PSK,* and champion in Germany, Luxemburg, and the Netherlands (Miniature). Owned by H. Gortemaker (Netherlands).

Ch. Berry von den Kleinen Strolchen, BH, AD—Int. Ch., *VDH-Sieger, Klubsieger PSK,* and champion in Germany, Austria, and Switzerland (left, black-and-silver Miniature). Owned by A. Grund (Germany). Ch. Jeff vom Rhedaer Tor—*Bundessieger, Europasieger, VDH-Sieger, Klubsieger PSK,* champion in Germany (right, white Miniature). Owned by A. Grund (Germany).

P.S.K.

Ch. Ygel Maskottchen—Int. Ch., *Klubsieger Psk, Bundessieger, VDH-Sieger, Jahressieger, ISPU-Sieger,* and champion in Germany, Luxemburg, Belgium, and the Netherlands (Miniature). Bred by L. Bergmeyer; owned by W. Testorf (Germany).

K.C.

Ch. Iccabod Olympic Gold (Miniature). Owned by S. Frost and D. Bates (Great Britain).

A.K.C.

Ch. Feldmar Nightshade (Miniature). Bred and owned by Marcia Feld (United States).

Table 14-10. (Miniature Schnauzer)

PSK (Germany)	KC (London)	AKC (United States)
SIZE AND WEIGHT HEIGHT AT WITHERS: For dogs and bitches between 30 and 35 cm. WEIGHT: For dogs and bitches between 4 to 6 kg. **FAULTS** Any departure from the foregoing standard points should be considered a fault and the seriousness with which the fault should be regarded should be in exact proportion to its degree. Body too plump, too light, too high or too low on the legs. Too coarse or too round skull, wrinkled forehead, low set, very long and differently carried ears. Eyes too light, too large, or too round. Strongly protruding cheeks or cheek bones. Loose skin at throat, dewlap. Ewe neck. Pincers bite. Short, pointed or narrow muzzle. Too long, roached, humped and soft back. Croup falling away. Tail carried too erect or hare's tail. Loose elbows, cow-hocked, steep rear, bowlegged. Too long under thigh, too short rear pastern. Long feet. Pacing gait. Coat too short, too long, soft, wavy, shaggy or silky. White or spotted hair in the black and pepper and salt Miniature; spotted hair in the black and silver and white Miniature; brown undercoat; trace or black saddle in the pepper and salt variety; the white triangles on the chest of the black and silver not clearly separated. Terrier expression. Over and under size. Obvious reversal of sex characteristics (for ex. bitchy dogs). Weak temperament. **DISQUALIFYING FAULTS** 1. Deformities of any kind. 2. Monorchids or cryptorchids. Dogs must have two clearly normal developed testicles, fully descended in the scrotum. 3. Insufficient type. 4. Overshot, undershot, or more than 2 missing teeth. 5. Severe faults in specific parts of the anatomy, coat and color. 6. Shy or vicious attitude.	**SIZE** Ideal height for dogs 14 ins (35.6 cm) and for bitches 13 ins (33 cm). Too small toyish appearing dogs are not typical and not desirable. **FAULTS** Any departure from the foregoing points should be considered a fault and the seriousness with which the fault should be regarded should be in exact proportion to its degree. Note: Male animals should have two apparently normal testicles fully descended in the scrotum.	**SIZE** From 12 to 14 inches (30.5 to 35.6 cm). He is sturdily built, nearly square in proportion of body length to height with plenty of bone, and without any suggestion of toyishness. Disqualifications: Dogs or bitches under 12 inches or over 14 inches. **FAULTS** Faults listed under descriptions. [NOTE. All-breed disqualification—monorchid or cryptorchid males.]  Ch. Malya Ushi and Feldmar Snow Crystal at Malya—both Int. Champions and champions in Italy (Miniatures). Owned by A. Torregiani (Italy).

Comment (Table 14-10). To maintain a clear distinction between Miniature, Standard, and Giant Schnauzers, it is essential that the size limits are respected. These measures have originally been expressed in metric measures.

The Germans don't specify preferred sizes for bitches or males. They feel that correct *type* and a perfectly proportioned conformation is more important than a preferred size. Of course, a bitch must remain feminine, and a dog must maintain his masculine appearance.

The size limits for bitches and males are stipulated as follows:

Miniature Schnauzers   between 30 and 35 cm

Standard Schnauzers   between 45 and 50 cm

Giant Schnauzers   between 60 and 70 cm

For the convenience of British and American fanciers, these measurements should be converted to actual imperial sizes, not to the nearest complete unit. To convert measures from metric to inches, multiply by 0.3937.

Miniature Schnauzers   between 11¾ and 13¾ in
(not 12 and 14 in)

Standard Schnauzers   between 17½ and 19½ in

Giant Schnauzers   between 23¾ and 27½ in

As far as weight is concerned, to convert from metric to English pounds, multiply the kg by 2.2.

Table 14-11. (Standard Schnauzer)

PSK (Germany)	KC (London)	AKC (United States)
GENERAL APPEARANCE Medium sized, robust, rather thickset than slim, wirehaired. **PROPORTIONS** Square-built; nearly square in proportion of body length to height at the withers. The length of the head (from tip of nose to occiput) is in proportion to the length of the back (from withers to set on of tail) in a ratio of 1 : 2. **BEHAVIOR AND CHARACTER** His typical traits are a lively temperament coupled with sound composure, a good natured character, playful, loyalty to his master, very fond of children, incorruptible alertness without being a yapper. Highly developed senses, intelligence, ability to be trained, undauntedness, endurance and resistance against weather and illness give the Standard Schnauzer all the prerequisites to be an exceptional watch- and companion dog which can also be used as a working dog.	**GENERAL APPEARANCE** Sturdily built, robust, sinewy, nearly square (length of body equal to height at shoulders). Expression keen and attitude alert. Correct conformation is of more importance than colour or other purely beauty points. **CHARACTER** Strong, vigourous dog capable of great endurance. **TEMPERAMENT** Alert, reliable, and intelligent. Primarily a companion dog.	**GENERAL APPEARANCE** The Standard Schnauzer is a robust, heavy-set dog, sturdily built with good muscle and plenty of bone; square-built in proportion of body length to height. His nature combines high-spirited temperament with extreme reliability. His rugged build and dense harsh coat are accentuated by the hallmark of the breed, the arched eyebrows, bristly moustache, and luxuriant whiskers.

Comment (Table 14-11). All parties agree on the general appearance. The PSK makes an important point when defining the way the head should be in proportion to the length of the back. This is simply to warn breeders against striving for overly elongated heads that enhance a terrier expression.

It is important to understand that, as far as the wirehaired coat is concerned, this description reflects on the whole coat—that is, not a wiry jacket with fluffy leg furnishings. This is directly linked with the fact that the Standard Schnauzer, although primarily a companion dog, always remains a watchdog, which may also be used as a working dog. One must not forget that the German breeder who wishes to obtain pedigrees with a *Leistungszucht* seal must train and qualify his Standard Schnauzer breeding stock in Schutzhund or IPO trials. Therefore, the Standard Schnauzer's general appearance must be in line with such requirements.

Personally, I believe—and this is based on many years of experience—that the Standard Schnauzer is a fantastic dog. The most typical feature of the schnauzer is not merely eyebrows and whiskers but his *personality*.

Ch. Jacky v.d. Ley—*Klubsieger PSK, Jahressieger, Bundessieger, Europasieger,* and champion in Germany (Standard). Bred by A. Schroder (Germany); owned by H. Weisz (Germany).

Ch. Siddley's Bargemaster (Standard). Owned by S. J. Hattrell-Brown (Great Britain). Best of breed at Crufts for six consecutive years (1987-1992).

Standard Schnauzer Standards

Ch. Harky de Ludolphi, Int Ch., Europasieger, Weltsieger, Winner in Amsterdam, and champion in Belgium, France, Luxemburg, and the Netherlands. Bred by Mrs. D. Gustin (Belgium).

Ch. Cara Bella's First Prize, Champion in the U. S. and Sweden. Bred by C. A. Richie (United States); owned by B. Perming (Sweden).

Table 14-12. (Standard Schnauzer)

PSK (Germany)	KC (London)	AKC (United States)
HEAD SKULL: The skull is strong and elongated, without pronounced occiput. The head is in harmony with the substance of the dog. The forehead is flat and unwrinkled and runs parallel to the ridge of the nose. STOP: The stop is markedly emphasized by the eyebrows. FOREFACE: • Nose: The tip of the nose is full and black. The ridge is straight. • Muzzle: Ends in a moderately blunt wedge. • Lips: Tight and black. • Jaws/Teeth: Strong and rounded. The complete scissors bite (42 teeth) is strong, meets perfectly and is pure white. • Jaw muscles: The masseters are strongly developed; however the cheeks should not be protruding to disturb the rectangular shape of the head (with beard). • Eyes: Of medium size, oval, directed forward, dark and lively. The dark eyelids are tight. • Ears: Set high, V-shaped, the inner sides touching the head. Carried symmetrically, turned forward in the direction of the temples, with the parallel folds not surfacing the upper-line of the skull. (In countries, where as yet no ban on cropping exists, cropped ears must be carried symmetrically in an upright poise).	**HEAD AND SKULL** Head strong and of good length, narrowing from ears to eyes and then gradually forward to end of nose. Upper part of the head (occiput to base of the forehead) moderately broad between ears. Flat, creaseless forehead; well muscled but not too strongly developed cheeks. Medium stop to accentuate prominent eyebrows. Powerful muzzle ending in a moderately blunt line, with bristly, stubby moustache and chin whiskers. Ridge of nose straight and running almost parallel to extension of forehead. Nose black with wide nostrils. Lips tight but not overlapping. MOUTH: Jaws strong with perfect, regular and complete scissors bite, i.e. the upper teeth closely overlapping the lower teeth and set square to the jaws. **EYES** Medium sized, dark, oval, set forward, with arched bushy eyebrows. **EARS** Neat, V-shaped, set high and dropping forward to the temple.	**HEAD** Strong, rectangular, and elongated; narrowing slightly from the ears to the eyes and again to the tip of the nose. The total length of the head is about one half of the length of the back measured from the withers to the set on of the tail. The head matches the sex and substance of the dog. The top line of the muzzle is parallel with the top line of the skull. There is a slight stop which is accentuated by the wiry brows. SKULL: (Occiput to stop). Moderately broad between the ears with the width of the skull not exceeding two thirds of the length of the skull. The skull must be flat, neither domed nor bumpy; skin unwrinkled. CHEEKS: Well-developed chewing muscles, but not so much that 'cheekiness' disturbs the rectangular head form. MUZZLE: Strong, and both parallel and equal in length to the top skull; it ends in a moderately blunt wedge with wiry whiskers accentuating the rectangular shape of the head. Nose is large, black and full. The lips should be black, tight and not overlapping. BITE: A full complement of white teeth, with a strong, sound scissor bite. The canine teeth are strong and well developed; with the upper incisors slightly overlapping and engaging the lower. The upper and lower jaws are powerful and neither overshot nor undershot. FAULTS: A level bite is considered undesirable but a lesser fault than an overshot or undershot mouth. EYES: Medium size, dark brown, oval in shape and turned forward; neither round nor protruding. The brow is arched and wiry, but vision is not impaired nor eyes hidden by too long an eyebrow. EARS: Evenly shaped, set high and carried erect when cropped. If uncropped, they are small, V-shaped button ears of moderate thickness and carried rather high and close to the head.

Domino De Manso Pelegri at Kanix (Standard). Bred by M. and A. Gil de Biedma (Spain); owned by K. Wilberg (Sweden).

Comment (Table 14-12). The PSK standard mentions that the skull is elongated—that is, not square but slightly rectangular, definitely not trapezoidal. However, the muzzle ends in a moderately blunt wedge. This means that the narrowing of the head starts from the eyes toward a blunt nose—not from ears to eyes and then from eyes to nose as common in many terrier heads. The AKC standard even enhances this tendency by stipulating that the width of the skull should not exceed two-thirds of its length, which describes an excessively long and narrow head. Considering that the length of the skull equals the length of the muzzle, the AKC description basically says that if the skull is 12 cm (4¾ in) long, it should not be more than 8 cm (just over 3 in wide. The total length of the head would then be 12 + 12 = 24 cm (9½ in) and narrow from the ears to eyes and, again, from eyes to tip of nose. This is a description of an extremely long head, which I doubt can hardly be in harmony with the substance of the dog.

Table 14-13. (Standard Schnauzer)

PSK (Germany)	KC (London)	AKC (United States)
NECK • Profile: The muscular nape is curved upward. The neck blends harmoniously into the withers. • Form: Powerfully fitted, slender, nobly crested, and in proportion to the substance of the dog. • Skin: Unwrinkled and fitting tightly to the throat (dry neck). **BODY** • Topline: Slightly sloping from withers to croup. • Withers: High and clearly defined. • Back: Short and firm. • Loin: The distance from the end of the ribcage to the pelvis is short, giving the impression of a short-coupled dog. • Croup: Slightly rounded, flowing over into the set on of the tail. • Chest: Moderately broad, ribs well sprung, in cross-section oval, brisket deep and reaching just below the elbows. The forechest is, because of the prosternum clearly extending beyond the shoulder joints, markedly pronounced. • Underline and belly: The under-chest raises slightly towards the loin. The belly is moderately drawn up. • Tail: Docked to 3 joints. Harmoniously continuing the slope of the croup and carried slightly raised. (In countries where tail docking is prohibited by law, it can be left in its natural state).	**NECK** Moderately long, strong and slightly arched; skin close to throat; neck set cleanly on the shoulders. **BODY** Chest moderately broad; deep with visible, strong breastbone reaching at least to height of elbow and rising slightly backward to loins. Back strong and straight, slightly higher at shoulder than at hindquarters, with short well developed loins. Ribs well sprung. Length of body equal to height from top of withers to ground. **TAIL** Set on and carried high, customarily docked to three joints.	**NECK** Strong, of moderate thickness and length, elegantly arched and blending cleanly into the shoulders. The skin is tight, fitting tightly to the dry throat with no wrinkles or dewlap. **CHEST** Of medium width with well-sprung ribs, and if it could be seen in cross-section would be oval. The breastbone is plainly discernible. The brisket must descent at least to the elbows and ascend gradually to the rear with the belly moderately drawn up. **BODY** Compact, strong, short-coupled and substantial so as to permit great flexibility and agility. The height at the highest point of the withers equals the length from the breastbone to point of buttock. Faults: Too slender or shelly; too bulky or coarse; excessive tuck-up. **BACK** Strong, stiff, straight and short, with a well developed loin section; the distance from the last rib to the hips as short as possible. The top line of the back should not be absolutely horizontal, but should have a slightly descending slope from the first vertebrae of the withers to the faintly curved croup and set-on of the tail. **TAIL** Set moderately high and carried erect. It is docked to not less than 1 inch nor more than 2 inches. Faults: Squirrel tail.

Comment (Table 14-13). One of the main features that gives the schnauzer an expression of nobility is a strong, well-muscled but, at the same time, elegantly crested neck that blends into the shoulders with a flowing line—that is, not set in a clear angle.

It is not enough to mention that the chest must be moderately broad and the brisket descend to the elbows. The most forward part of the breastbone—that is, the prosternum—must be clearly discernible beyond the line formed by the shoulder blades and the upper arms. Such a forechest, together with correct angulation of the forequarters, is an absolute for the well-constructed schnauzer. It differentiates the schnauzer from the terrier, and this detail should never be omitted from any schnauzer breed standard.

The KC standard mentions a strong and straight back without giving any specification for the croup. Therefore, I presume that they require a flat croup in line with the straight back. It is anatomically and physiologically extremely important that the spinal column is not composed of straight segments. In addition to containing the spinal cord, the spine functions as a flexible chassis to which the whole motive system is linked. It is extremely important that the spine, over its entire length, maintains its normal anatomical curves to fulfill its function of flexible shock absorber and spring.

The angle of the croup is defined by the position of the sacrum, to which the caudal vertebrae (tail) are linked. The lay of the croup is determined by the way in which the dog wants to express his mood by holding or moving his tail in a certain manner. A lively schnauzer, when in a situation requiring alertness will instinctively tighten the muscles running over the sacrum to the tail, raise the tail, and level the croup. To please the judge, a level croup may be achieved by making your schnauzer stand alertly.

Ch. Negus-Volker van Hilbelinkhof—Int. Ch., *Jahressieger, Europasieger, Weltsieger,* and champion in Spain, Portugal, France, Monaco, and Germany (Standard). Bred by H. J. Lutjenkossink (Netherlands); owned by M. and A. Gil de Biedma (Spain).

Ch. Madame v. d. Ley—Int. Ch. and champion in Denmark (Standard). Bred by A. Schröder (Germany); owned by S. Rabjerg (Denmark).

Ch. Hauke v. Grafen zu Moers AD, BH, FH, WH, SchH III—Int. Ch., *Klubsieger, Jahressieger, ISPU-Sieger, VDH-Sieger,* and champion in Germany (Standard). Bred by M. Welge and R. Backhaus (Germany); owned by Longert family (Germany).

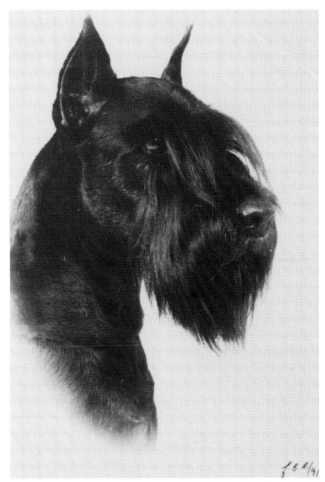

A head study of Ch. Negus-Vokler van Hilbelinkhof, a black Standard with cropped ears. Bred by H. J. Lutjenkossink (Netherlands); owned by M. and A. Gil de Biedma (Spain).

A standard Schnauzer puppy with a natural sabre tail.

Ch. Lisser de Ludolphi—Int. Ch., *VDH-Sieger, Klubsieger PSK, Europasieger,* and champion in Italy, France, Germany, Austria, Switzerland, and Yugoslavia (Standard). Bred by D. Gustin (Belgium); owned by F. Meneghello (Italy).

Ch. Amethyst v. Napoleonstock—*Weltsieger, Europasieger, Klubsieger PSK, Bundessieger, VDH-Sieger, Jahressieger,* and champion in Germany. (Standard). Bred and owned by M. Loh (Germany).

Dedicado de Manso Pelegri at Kanix (Standard). Bred by M. Gil de Biedma (Spain); owned by C. Staunskaer (Sweden). This black Standard Schnauzer is an excellent example of balanced front and rear angulation.

Ch. Benjamin v. Scharzwaldhaus, AD, BH—Int. Ch., *Europajugendsieger, Weltsieger, Klubsieger PSK, VDH-Sieger, Jahressieger,* and champion in Germany and Switzerland (Standard). Bred by T. Huck (Germany); owned by D. Henne (Germany).

Pepsy de Ludolphi and Mascar's Morella (Standards). Both ten months of age, Morella illustrates the saber tail.

Pepsy de Ludolphi (Standard). Bred by D. Gustin (Belgium); owned by M. Gale (Republic of South Africa).

Table 14-14. (Standard Schnauzer)

PSK (Germany)	KC (London)	AKC (United States)
FOREQUARTERS • General: The forelegs are constructed as strong supports, they are straight viewed from all sides and stand moderately wide (neither too narrow nor too wide. • Shoulders: The shoulder blade is long, well angulated, lying close and flat. The shoulder is well muscled. • Upper arms: Long, well angulated, and strongly muscled. • Elbows: Close to body. • Forearms: The length of the forearm must correspond with the length of the upper arm. Viewed from all sides they must be straight. • Wrists: These joints may not be broadened. • Pasterns: Firm, vertical when viewed from the front and slightly angulated to the ground when seen from the side. • Forefeet: Short and round. They have tightly closed, well arched toes (cat's paws), with dark nails, and hard, tough pads.	**FOREQUARTERS** Shoulders flat and well laid. Forelegs straight when viewed from any angle. Muscles smooth and lithe rather than prominent; bone strong, straight and carried well down to feet; elbows close to body and pointing directly backwards.	**SHOULDERS** The sloping shoulder blades are strongly muscled, yet flat and well laid back so that the rounded upper ends are in a nearly vertical line above the elbows. They slope well forward to the point where they join the upper arm, forming as nearly as possible a right angle when seen from the side. Such angulation permits the maximum forward extension of the forelegs without binding or effort. **FORELEGS** Straight, vertical, and without any curvature when seen from all sides; set moderately far apart; with heavy bone; elbows set close to the body and pointing directly to the rear.

Comment (Table 14-14). The ideal angulation of the forequarters consists of the shoulder blades sloping forward at an angle of nearly 45 degrees toward an imaginary horizontal line and the upper arms sloping back at a similar angle. Such balanced angulation will allow the required reach of the forequarters.

It is also essential that the front pasterns are slightly angled—about 10 degrees—at the carpal joint (wrist) to give the necessary kick.

Provided that this picture is in harmony with correctly angulated hindquarters, the schnauzer will be equipped with a kinetic system allowing him to walk, trot, or gallop in a free and balanced way.

Mascar's Morella (Standard). Bred by A. Radberg (Sweden); owned by E. Gallant (Republic of South Africa).

Ch. Arko v.d. Goliathhöhe—Int. Ch., *Bundesjugendsieger, VDH-Sieger, Klubsieger PSK, Bundessieger, Jahressieger, Weltsieger,* and champion in Germany (Standard). Bred by H. Weisz (Germany); owned by F. Brocks (Germany).

Table 14-15. (Standard Schnauzer)

PSK (Germany)	KC (London)	AKC (United States)

HINDQUARTERS

- General: Viewed from the side they are slanting, seen from behind, the hindquarters are parallel.
- Upper thighs: Long, in harmony with the substance of the dog, directed forward, broad and strongly muscled.
- Knee: Clearly angulated, situated straight between upper and under thigh, without pointing inward nor outward.
- Under thighs: Long and strong, length in correct proportion to the whole build of the hindquarters.
- Hock joint: Angulation well pronounced.
- Rear pasterns: Longer than the front pasterns, yet not too long, not disturbing the harmony.
- Hind feet: As forefeet, only longer. No rear dewclaws.

GAIT

- Dogs move in three different ways: walk, trot and gallop. When on lead, the dog will normally walk, although the most frequent movement is the trot. Gallop is possible. Walk and trot have to be performed in diagonal sequence. Typical for the trot is an ample ground covering free and smooth movement, with powerful drive from the rear and good reach in the front. Viewed from the front or the rear the legs move in straight lines.

HINDQUARTERS

Thighs slanting and flat but strongly muscled. Hind legs (upper and lower thighs) at first vertical to the stifle; from stifle to hock in line with the extension of the upper neck line; from hock vertical to ground.

FEET

Short, round, cat-like, compact with closely arched toes, dark nails, firm black pads, feet pointing forwards.

GAIT/MOVEMENT

Free, balanced and vigourous, with good reach in forequarters and good driving power in hindquarters. Topline remains level in action.

HINDQUARTERS

Strongly muscled, in balance with the forequarters, never appearing higher than the shoulders. Croup full and slightly rounded. Thighs broad with well-bent stifles. The second thigh, from knee to hock, is approximately parallel with an extension of the upper-neck line. The legs, from the clearly defined hock joint to the feet, are short and perpendicular to the ground and when viewed from the rear are parallel to each other.

Feet—Small and compact, rounded with thick pads and strong black nails. The toes are well closed and arched (cat's paws) and pointing straight ahead.

Dewclaws, if any on the hind legs are generally removed. Dewclaws on the forelegs may be removed.

GAIT

Sound, strong, quick, free, true and level gait with powerful well angulated hindquarters that reach out and cover ground. The forelegs reach out in a stride balancing that of the hindquarters. At a trot, the back remains firm and level, without swaying, rolling or roaching. When viewed from the rear, the feet, though they may appear to travel close when trotting, must not cross or strike. Increased speed causes feet to converge toward the center line of gravity.

Comment (Table 14-15). The provision in both the KC and AKC standards that the line running from stifle to hock should be parallel to the extension of the neck line can, in my opinion, only be considered as far as a schnauzer is positioned in the show ring. As I have already pointed out, movement is an integral function of front and hindquarters. The show-ring stance is aimed at fashion and pleasing the eye of the judge. Any judge should make a definite correlation between the manner in which a schnauzer stands and moves.

To specify that the upper thigh should be vertical is somehow delusive, as it may lead to the conclusion that in a show stance, the femur should be perpendicular to the ground. Moreover, many schnauzers are posed with the upper thighs extended to rear to convey the impression of a sloping topline. It is my experience that a schnauzer, standing naturally, prefers to place his hind legs slightly apart. The femur of the leg placed farthest back extends slightly to the rear. The femur of leg that carries the weight of the pelvis will, correctly, slant slightly forward to allow the hip joint to function normally—that is, allow flexion of the hip joint to absorb weight or pressure on the pelvis and to allow extension from the hip joint to move the body forward.

Table 14-16. (Standard Schnauzer)

PSK (Germany)	KC (London)	AKC (United States)

SKIN

Tight fitting over the whole body (dry dog). In black dogs rather medium grey, the pepper and salt has a lighter pigmentation.

COAT

TEXTURE

The coat is wirehaired. It should be wiry and close. It consists of a thick undercoat and a harsh flat-lying topcoat, which under no circumstances should be too short. The topcoat is wiry, never shaggy or wavy. The hair at the head and the legs is also harsh, on the forehead and the ears slightly shorter. The typical hallmarks are a not too soft beard and the bushy eyebrows which slightly overshadow the eyes.

COLOR

a. Solid black with black undercoat.

b. Pepper and salt.

The breeding aim for the pepper and salt color is a medium shade, with an evenly distributed and intensely pigmented "peppering," and a grey undercoat. Admissible are the shades ranging from dark iron-grey to silver-grey. All shades must have a dark mask which harmoniously fits the particular shade and emphasizes the expression. Lighter marks on the head, chest and legs are undesirable.

SIZE AND WEIGHT

HEIGHT AT WITHERS: For dogs and bitches between 45 and 50 cm.

WEIGHT: For dogs and bitches between 13 to 20 Kg.

COAT

Harsh, wiry and short enough for smartness. Closer on neck and shoulders; clean on throat, skull and ears. Harsh hair on legs. Dense undercoat essential.

COLOUR

Pure black (white markings on head, chest and legs undesirable) or pepper and salt.

Pepper and salt shades range from dark iron grey to light grey; good pigmentation. Hairs banded dark/light dark. Facial mask to harmonize with corresponding coat colour.

SIZE

Ideal height at the withers for dogs 19 ins (48.3 cm) and for bitches 18 ins (45.7 cm). Any variations of more than 1 inch in these heights undesirable.

COAT

Tight, hard, wiry and as thick as possible, composed of a soft, close undercoat and a harsh outer coat which, when seen against the grain, stands up off the back, lying neither smooth nor flat.

The outer coat (body coat) is trimmed (by plucking) only to accent the body outline. When in show condition, the outer coat's proper length is approximately 1½ inches (3.8 cm), except on the ears, head, neck, chest, belly and under the tail where it may be closely trimmed to give the desired typical appearance of the breed. On the muzzle and over the eyes the coat lengthens to form luxuriant beard and eyebrows; the hair on the legs is longer than that on the body. These furnishings should be of harsh texture and should not be so profuse so as to detract from the neat appearance or working capabilities of the dog.

COLOR—Pepper and salt or pure black.—The typical pepper and salt color of the top coat results from the combination of black and white hairs, and white hairs banded with black. Acceptable are all shades of pepper and salt from dark iron-gray to silver-gray. Ideally, pepper and salt Standard Schnauzer have a gray undercoat, but a tan or fawn undercoat is not to be penalized. It is desirable to have a darker facial mask that harmonizes with the particular shade of coat. Also, in pepper and salt dogs, the pepper and salt mixture may fade out to light gray or silver-white in the eyebrows, whiskers, cheeks, under throat, across chest, under tail, leg furnishings, under body and inside legs.

Black.—Ideally the black Standard Schnauzer should be a true rich color, free from any fading or discoloration or any admixture or gray or tan hair. The undercoat should also be solid black. However, increased age or continued exposure to the sun may cause a certain amount of fading and burning. A small white smudge on the chest is not a fault. Loss of color as a result of scars from cuts or bites is not a fault.

HEIGHTS

Ideal height at the highest point of the shoulder blades, 18½ to 19½ inches for males and 17½ to 18½ inches for females. Dogs measuring over or under these limits must be faulted in proportion to the extent of the deviation. Dogs measuring more than ½ inch over or under these limits must be disqualified.

Ch. Argenta's Flemming. Bred by B. Niklasson, B. Andersson, and G. Garpas; owned by R. Kierrman (Sweden).

Table 14-16. (Standard Schnauzer) *Continued*

FAULTS

Any departure from the foregoing standard points should be considered a fault and the seriousness with which the fault should be regarded should be in exact proportion to its degree.

Body too plump, too light, too high or too low on the legs. Too coarse or too round skull, a proportionwise too big or too small head, wrinkled forehead. Low set, too long and differently carried ears. Light, too large, or too round eyes. Strongly protruding cheeks and cheek bones. Loose skin at throat, dewlap. Ewe neck. Pincers bite. Short, pointed or narrow muzzle. Too long, roached, humped and soft back. Croup falling away. Tail carried over-erect or hare tail. Loose elbows, cow-hocked, steep rear, bowlegged. Long feet. Coat too short, too long, soft, wavy, shaggy or silky. White or spotted hair, or any other additional shade, brown undercoat, trace and black saddle. Terrier expression. Over and under size. Obvious reversal of sex characteristics (for ex. bitchy dogs and the reverse). Pacing gait. Weak temperament.

DISQUALIFICATIONS

1. Deformities of any kind.
2. Monorchids or cryptorchids. Dogs must have two clearly normal developed testicles, fully descended in the scrotum.
3. Insufficient type.
4. Overshot, undershot or more than 2 missing teeth.
5. Severe faults in specific parts of the anatomy, coat and color.
6. Shy or vicious attitude.

FAULTS

Any departure from the foregoing points should be considered a fault and the seriousness with which the fault should be regarded should be in exact proportion to its degree.

Note: Male animals should have two apparently normal testicles fully descended into the scrotum.

FAULTS

Level bite is considered undesirable but a lesser fault than an undershot or overshot mouth.

Body: Too light, too plump.

Tail: Squirrel tail.

Coat: Soft, smooth, curly, wavy or shaggy; too long or too short; too sparse or lacking undercoat; excessive furnishings; lack of furnishings.

Color: Any colors other than specified, and any shadings or mixtures thereof in the topcoat such as rust, brown, red, yellow or tan; absence of peppering; spotting or striping; a black streak down the back; or a black saddle without typical salt and pepper coloring; gray hairs in the coat of the black; in blacks any undercoat other than black.

Gait: Crabbing or weaving; paddling, rolling, swaying; short, choppy, stiff, stilted rear action; front legs that throw out or in (East and West movers); hackney gait; crossing over, or striking in the front or rear.

Others: Any deviation from the specifications in the standard is to be considered a fault and should be penalized in proportion to the extent of the deviation. In weighing the seriousness of a fault, greatest consideration should ge given to deviation from the desired alert, highly intelligent, spirited, reliable character of the Standard Schnauzer, and secondly to any deviation that detracts from the Standard Schnauzer's desired general appearance of a robust, active, square-built, wire-coated dog. Dogs that are shy or appear to be highly nervous should be seriously faulted and dismissed from the ring.

Disqualifications: Vicious dogs shall be disqualified. Males under 18 inches or over 20 inches in height. Females under 17 or over 19 inches in height.

[NOTE. All-breed disqualification—monorchid or cryptorchid males.]

Comment (Table 14-16). It is my experience (a) that any schnauzer with a correct wirehaired coat will not develop excessively long hair or furnishings on the legs, (b) that excessively long furnishings are *never* wiry and impair the working capability of a schnauzer.

It is also my experience that, by allowing silver-white fading on the legs of the salt-and-pepper schnauzer, one tries to accommodate the furnishings, as these white hairs are always longer and softer. It is, therefore, much better to strive for a salt-and-pepper color that is evenly distributed over the whole body. The same applies to leniency in allowing tan or fawn undercoat, which also enhances incorrect coat structure.

Giant Schnauzer Standard

Ch. Kobold von Lobbachtal, PD—Int. Ch., *Klubsieger PSK*. Winner Amsterdam, and champion in Denmark, Sweden, Luxemburg, and the Netherlands (Giant). Bred by J. Senitwany; owned by Mrs. V. Rune (Denmark).

K.C.

Ch. Sandridge Olympic Gold. Bred and owned by L. Steele (Great Britain).

A.K.C.

Ch. Keay's I'm a Jetsetter—champion in the United States, Canada, and Bermuda (Giant). Bred and owned by N. and J. Keay (Canada).

Giant Schnauzer Standards

When comparing the different ways the Giant Schnauzer has been described on paper, one must conclude that there are no fundamental differences. However, reality proves that despite such compatible descriptions, the American and European Giant Schnauzer are totally different dogs. The American Giant Schnauzer champion, in many respects, does not conform with that is laid down in his very own AKC breed standard. The reason, therefore, can only be found in the American preference for fashion.

Nobody can deny that most of the Giants that became American champions during the 1980s do not conform with the following statement: The sound, reliable temperament, rugged build, and dense wiry weather-resistant coat make for one of the most useful, powerful, and enduring working breeds. It is my belief that nobody should breed Giant Schnauzers unless he is prepared to work them so that he can establish the working value of his breeding stock. In the case of a Giant Schnauzer, working entails nose work (tracking), control work (obedience), and protection work. The combined abilities required during these disciplines will guarantee a balanced, well-behaved, and reliable modern working dog.

Table 14-17. (Giant Schnauzer)

PSK (Germany)	KC (London)	AKC (United States)
GENERAL APPEARANCE Large, strong, rather thickset, not slim, wirehaired; the enlarged and stronger version of the Standard Schnauzer. A proud and courageous dog with a respect-imposing appearance. **IMPORTANT PROPORTIONS** Square-built; nearly square in proportion of body length to height at the withers. The length of the head (from tip of nose to occiput) is in proportion to the length of the back (from withers to set on of tail) in a ratio of 1 : 2. **BEHAVIOR AND CHARACTER** His typical traits are a good natured, well balanced character, with an unconditional loyalty to his master. He possesses highly developed senses, intelligence, adaptability to training, strength, endurance, speed and resistance against weather and illness. Through his inborn readiness to defend, he has all the prerequisites to be an outstanding service and working dog. **HEAD** SKULL: The skull is strong and elongated, without a clearly pronounced occiput. The head is in harmony with the substance of the dog. The forehead is flat and unwrinkled and runs parallel to the ridge of the nose. STOP: The stop is markedly emphasized by the eyebrows. FOREFACE: • Nose: The tip of the nose is full and black. The ridge is straight. • Muzzle: Ends in a moderately blunt wedge. • Lips: Tight and black.	**GENERAL APPEARANCE** Powerfully built, robust, sinewy, appearing almost square. Imposing, with keen expression and alert attitude. Correct conformation of the utmost importance. **CHARACTERISTICS** Versatile, strong, hardy, intelligent and vigourous. Adaptable, capable of great speed and endurance and resistant to weather. **TEMPERAMENT** Bold, reliable, good natured and composed. **HEAD AND SKULL** Head strong and of good length, narrowing from ears to eyes and then gradually toward toward end of nose. The overall length (from nose to occiput) is in proportion to the back (from withers to set on of tail) approximately 1 to 2. Upper part of the head (occiput to the base of forehead) moderately broad between ears, with flat creaseless forehead. Well muscled but not over developed cheeks. Medium stop accentuated by bushy eyebrows. Powerful muzzle ending in a moderately blunt wedge, with bristly, stubby moustache and chin whiskers. Ridge of nose straight, running parallel to extension of forehead. Nose black with wide nostrils. EYES: Medium sized, dark, oval, set forward, with lower lid fitting closely. EARS: Neat, V-shaped, set high, and dropping forward to temple. MOUTH: Jaws strong, with perfect, regular and complete scissors bite, i.e. the upper teeth closely overlapping lower teeth and set square to the jaws. Lips black, closing tightly but not overlapping.	**GENERAL DESCRIPTION** The Giant Schnauzer should resemble, as nearly as possible, in general appearance, a larger and more powerful version of the Standard Schnauzer. On the whole a bold and valiant figure of a dog. Robust, strongly built, nearly square in proportion of body length to height at withers, active, sturdy, and well muscled. Temperament which combines spirit and alertness with intelligence and reliability. Composed, watchful, courageous, easily trained, deeply loyal to family, playful, amiable in repose, and a commanding figure when aroused. The sound, reliable temperament, rugged build and dense weather-resistant wiry coat make for one of the most useful, powerful, and enduring working breeds. **HEAD** Strong, rectangular in appearance, and elongated; narrowing slightly from the ears to the eyes, and again from the eyes to the tip of the nose. The total length of the head is about one-half of the length of the back (withers to set on of tail). The head matches the sex and substance of the dog. The top line of the muzzle is parallel to the top line of the skull. There is a slight stop which is accentuated by the eyebrows. SKULL: (Occiput to stop). Moderately broad between the ears, occiput not too prominent. Top of skull flat, skin unwrinkled. CHEEKS: Flat, but with well-developed chewing muscles; there is no cheekiness to disturb the rectangular head appearance (with beard). MUZZLE: Strong and well filled under the eyes; both parallel and equal in length to the top skull; ending in a moderately blunt wedge. The nose is large, black and full. The lips are tight and not overlapping, black in color.

Table 14-17. (Giant Schnauzer) *Continued*

- Jaws/Teeth: Strong and rounded. The complete scissors bite is strong, perfectly locking and pure white. It totals 42 teeth.
- Jaw muscles: The masseters are strongly developed; however the cheeks should not be protruding to disturb the rectangular shape of the head (with beard).
- Eyes: Of medium size, oval, directed forward, dark and lively. The lower eyelid is tight.
- Ears: Set high, V-shaped, the inner-sides of the ear touching the head. Carried symmetrically, turned forward in the direction of the temples, with the parallel folds not surfacing the upper-line of the skull. (In countries where as yet no ban on cropping exists, cropped ears must be carried symmetrically in an upright poise).

BITE: A full complement of sound white teeth (6/6 incisors, 2/2 canines, 8/8 premolars, 4/6 molars) with a scissors bite. The upper and lower jaws are powerful and well formed. Disqualifying faults: Overshot or undershot.

EARS: When cropped, identical in shape and length with pointed tips. They are in balance with the head and are not exaggerated in length. They are set high on the skull and carried perpendicularly at the inner edges with as little bell as possible along the other edges. When uncropped the ears are V-shaped button ears of medium length and thickness, set high and carried rather high and close to the head.

EYES: Medium size, dark brown, and deep-set. They are oval in appearance and keen in expression with lids fitting tightly. Vision is not impaired nor eyes hidden by too long eyebrows.

Comment (Table 14-17). When discussing the Miniature and the Standard Schnauzer, I have already mentioned that the schnauzer's skull should be slightly rectangular but not narrowing from ears to eyes. The muzzle narrows from eyes to a moderately blunt nose; but, because of the moustache and chin whiskers, this narrowing is camouflaged, and the whole head seems rectangular.

Although the majority of American Giant Schnauzers have their ears cropped, the standard makes provision for an uncropped ear. To describe this as a V-shaped button ear is not ideal. The natural hanging ear must be set high, the fold for the pendant should be level with the skull, the ears then drop forward with the inner edge of the V touching the temple.

Ch. Daya van't Wareheim (Giant). Bred by J. and E. Gallant (Republic of South Africa); owned by P. Pauwels (Belgium).

Ch. Otti van't Wareheim (Giant). Bred and owned by J. and E. Gallant (Republic of South Africa.)

Table 14-18. (Giant Schnauzer)

PSK (Germany)	KC (London)	AKC (United States)
NECK • Profile: The strong, muscular nape is curved upward. The neck blends harmoniously into the withers. • Form: Powerfully fitted, slender, nobly crested and in proportion to the substance of the dog. • Skin: The skin of the throat is unwrinkled and fits tightly (dry neck). **BODY** • Topline: Slightly sloping from withers to croup. • Withers: High and clearly defined. • Back: Short and firm. • Loin: The distance from the end of the ribcage to the pelvis is short, giving the impression of a short-coupled dog. • Croup: Slightly rounded, flowing over into the set on of the tail. • Chest: Moderately broad, ribs well sprung, in cross-section oval, brisket deep and reaching just below the elbows. The forechest is, because of the prosternum clearly extending beyond the shoulder-joints, markedly pronounced. • Underline and belly: The under-chest raises slightly. The belly is moderately drawn up. • Tail: Docked to 3 joints. Harmoniously continuing the slope of the croup and carried slightly raised. (In countries where tail docking is prohibited by law, it can be left in its natural state).	**NECK** Moderately long, strong, and slightly arched; skin close to the throat; neck set cleanly on shoulders. **BODY** Chest moderately broad and deep, reaching at least to height of elbow, rising slightly backward to loins. Breastbone clearly extends to beyond joint of shoulder and upper arm, forming the conspicuous forechest. Back strong and straight, slightly higher at shoulders than at hindquarters, with short, well-developed loins. Slightly sloping croup. Ribs well sprung. Length of body equal to height at top of withers to ground. TAIL: Set on high and carried at an angle slightly above the topline, customarily docked to two joints.  Note the clean, arched neck.	**NECK** Strong and well arched, of moderate length, blending cleanly into the shoulders, and with the skin fitting tightly at the throat; in harmony with the dog's weight and build. **BODY** Compact, substantial, short-coupled, and strong with great power and agility. The height at the highest point of the withers equals the body length from breastbone to point of rump. The loin section is well developed, as short as possible for compact build. CHEST: Medium in width, ribs well sprung but with no tendency toward a barrel chest; oval in cross section; deep through the brisket. The breastbone is plainly discernible, with strong forechest; the brisket descends at least to the elbows, and ascends gradually toward the rear with the belly moderately drawn up. The ribs spread gradually from the first rib so as to allow space for the elbows to move close to the body. BACK: Short, straight, strong and firm. TAIL: The tail is set moderately high and carried high in excitement. It should be docked to the second or not more than the third joint (approximately 1 ½ to about 3 inches long at maturity).

Comment (Table 14-18). With regard to this particular section, I would like to refer to what I wrote on this subject for the Standard Schnauzer.

I must, however, emphasize one point in particular. In the United Kingdom during the 1970s, before the Giant Schnauzer was transferred from the utility to the working group, in addition to the tendency to exaggerate the leg furnishings, there was also a trend to strive for a neck that was set at a neat angle to the back, with the neck line running parallel to the line from the stifle to the hock (see description of the hindquarters). Although the furnishings have disappeared and the British Giant has become closer to the German type, I feel there is still an obvious difference where the smooth blending of the neck into the shoulders is concerned. This is probably due to the British tendency to adhere to common standards and to see the necks of Dobermans, Boxers, Rottweilers, schnauzers, and so forth all set in the same clean way on the shoulders. The ideal picture for the Giant Schnauzer, which at the same time gives an impression of power and nobility, is a well-muscled and elegantly crested neck that blends into the shoulders in a flowing line.

Ch. Sanio v. d. Lederhecke—*ISPU-Sieger, Klubsieger PSK, Bundessieger,* and a champion in Germany (Giant). Bred and owned by W. Büschel (Germany). Observe the distinct forechest and the depth of the brisket, completely in harmony with the angle of the shoulder and upper arm.

Titan v. Bartenwetzer (Giant). Bred and owned by W. Schicker (Germany). A very promising puppy at eight months, with good hindquarters.

Telchines Appolo at van't Wareheim (Giant). Bred by M. Ambrosi (Italy); owned by J. and E. Gallant (Republic of South Africa). At four months, this puppy demonstrates a balanced, single-tracking trot while retrieving his toy.

Ch. Sandridge Kirry (Giant). (Great Britain)

Ch. Enak van't Wareheim, IPO III (Giant). Bred and owned by J. and E. Gallant (Republic of South Africa). A powerful and compact body.

Arlet van't Wareheim (Giant). Relaxed, with a normally positioned croup and lowered tail.

Arlet van't Wareheim (Giant). On alert a few seconds later, with a flattened croup and raised tail.

Ch. Free de Pichera—*ISPU Sieger* and champion in Italy (Giant). Bred by D. Vincente Y D Jesus Giner Barat (Spain); owned by Casali Lucillo (San Marino).

Ch. Regal Cora at van't Wareheim, CQN, CACIB/IPO—Int. Ch., *Klubsieger PSK,* and champion in Germany, Belgium, France, Netherlands (Giant). Bred by A. Kirsten (Denmark); owned by J. and E. Gallant (Republic of South Africa).

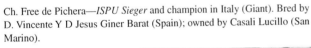

Table 14-19. (Giant Schnauzer)

PSK (Germany)	KC (London)	AKC (United States)
FOREQUARTERS • General: The forelegs are constructed as strong supports, they are straight viewed from all sides and stand moderately wide (neither too narrow nor too wide. • Shoulder: The shoulder blade is long, well angulated, lying close and flat. The shoulder is well muscled. • Upper arm: Long shaped, well angulated, and strongly muscled. • Elbows: Close to body. • Forearm: The length of the forearm must correspond with the length of the upper arms. The forearm must be straight, viewed from all sides. • Wrist: These joints may not be broadened. • Shoulders: above the elbows. They slope **well** forward. • Pastern: Firm, vertical when viewed from the front and slightly angulated to the ground when seen from the side. • Forefeet: Short and round. They have tightly closed, well arched toes (cat's paws) with dark nails and hard, tough pads. **HINDQUARTERS** • General: Viewed from the side slanting, seen from behind parallel. • Upper thigh: Long, in harmony with the substance of the dog, directed forward, broad and strongly muscled. • Knee: Clearly angulated, is situated straight between the upper and under thigh, without pointing inward nor outward. • Under thigh: Long and strong, in length in correct proportion to the whole build of the hindquarters. • Hock joint: Angulation well pronounced. • Rear pasterns: Longer than the front pasterns, yet not too long. Not disturbing the harmony. • Hind feet: As forefeet, only longer. No rear dewclaws. **GAIT** Dogs move in 3 different ways: walk, trot and gallop. When on lead the dog will normally walk, although the most frequent movement is the trot. Gallop is possible. Walk and trot have to be performed in diagonal sequence. Typical for the trot is an ample ground covering, free and smooth movement, with powerful drive from the rear and good reach in the front. Viewed from the front or the rear the legs move in straight lines.	**FOREQUARTERS** Shoulders flat, well laid back. Forelegs straight when viewed from any angle. Muscles smooth and lithe rather than prominent, bone strong, carried straight to feet. Elbows set close to body and pointing directly backwards. **HINDQUARTERS** Strongly muscled. Stifles forming a well defined angle. Upper thighs vertical to stifle, from stifle to hock in line with extension of upper neck line, from hock vertical to ground. When viewed from rear, hind legs parallel. FEET: Pointing directly forward, short, round, compact with closely arched toes. Deep, dark and firm pads. Dark nails. **GAIT/MOVEMENT** Free, balanced and vigourous, with good reach of forequarters and good driving power from hindquarters. Topline remains level in action.	**FOREQUARTERS** The forequarters have flat, somewhat sloping shoulders and high withers. Forelegs are straight and vertical when viewed from all sides, with strong pasterns and good bone. They are separated by a fairly deep brisket which precludes a pinched front. The elbows are set close to the body and point directly backwards. SHOULDERS: The sloping shoulderblades (scapula) are strongly muscled, yet flat. They are well laid back so that from the side the rounded upper ends are in a nearly vertical line above the elbows. They slope well forward to the point where they join the upper arm (humerus), forming as nearly as possible a right angle. Such an angulation permits the maximum forward extension of the forelegs without binding or effort. Both shoulder blade and upper arm are long, permitting depth of chest at the brisket. **HINDQUARTERS** The hindquarters are strongly muscled, in balance with the forequarters; upper thighs are slanting and well bent at the stifles, with second thighs (tibia) approximately parallel to an extension of the upper neck line. The legs from the hock joints to the feet are short, perpendicular to the ground while the dog is standing naturally, and from the rear parallel to each other. The hindquarters do not appear over-built or higher than the shoulders. Croup full and slightly rounded. Feet—well-arched, compact and catlike, turning neither in nor out, with thick tough pads and dark nails. Dewclaws, if any, on hind legs should be removed; on the forelegs may be removed. **GAIT** The trot is the gait at which movement is judged. Free, balanced and vigorous, with good reach in the forequarters and good driving power in the hindquarters. Rear and front legs are thrown neither in nor out. When moving at a fast trot, a properly built dog will single track. Back remains strong, firm and flat.

Comment (Table 14-19). As far as the description of the forequarters and hindquarters and my comment thereon is concerned, I must simply refer to what I wrote for the Standard Schnauzer.

Immediately linked to this is the description of the gait.

The trot is performed in a diagonal sequence—that is, no pacing gait—and the forward moving hind paw reaches a place level with the spot where the opposite front paw touched down. As the speed increases, the feet converge toward a single track.

Table 14-20. (Giant Schnauzer)

PSK (Germany)	KC (London)	AKC (United States)
SKIN Tight fitting over the whole body (dry dog). In black dogs rather medium grey, the pepper and salt has a lighter pigmentation. **COAT** TEXTURE The coat is wirehaired. It should be wiry and close. It consists of a thick undercoat and a hard flat-lying topcoat, which under no circumstances should be too short. The topcoat is wiry, never shaggy or wavy. The hair at the head and the legs is also harsh; on the forehead and the ears slightly shorter. The typical hallmarks are a not too soft beard and the bushy eyebrows which slightly overshadow the eyes. **COLOR** Black is permitted; any other markings are disqualifying faults. Pepper and salt — but include "peppering." Markings are disqualifying faults. a. Solid black with black undercoat. b. Pepper and salt: The breeding aim for the pepper and salt color is a medium shade, with an evenly distributed and intensely pigmented "peppering," and a grey undercoat. Admissible are the shades ranging from dark iron-grey to silver-grey. All shades must have a dark mask which harmoniously fits the particular shade and emphasizes the expression. Lighter markings on the head, chest and legs are undesirable.	**COAT** Top coat harsh and wiry, just short enough for smartness on body. Slightly shorter on neck and shoulders but blending smoothly into body coat. Clean on throat, skull, ears and under tail. Good undercoat. Harsh hair on legs. **COLOUR** 1. Pure black. 2. Pepper and salt; shades range from dark iron grey to light grey; hairs banded blark/light/black. Dark facial mask essential, harmonizing with corresponding body colour. On both colours white markings on head, chest and legs undesirable. Good pigmentation essential.	**COAT** Hard, wiry, very dense; composed of a soft undercoat and a harsh outer coat which, when seen against the grain, stands slightly up off the back, lying neither smooth nor flat. Coarse hair on top of head; harsh beard and eyebrows, the schnauzer hallmark. **COLOR** Solid black or pepper and salt. Black—A truly pure black is permitted; any other markings are disqualifying faults Pepper and salt—Outer coat of a combination of banded hairs (white with black and black with white) and some black and white hairs, appearing gray from a short distance. Ideally an intensely pigmented medium gray shade with 'peppering' evenly distributed throughout the coat, and a gray undercoat. Acceptable all shades of pepper and salt from dark iron-gray to silver-gray. Every shade of coat has a dark facial mask to emphasize the expression; the color of the mask harmonizes with the shade of the body coat. Eyebrows, whiskers, cheeks, throat, chest, legs, and under tail are lighter in color but include "peppering." Markings are disqualifying faults.

Comment (Table 14-20). In the introduction to the discussion of the Giant Schnauzer's breed standard, I have already pointed out why a correct dense, wiry, weather-resistant coat is so important for the Giant Schnauzer.

Nobody will deny that a Giant with a correct wiry coat is equipped with a suitable work-oriented outfit that requires only basic grooming. A correct coat is not appropriate for fashionable grooming. The show ring loves glamour and fashion, and it is only human to strive for what one wants to see even if this appearance conflicts with what it should be. We must not, a priori, blame judges for awarding CCs to long, wavy-haired Giant Schnauzers with plenty of leg furnishing. The problem starts with the breeder, who should endeavor to select for a correct coat. That the public prefers soft and fluffy coats is another excuse. In countries where wirehaired Giant Schnauzers are available and where the public can find out for itself how practical such a coat is, the breeder will have no difficulty advertising the right product.

Table 14-21. (Giant Schnauzer)

PSK (Germany)	KC (London)	AKC (United States)

PSK (Germany)

SIZE AND WEIGHT

HEIGHT AT WITHERS: For dogs and bitches between 60 and 70 cm.

WEIGHT: For dogs and bitches between 35 to 42 Kg.

FAULTS

Any departure from the foregoing standard points should be considered a fault and the seriousness with which the fault should be regarded should be in exact proportion to its degree.

Body too plump, too light, too high or too low on the legs. Too coarse or too round skull, a proportionwise too big or too small head, wrinkled forehead. Low set, too long and differently carried ears. Eyes too light, too large, or too small. Strongly protruding cheeks or cheek bones. Loose skin at throat, dewlap. Ewe neck. Pincers bite. Short, pointed or narrow muzzle. Too long, roached, humped and soft back. Croup falling away. Tail carried over-erect or hare tail. Loose elbows, cow-hocked, steep rear, bowlegged. Long feet. Coat too short, too long, soft, wavy, shaggy or silky. White or spotted hair, or any other additional shade; brown undercoat; in the pepper and salt variety: trace and black saddle. Terrier expression. Over and under size. Obvious reversal of sex characteristics (bitchy dogs and the reverse). Pacing gait. Weak temperament.

DISQUALIFICATIONS

1. Deformities of any kind.
2. Monorchids or cryptorchids. Dogs must have two clearly normal developed testicles, fully descended in the scrotum.
3. Insufficient type.
4. Bite faults such as overshot, undershot. Or more than 2 missing teeth.
5. Severe faults in specific parts of the anatomy, coat and color.
6. Shy or vicious temperament.

KC (London)

SIZE

Dogs: 25½ to 27½ ins (65 to 70 cm)
Bitches: 23½ to 25½ ins (60 to 65 cm)
Variations outside these limits undesirable.

FAULTS

Any departure from the foregoing points should be considered a fault and the seriousness with which the fault should be regarded should be in exact proportion to its degree.

DISQUALIFICATIONS

Overshot or undershot.

Note: Male animals should have two apparently normal testicles fully descended into the scrotum.

AKC (United States)

HEIGHT

The height at the withers of the male is 25½ to 27½ inches, and of the female, 23½ to 25½ inches, with the mediums being desired.

Size alone should never take precedence over type, balance, soundness and temperament. It should be noted that too small dogs generally lack the power and too large dogs, the agility and maneuverability, desired in a working dog.

FAULTS

The foregoing description is that of the ideal Giant Schnauzer. Any deviation from the above described dog must be penalized to the extent of the deviation.

The judge shall dismiss from the ring any SHY or VICIOUS Giant Schnauzer.

Shyness: A dog shall be judged fundamentally shy if, refusing to stand for examination, it repeatedly shrinks away from the judge; if it fears unduly any approach from the rear; if it shies to a marked degree at sudden and unusual noises.

Viciousness: A dog that attacks or attempts to attack either the judge or its handler, is definitely vicious. An aggressive or belligerent attitude towards other dogs shall not be deemed viciousness.

DISQUALIFICATIONS

Overshot or undershot.
Markings other than specified.

Left: Ch. Bastian van 't Wareheim, IPO III (Giant) and Ch. Mascars Morella (Standard with natural sabre tail and natural ears) owned by J. & E. Gallant.

Comment (Table 14-21). It is a matter of fact that it is easy to breed Giant Schnauzers that are taller than the limits set by the breed standard. It is probably again the uninformed public or the macho-oriented fancier wanting the biggest male out of the litter who have stimulated some breeders to go for more size.

It is my experience that to maintain functional agility and working ability in general, the ideal Giant Schnauzer should not exceed the limits laid down in the PSK standard.

Ch. Scedir Ares with his owner, A. Torreggiani (Italy), during an agility competition. Holder of thirty-two breed championship titles, this Miniature is in the *Guiness Book of World Records*.

15

Performance Tests and Related Activities

Most national dog organizations have, within the framework of their constitutions, made provisions for rules and regulations for obedience classes, working trials, dog jumping, agility, carting, and so forth. This is extremely important as it emphasizes the dog's ability to perform within a human-canine companionship.

Most of these activities are competitive. The description of exercises and the programs differ from country to country. To describe in detail all disciplines throughout the world would constitute a book. We may, however, consider that as a general rule all countries differentiate the different disciplines into various grades. For example, obedience classes start with beginners, move through novice, and then provide for one, two, or three more difficult classes. The same applies for working titles where the stakes are graded from companion dog through utility dog, tracker dog, and finally police dog or something similar.

Mankind, over the past few decades, has undoubtedly developed a better understanding of the dog as a companion. The development of urban means and the towering presence of dogs in this hectic twentieth-century society has called for structures by which the presence of dogs and the mutual understanding of people and dogs could be improved. There are people who dislike dogs and the nuisance that many of them create. To counteract such feeling, it is necessary to educate the dog fancier on how to understand and train his pet so that the dog is no longer a public nuisance. The classical obedience classes and working-trial training sessions provided by dog clubs reach only a very limited part of the canine population. It was, therefore, necessary that something more efficient and far reaching in terms of the canine population be introduced. I cannot stress enough how important it is that *any* schnauzer fancier should endeavor to learn how to train his schnauzer and make it a question of principle to work toward successful completion of at least one of these elementary tests.

The AKC's Canine Good Citizen Test

The AKC's Canine Good Citizen Test, next to the classical obedience classes and the companion dog stake (CD) as the most elementary working trial, is offered throughout the United States by AKC affiliated all-breed and specialty clubs and judged by a qualified evaluator. Schnauzer owners can prove their dogs have been trained to the elementary level of good social behavior, and a certificate is issued to those who pass the following requirements.

1. Appearance and grooming. Demonstrate that the dog will welcome being groomed and examined and will permit a stranger, such as a Veterinarian or his/her assistant or someone other than the owner to do so.
2. Accepting a stranger. The Evaluator and handler will shake hands and exchange pleasantries. The dog must show no sign of resentment or shyness, and must not break position or try to go to the evaluator.
3. Walk on loose lead—out for a walk. Demonstrates that the handler is in control. The dog must be on the left side of the handler. The dog need not be in the "heel position" as required by AKC Obedience tests.
4. Walk through a crowd. Demonstrates that the dog should have no difficulty in moving about in pedestrian traffic. The dog and handler will walk around and pass close to several persons (at least 3). The dog must show some interest in the strangers, but should continue to walk with the handler without evidence of shyness or resentment. The dog should not be straining at the leash.
5. Sit for exam. Demonstrates that the dog will allow the approach of a stranger and permit petting. The dog must not show shyness or resentment.
6. Sit and down on command. Demonstrates that the dog has had some formal training and will respond to the handler's command. The Evaluator must determine if the dog does respond to the handler's command. The handler must not force the dog into either position. The handler may use more than one command.
7. Stay in position (sit or down). Demonstrates that the dog will assume and remain in the position commanded by the handler. The dog must maintain the position in which it was left until the handler returns and until the Evaluator instructs the handler to release the dog.
8. Reaction to another dog. Demonstrates the proper behavior when in the presence of other dogs. The dogs should demonstrate no more than casual interest. Neither dog should go to the other dog or handler.
9. Reactions to distractions. Demonstrates that the dog is confident at all times when faced with distracting conditions. the dog may express natural interest and curiosity, may startle but should not panic, try to run away, show aggressiveness, or bark.
10. Dog left alone. Demonstrates that the dog may be left alone, demonstrating training and good manners. The dog should not bark, whine, howl or pace unnecessarily or register anything other than mild agitation or nervousness.

Some German Qualifying Tests

Traffic-Tested Companion Dog

The VDH has developed what they call *Verkehrssichere Begleithund* (BH), which roughly translates as traffic-tested companion dog. Schnauzer fanciers should be aware that the PSK strongly promotes this test, which is a first step and a requirement for any further training. For example, in May 1992, it was decided that any handler wishing to compete in Schutzhund must first qualify with his dog in the BH test. The test is open to dogs of all breeds and sizes and over the age of 12 months. Test results are not given as points or scores—only a pass or fail is given by the judge. To pass, 70 percent of the marks (points) in Part A must be achieved and the exercises in Part B carried out to the satisfaction of the judge.

An overview of the different exercises.

Part A. To be carried out on a training area or open ground.

1. Heel on lead in an unreserved way (15 marks). A classical heeling pattern is done at normal pace, with changes of direction and walking through an intermingling group of at least four people.
2. Heel free (15 marks). The same heeling pattern is repeated with the dog off lead. During this exercise, two shots are fired (not while the dog is passing through the group). The dog must show complete indifference to the gunshots. Gun-shy dogs may not continue the test.
3. Sit and stay for one minute (10 marks). The handler gives the command to sit while on the move and continues for another twenty paces where he waits until a minute has passed before returning to the dog.
4. Down and stay with recall (10 marks). The handler gives the command to down while on the move and continues for another twenty paces before turning about and calling the dog.
5. Down and stay with diversion (10 marks). The handler commands his dog to down and walks away to a distance of about forty paces, remaining in sight. The dog must maintain the down position until another team has completed exercises 1 to 4. The handler returns and commands the dog to sit.

Part B. Practical traffic safety test carried out in a public traffic zone with moderate traffic flow. On this test, only the dog, the handler, and the judge participate. No points are awarded. The judge establishes whether the dog can behave competently in traffic conditions.

1. Movement and behavior in street traffic. The judge follows and observes the handler with the dog on lead, walking on the pedestrian sidewalk. By prearrangement, a running passerby crosses the path, and a bicyclist overtakes the team from behind, ringing his bell. The team then turns about and returns toward the judge, where they stop. The handler greets the judge with a shake of hands and conversation.
2. Behavior under more difficult traffic conditions. This walk on lead is done in heavy passing traffic. The handler halts twice, once with a sit command and the other with a down command. During this exercise, a brief halt is made at a place with a high noise level such as a passing train or tramway.
3. Behavior when left alone for a short period in ongoing traffic. The dog is tied to a fence of other fixed object, and the handler moves out of sight to the entrance of a nearby shop. The dog may stand, sit, or lay down for a period of two minutes. Another handler with a nonaggressive dog on lead passes by at a distance of about five paces.

Endurance Test

The purpose of the *Ausdauerungsprüfung* (AD) is to determine whether the dog has the physical stamina for a long-distance run without showing excessive signs of fatigue. This—together with other qualities related to temperament, character, and conformation—will recommend the dog for breeding purposes. To be eligible, the dogs must be between the ages of fourteen months and eight years and must appear to be in good health. Bitches may not be in season or in whelp. For assessment, no marks are awarded. The judge only indicates whether the dog has passed or failed.

For the test, the dog runs on a loose lead next to the handler, who rides a bicycle over different surfaces at an average speed of 10 to 15 km/hour (6.2 to 9.3 mph). The total distance is adjusted to the dog's size, and schnauzers must cover the following: Giants, 20 km (12.4 mi); Standards, 15 km (9.3 mi); and Miniatures, 10 km (6.2 mi). At the halfway point, there is a fifteen-minute break, during which the dog's condition is checked—for example, condition of the pads. At the completion of the test, a small amount of heeling work is required, and the dog's condition is checked again.

Breed Survey

The purpose of the PSK breed survey is to select Giant Schnauzers, Standard Schnauzers, and German Pinschers with a steadfast character. After qualification and subject to the conditions with regard to HD, show results, and endurance test being met, they will be eligible for selected breeding *(Körzucht)*. (See Chapter 13, The Pinscher-Schnauzer Klub.)

The breed survey consists of two well-defined elements:
1. Character test in practical traffic conditions.
2. Testing the ability to take pressure, aptitude for courage, self-confidence, and lack of fear.

Character test procedure. This consists of all the second part of the traffic-tested companion dog (BH) test, combined with steadiness to gunshots. The steadiness to gunshot test is carried out while the dog is heeling off lead. Two shots are fired from a distance of about twenty paces.

Schutzhund—Int. Working Trials

Tracking

Edith Gallant and her Giant Schnauzer Ch. Bastian van't Wareheim, IPO III demonstrate the exercises during an IPO III training session. Bastian is given sufficient time to take scent. He should do this calmly and with his nose close to the ground.

Bastian follows the track calmly, nose down.

The handler follows at the end of the completely unrolled tracking leash.

Each article found is shown to the judge.

Obedience

Heel free is performed at normal, fast, and slow pace.

Send away.

FIGURE 15-3

Gunshot Response

Evaluation.
Steadiness to gunshot—responses.
1. Completely calm, free, and unimpressed
2. Impressed at the outset but quickly regains confidence
3. Barks and/or presses against the handler
4. Barks and/or pulls on the lead, demonstrating flight tendency
5. Barks and/or becomes aggressive toward other dogs or people and can hardly be calmed down

Interpretation.
• Response 1 and 2 are acceptable
• Response 3, test to be repeated in another area
• Response 4 and 5 are failures

Courage test procedure. (This requires the help of a qualified "decoy" in a protective outfit and carrying a padded, leather-covered, flexible stick).
1. Attack on dog. From a distance of about fifty paces, the handler and dog (on lead) walk toward a blind where the decoy is concealed. On the judge's command, the decoy launches an attack in the direction of the dog. The handler drops the lead, and the dog must immediately foil the attack by taking a firm hold of the decoy's protected arm. At this point, the decoy strikes the dog's withers twice with the stick. On command from the judge, the decoy stops his action and stands immobile. The handler takes his dog under control and restrains him by the collar.
2. Pursuit and test of courage. The decoy then drops his stick and, on command from the judge, runs away. At a distance of about fifty paces, he turns and makes threatening gestures toward the handler and dog. On the judge's command, the handler releases the dog. When the dog has approached to about twenty paces, the decoy runs toward the dog. Without hesitation, the dog should take a firm hold of the decoy's protected arm. In the event that the dog hesitates, the decoy makes a slight backward escape maneuver, and the dog should then take hold immediately.

Standard of value—*Wertmessziffer* (WMZ). (The *stimulus threshold* is the precise limit beyond which a stimulus will pass the threshold of awareness; a medium threshold stimulus is required for schnauzers.)

WMZ-1—reserved, hesitant, demonstrating lack of self-confidence, does not bite or hardly takes hold of the arm guard with the front teeth (threshold stimulus too low)

WMZ-2—high drive to attack, too strong, release only with physical intervention of the handler (low threshold stimulus)

WMZ-3—takes hold in a hard and strong way, energetic urging toward assistant, full bite (good tempered, medium threshold stimulus)

WMZ-4—not so hard but self-confident, takes hold (threshold stimulus high)

WMZ-5—avoids under pressure, confronts but does not bite, insufficient defensive behavior (threshold stimulus too high)

Qualification. Dogs receiving a WMZ-2, 3, or 4 qualify. Dogs with a pronounced sound sensitivity or a WMZ-1 or 5 fail. The same applies to dogs that cannot be considered good-natured and that are not safe in a practical traffic situation.

Schutzhund and International Working Regulations

Schutzhund and international working regulations (*Internationale Prüfungsordnung* or IPO) are controversial in most English-speaking countries. The KC and the AKC do not regulate these disciplines. The American Working Dog Federation, however, promotes the so-called Schutzhund training. It cannot be ignored that just as some breeds have been developed for hunting others have been selected for protection and modern security work. If breeders and specialty clubs show interest only in conformation and are careless where character is concerned, the breed will quickly lose this part of its natural heritage and become unsuitable for what it was selected for.

Schnauzer fanciers who have not been involved in Schutzhund work will pretend that the section that teaches defense work is aimed at rendering a dog aggressive. Such a claim will easily be accepted by any lay man. Next to tracking and obedience, which are also an integral part of Schutzhund training, the defense work is fully based on canine psychology and behavior as described by Konrad Lorenz and others. The aim of the defense work section in Schutzhund is to manipulate and develop certain inherent drives *and to lead them in the right direction*. A trained assistant knows exactly what he is doing, and there is no question of developing any form of viciousness. As a pack animal, each canine is born with a certain amount of prey and defensive drive. In working breeds, these drives have been developed by selective breeding and must simply be maintained so that the breed does not lose its ancestral status. To elaborate here on the principles and the techniques that are used in Schutzhund defense training would consist of a book in itself. Trust me, I have taught many hundreds of working dogs when and how to bite my protected arm. They are taught self-confidence and the ability to differentiate between threat and a normal situation. I dare state that of all the dogs I have trained, I could trust them with children, even immediately after a defense work training

Sit on the move.

Down on the move with recall.

Stand stay at a fast pace, with recall.

←——————————→

Send away.

Retrieve Over Hedge

session. I can only warn you against people who pretend that outside Germany Giant Schnauzers used for breeding don't have to do Schutzhund training and that it should be enough to import some occasional German stock to maintain the breed's qualities.

Modern dogs are, in essence, companions of man. The best companion and most reliable dog is the one with a solid nervous system and a steady character and temperament. In other words, a dog that displays all normal canine traits in a balanced way. These qualities cannot be evaluated in the breed ring, and therefore, we need character tests or Schutzhund trials. It is the breeder's responsibility to produce well-balanced offspring. The way in which to achieve this is to use breeding stock that has been proven to possess the required qualities in a specific character test or in Schutzhund training. Statements that Schutzhund work makes a dog vicious can be made only by people who have never been involved in it. I would like to recommend that if you have a feeling for it, join a Schutzhund club, and both you and your schnauzer will thoroughly enjoy the experience.

The exercises for Schutzhund and IPO are identical. The difference is that Schutzhund is regulated by the German DHV (German Dog Sport Association), which is a national organization, and the IPO is regulated and controlled by the FCI commission for working dogs in which many countries are represented.

The tests have three levels of progressive difficulty, and each level consists of three different subjects—tracking, obedience, and defense.

Selection for modern protection dogs mainly occurred on the European continent around the turn of the century. In Germany, the following native breeds qualified as protection dogs: German Shepherd Dog, Doberman Pinscher, Boxer, Rottweiler, Hovawart, Standard Schnauzer, and Giant Schnauzer. To maintain the working ability for which these breeds were selected, suitable training methods and tests had to be developed. Schutzhund and IPO are not primarily spectator sports but are basic tests in which a working dog can prove that he possesses the natural qualities and drives required for his breed. It is absolutely ridiculous to believe that, because a breed has been selected for protection a hundred years ago, it will continue to retain that aptitude indefinitely. Based on long-standing experience, it is my conviction that the schnauzer's temperament and the working ability of the Standard and Giant must be an intrinsic part of every schnauzer breeder's ambition. It is in light of this that the PSK advocates the BH degree, the breed survey, and the Schutzhund test. In Germany alone, there are 150,000 fanciers cherishing and training their working dogs. It is my belief that, for the essence of the breed, this is much more important than all the grooming parlors in the world. I can assure you and prove to you that a Standard and Giant Schnauzer can simultaneously be a lovely pet, a breed

champion, and a tough working dog. Such results cannot be achieved by dreaming and referring to results achieved by fanciers of the past. It will be accomplished by putting one's act together and by doing what is right for the breed—love it, select it, show it, work it, and improve it.

I guess that the 1991 formation of the Working Schnauzer Federation and its affiliation with the American Working Dog Federation (AWDF) found its origin in the above principles. American Giant Schnauzers may soon be seen as competitors in the IPO world championships. This is not surprising if one realizes that in the 1992 WUSV world championships (reserved for German Shepherds), the Americans took second and third place and won the cup for the best national team. This proves that the AWDF is a competent and strong organization, able to beat the Germans and over fifty other countries in a discipline that is relatively new in the United States.

Erling Gornitzka and Ch. Farouk van't Wareheim, Apt., CD EX, IPO III (Giant), demonstrate heel off lead as an obedience exercise.

156

Scaling a Sloping Stockade and Retrieving an Object

Ch. Evan Van Schaden. Owned by Elaine (Walton) Chambers and Maxine Petteway. Evan set a record for Standard Schnauzers, with twelve best-in-show wins, always handled by Elaine.

16

The Standard Schnauzer in the United States

by Cynthia Lorr

The first Standard Schnauzer registered by the AKC was registered in 1904 as a German Pinscher—Norwood Victor, sired by Schnauzer out of Schnauzerl. There is no written record of any schnauzers that might have reached the United States earlier.

Early History

The Standard Schnauzer had a confusing early history in this country, going through several name changes and bouncing back and forth between the terrier and working groups. The quality seems to have been high, however, as they did a lot of winning.

The Wirehaired Pinscher Club of America was founded in 1925 by fanciers of both Miniature and Standard Schnauzers. The Swiss import Resy Patricia won the breed at the 1925 Westminster Kennel Club show and became the breed's first champion; her daughter Fracas Franconia became breed's first American-bred champion. That same year, two Standards went all the way to best in show—Fred Gamundia, followed by Butz Saldan.

By 1926, Standard Schnauzers had really taken off in the American show world. More Standard Schnauzers were exhibited that year than in 1992. Four dogs were required for a single point, and ten were required for a three-point major.

Confusion about which group the Standard Schnauzer should be shown in was evident. During 1926, the breed moved to the terrier group from working, enabling Ajax v. Paderquell to win both groups that April.

Pity the 1926 exhibitor filling out a show entry. The breed started the year as Wirehaired Pinschers, becoming Pinscher (Schnauzer) by June, Schnauzer-Pinscher by July, and finally Schnauzer by October.

Standard Schnauzers continued to win groups and best-in-show awards. Claus v. Furstenwall had four best-in-show and three more group wins that year, on his way to a lifetime record of ten best-in-show wins. His record held until the 1980s when Ch. Charisma Cafe Diable won eleven, and Ch. Evan Von Schaden set a new all-time high of twelve.

In 1929, a new breed standard raised the minimum height from 15¾ to 16¾ inches. It also disqualified cropped ears. In 1931, the AKC cancelled all wins by dogs with cropped ears that were whelped after September 1, 1929. This was as big

a controversy in those days as it would be today. Many breeders cropped ears but just didn't show their dogs. There was a great decline in entries.

Before the controversy, Standard Schnauzers had been consistent group and best-in-show winners. With the sudden drop in entries, the momentum was lost, not to be retained for more than half a century, if then.

Sometimes, Miniatures and Standards competed together for best of breed, and other times separately for two breed awards. This continued until 1933 when the Schnauzer Club of America divided into the Miniature Schnauzer Club of America and the Standard Schnauzer Club of America (SSCA).

The national club was basically inactive, however, until a group of fanciers reactivated it in 1935. A 1936 membership list shows twenty-three members. A new breed standard was approved in 1939, but until after World War II, the Midwest Standard Schnauzer Club was more active than the national club.

The Second World War brought profound change to the world of Standard Schnauzers. Before the war, most exhibitors were wealthy and hired professional handlers and kennel managers to oversee their dogs. By 1945, when the Standard Schnauzers moved back to the working group, with few exceptions breed fanciers were people new to the breed who kept the dogs as family pets. Most people showed their own dogs, even after the SSCA instituted annual awards in 1957. Today, while kennels still tend to be small, more top specials are handled by professionals, though there are always the exceptional owners who show their dogs with professional skill.

Some Early Kennels

Many dogs important to the breed came from the Winalesby Kennels of Mrs. Winifred Atkinsom. The first litter, whelped in January of 1930, included Ch. Winalesby Skulda, CD, who earned the breed's first obedience title. The Winalesby continued to be important winners for over a decade.

Ch. Winalesby Reital, CD was the important foundation sire for Helen Boynton's Von Volken dogs. The Von Volken line has been extremely important in both this country and, through the Von Hahlweg line, in Europe.

Ch. Nickel St. Gallus, owned by Sophronia Bunker, was another important sire. He is known especially for producing Ch. Chief of Staff when bred to his daughter Angel of Thimble Farm.

Ch. Chief of Staff, owned by B. B. Berman, sired the great Ch. Major Pfeffer, owned by Mary Nelson (Stephenson). Major Pfeffer was bred to at least four of Chief of Staff's daughters (his half sisters), producing a number of champions with the Pfeffer prefix and the great producer Ch. BBB's Baghdad by the Bay.

Bred to Gretchen Von Volken, Ch. BBB's Baghdad by the Bay produced the Stone Pine champions Nickel, Frisco, and Swaps, among others. His daughter Ch. Bobuberm Bussy, CD was the dam of Ch. Ricknpat's Royal Rogue, CDX—four times the SSCA dog of the year and once dog of the year of opposite sex between 1959 and 1963. Bred to Nickel, he produced the Stone Pine champions Smoke, Storm, Spunk, Spark, Sabre, and Spice for the Aronstams as well as multiple Ricknpat champions and others. His daughter Ch. Jimay's Princess Pooka, CD was the foundation for Gail Mackiernan's Katahdin line; bred to Ch. Erik Von Hahlweg, she produced the Katahdin champions Tsunami and Meteor.

Liz Hanrahan's Patundlis Kennels produced a number of influential dogs, including Ch. Patundlis Erich, the sire of Ch. Badger's Balderdash, owned by Alice Vandergrift,

Ch. Badger's Balderdash was bred to four daughters of Ch. Stone Pine Stacatto, producing many champions. His son Ch. Badger's Whippersnapper appears in many of today's pedigrees because he is the sire of Ch. Drehil Whiplash of Williams and Ch. Flashback of Williams, the foundation sire and dam of Pat Korn's Drehil Kennels.

Sue Baines' Ch. Anne Von Breitenloh, bred to Int. Ch. Furst Von Hahlweg, produced Ch. La Marka's Diva Von Heidi. Owned by Mary Hoenig, she produced five champions for Klinahof, including Ch. Klinahof's Furst v. Frisco.

One of the longest-running kennels in America was the Schumachers' Von Helgoland line, active from the 1940s into the 1970s. Ch. Fritz v. Helgoland was a specialty winner of the 1940s. The last champion, Ch. Hildur Derfuhrer Von Helgoland, finished in 1980, which is quite a span of activity for any kennel.

Imports

Imports from Germany and Switzerland have been important since the earliest days. The v. d. muntern Gesellen dogs bred by Gisela Gerth have been noteworthy, particularly the multititled Joschi v. d. muntern Gesellen, who sired Ch. Andy v. d. muntern Gesellen, the foundation sire for Eula Lambert's Artula line. He also sired Ch. Negus v. Falkenhaus. Negus had a tremendous impact through his son Ch. Drehil Phantom, who produced many champions for Pat Korn's Drehil Kennels and for Oakwood.

The Von Hahlweg dogs of the Rothes have also been very important for years. Because the Rothes lived in the United States for years and speak English, their dogs have more accessible for monolingual Americans. The import Ch. Erik Von Hahlweg was not only the SSCA dog of the year in 1965 but also sired forty-six champions. His daughter Ch. Katahdin Tsunami was the foundation of Carol Davie-Earle's Tsunami line. Ch. Katahdin Meteor, his son, is behind many of today's show dogs, especially through his own son Ch. Katahdin Kon-Tiki, the all-time leading sire. Kon-Tiki also helped to establish the Yamada line. Ch. Kinderwachter

Abban v. Link, another Erik offspring, is behind Cecelia Link's Von Link line, and Ch. Tru-Lov's Artig Kinderwachter, from the same litter, is the foundation sire of Jane Wilson's Liebevoll schnauzers.

Contemporary breeders are also looking to England and Scandinavia for new bloodlines.

Interest in Russian schnauzers was heightened in 1991 when Madge Fish judged the breed (the most popular show dog) in Moscow, accompanied by Barbara Dille, SSCA president. They came back with many photographs of outstanding dogs. Russian imports, however, are not eligible for AKC registration. They are eligible for listing and may be used for breeding. Since few Standard Schnauzer breeders have the facilities to keep more than a few dogs, this option has limited appeal.

The flow of dogs has not been entirely one way by any means. When the Rothes (Von Hahlweg) took Ch. Pfeffer Von Volken to Switzerland, she was an immediate sensation, and she proved her worth as a brood bitch. Recently, breeders have sent dogs to Europe, Australia, and Latin America. The major barrier is one of language; the quality of the best dogs everywhere is very high.

Modern Show Winners

Group placements and best-in-show wins for Standard Schnauzers were very rare for many years.

Ch. August Von Volweg, owned by the Paynes and shown by Henry McGill, was SSCA dog of the year in 1968 and 1969. He garnered six bests in his career, the only Standard who won that award in the 1960s. August was also a *Leading Producer*—a title SSCA awards to dogs producing six champions and bitches producing four.

After a hiatus of ten years, the bitch Ch. Skico's Alpine Glow, handled by her owner Penny Duffee, took a best in show in 1979. A month later, Ch. Peajay's Charlie Waters took a best-in-show award. Alpine Glow, a Leading Producer, was SSCA's dog of the year of opposite sex in 1977 and 1979.

Another star of the 1970s was the top-winning black Standard Schnauzer Int. Ch. Pavo de la Steingasse, owned by Margaret Smith and shown by Sue Baines. He was SSCA dog of the year in 1970 and 1971 but never had a best in show. Pavo sired fourteen champions, a considerable number for a black, and he is behind many of the best blacks seen today.

In the 1980s, Standard Schnauzers made more frequent appearances in the group and best winners circle.

Ch. Karyon Konrad Von Eddy (owned by Dot Bourdin and shown by Houston Clark) and Ch. Heidi's Christmas Bell (owned by Joan and Jeff Hodges and shown by Maripi Woolridge) each took a best in show. Ch. Bengal Von Siegerhaus, owned by the Caldwells and the Yamadas, had four.

Figure 16-3

SSCA DOG OF THE YEAR

1958 Ch. Roberto's Conquistador (Dr. & Mrs. Gebhardt)
1959 Ch. Ricknpat's Royal Rogue, CDX (Pricilla Danckwerth)
1960 Ch. Ricknpat's Royal Rogue, CDX (Pricilla Danckwerth)
1961 Ch. Ricknpat's Pfeffer Too (R. & P. Danckwerth)
1962 Ch. Ricknpat's Royal Rogue, CDX (Pricilla Danckwerth)
1963 Ch. Ricknpat's Royal Rogue, CDX (Pricilla Danckwerth)
1964 Ch. Stone Pine Staccato (R. V. & S. K. Lothrop)
1965 Ch. Erik Von Hahlweg (Sue Baines)
1966 Ch. Klinahof's Furst v. Frisco (Mary Hoenig)
1967 Ch. Stuart's Storm Cloud (S. O. & J. R. Anderson)
1968 Ch. August Von Volweg (Mr. & Mrs. Arthur Payne)
1969 Ch. August Von Volweg (Mr. & Mrs. Arthur Payne)
1970 Int. Ch. Pavo de la Steingasse (Margaret Smith)
1971 Int. Ch. Pavo de la Steingasse (Margaret Smith)
1972 Ch. Salzundpfeffer's Bibi (Fran Reynolds)
1973 Ch. Artula Christopher Von Gurlin (Timothy Spurlock)
1974 Ch. Artula Christopher Von Gurlin (Timothy Spurlock)
1975 Ch. Artula Lord Greystone (Timothy Spurlock)
1976 Ch. Artula Lord Greystone (Timothy Spurlock)
1977 Ch. Artula Lord Greystone (Timothy Spurlock)
1978 Am./Can. Ch. Heren's Nitsche Yonan, CD, Can. CD (Harold Jess)
1979 Am./Can. Ch. Heren's Nitsche Yonan, CD, Can. CD (Harold Jess)
1980 Ch. Pepper Tree's Victor's Vanity (Sue Culbertson)
1981 Ch. Yamada's Star of Taurus (B. & E. Walton)
1982 Ch. Charisma Cafe Diable (T. & C. Adel)
1983 Ch. Charisma Cafe Diable (T. & C. Adel)
1984 Ch. Charisma Cafe Diable (T. & C. Adel)
1985 Ch. Yamada's Bosker Star Strider (J. & J. Hodges, B. & E. Yamada)
1986 Ch. Snowshoes Gusto of Charisma (Constance Adel)
1987 Ch. Evan Von Schaden (E. Walton and M. Petteway)
1988 Ch. Evan Von Schaden (E. Walton and M. Petteway)
1989 Ch. Evan Von Schaden (E. Walton and M. Petteway)
1990 Ch. Morganwald's Izod (Christa Duffee)
1991 Ch. Morganwald's Izod (Christa Duffee)
1992 Ch. Morganwald's Izod (Christa Duffee)
1993 Ch. Kennebunk Special Beau (Ruth Black, Dr. Catherine Black-Lee, and Ramona Fine)
1994 Ch. Cortaillod Ubeda (Carol Boehm)
1995 Ch. Oregonized Country Karisma (Catherine Lord)

Ch. Arjo's Siegfried Von Erivic, owned by the McCulloughs, garnered three top awards. Siegfried retired early after an embolism, though he continued to live a long and happy life.

Two outstanding show stars broke Standard Schnauzer records. The first, Ch. Charisma Cafe Diable, owned by Trevor and Connie Adel, was piloted to eleven best-in-show wins by Tim Spurlock. Diable was SSCA dog of the year in 1982, 1983, and 1984. His dam Ch. Princess Schatzi of Tanterra had been SSCA dog of the year of opposite sex in 1978, an honor his sister Ch. Charisma Cappucino repeated in 1980. All three of these schnauzers are SSCA Hall of Fame producers. According to the Adels, Diable defeated more Standard Schnauzers than any other in history.

The all-time record of twelve best-in-show awards for the breed is held by Ch. Evan Von Schaden, owned by Elaine (Walton) Chambers and Maxine Petteway and shown by Elaine. Evan often showed in his home area where Standard Schnauzer entries are sparse, so he did a lot of his winning at the group level to become the SSCA dog of the year for 1987, 1988, and 1989. Evan's dam, Ch. Tu-B's Brandy Von Schonheit, was SSCA dog of the year of opposite sex in 1985, and his sire, Ch. Yamada's Star of Taurus, was SSCA dog of the year in 1981.

In 1990, Ch. Lindal's Storm Shadow, a son of Ch. Bengal Von Siegerhaus, went best in show, making it the first time—at least in recent history—that a best-in-show winner sired another winner.

Am./Can. Ch. Oakwood Carolina Rebel, bred and owned by Anne Miller and A. H. Welch and shown by Robert Fisher had two best-in-show wins, both in 1990. He also topped the national specialty twice in his career.

Figure 16-4

SSCA DOG OF THE YEAR OF THE OPPOSITE SEX

1958 Ch. Ricknpat's Rich Reward (Mr. & Mrs. Wallace Butler)
1959 Ch. Stone Pine Smoke (R. V. & S. K. Lothrop, Jr.)
1960 Ch. Stone Pine Spice (Mr. & Mrs. S. Robinson)
1961 Ch. Ricknpat's Royal Rogue, CDX (Pricilla Danckwerth)
1962 Ch. Stone Pine Spark (Mrs. G. Fiedler)
1963 Ch. Sin-der Von Fleck (G. H. McGeary)
1964 Ch. Honor Von Volken (Maj. J. B. Schofield)
1965 Ch. Honor Von Volken (Maj. J. B. Schofield)
1966 Ch. Honor Von Volken (Maj. J. B. Schofield)
1967 Ch. Madeline's Gretchen (Madeline Condon)
1968 Ch. Honor Von Volken (Maj. J. B. Schofield)
1969 Ch. Honor Von Volken (Maj. J. B. Schofield)
1970 Ch. Gei-San's Gina Gee (Dr. & Mrs. S. C. Johnson III)
1971 Ch. Toxi Von Hahlweg (J. & J. Wood)
1972 Ch. Cliffside Schon (Mr. & Mrs. Carl Fisher)
1973 Ch. Salzundpfeffer's Bibi (Fran Reynolds)
1974 Ch. Artula Esme Von Gurlin (R. & A. Smith, E. & J. Hagadorn)
1975 Ch. Tonsa Von Hahlweg, CD (J. & H. Tabaczynski)
1976 Ch. Pepper Tree Love Song (E. & A. Holst)
1977 Ch. Skico's Alpine Glow (B. & P. Duffee)
1978 Ch. Princess Schatzi of Tanterra (T. & C. Adel)
1979 Ch. Skico's Alpine Glow (B. & P. Duffee)
1980 Ch. Charisma Cappucino (T. & C. Adel)
1981 Ch. Liebevoll's Pfennig Von Geld (D. & S. Knobel)
1982 Ch. Bardwood's Lady Dulcinea (R. & P. Lombardi)
1983 Ch. Tu-B's Dyn-O-Mite, CD (Lana Brinkmeyer)
1984 Ch. Drehil Revelry (Anne Miller)
1985 Ch. Tu-B's Brandy Von Schonheit (E. Salton and D. Betsill)
1986 Ch. Heidi's Christmas Bell (Drs. J. & J. Hodges)
1987 Ch. Heidi's Christmas Bell (Drs. J. & J. Hodges)
1988 Ch. Morganwald's Instant Winner (C. & A. Smith and P. Duffee)
1989 Ch. Morganwald's Instant Winner (C. & A. Smith and P. Duffee)
1990 Ch. Camino Oregonized Glory Days (D. & B. Kusch)
1991 Ch. Jan-Rex Princess Katarina (R. & J. Smith)
1992 Ch. Katon's Anastasia V Deepdale (Catherine Lord)
1993 Ch. Oregonized Country Karisma (Catherine Lord)
1994 Ch. Oregonized Country Karisma (Catherine Lord)
1995 Ch. Morgenwald's Knockout V Skico (Penny Duffee)

Ch. Charisma Cafe Diable. Bred and owned by Trevor and Connie Adel. Diable had a career record of eleven best-in-show awards. He defeated more Standard Schnauzers than any other in breed history.

Ch. Bengel Von Siegerhaus. Owned by Robert and Linda Caldwell and Burton and Ellen Yamada. Winner of four best-in-show awards, Bengel is the only winner to have best-in-show offspring.

Ch. Lindal's Storm Shadow. Bred and owned by Robert and Linda Caldwell. The best-in-show son of Ch. Bengel Von Siegerhaus.

Ch. Oakwood Carolina Rebel. Anne Miller and A. H. Welch.

Ch. Katahdin Kon-Tiki. Bred by Gail Mackiernan; owned by Carol Davis-Earle and Gail Mackiernan. Kon-Tiki is the sire of seventy-eight champions, the breed record.

Ch. Peajay's Charlie Waters. Owned by Elaine Walton. Winning best in show in 1979.

Ch. Skico's Alpine Glow. Owned by Bill and Penny Duffee. Shown by Penny, Alpine Glow was the first Standard Schnauzer in a decade to win best in show and the first bitch in forty years.

Another Standard Schnauzer emerged in 1992 as a multiple best-in-show dog. Christa Duffee's Ch. Morganwald's Izod, bred by Bill and Penny Duffee, took four top awards that year as well as going best of breed at the national specialty show. Izod was Christa's junior showmanship dog for several years, and when he won the national, she was only 20, making her the youngest handler to come away with that award. Izod was shown throughout his career by Christa or by Penny.

Showing at the group level being what it is, the momentum may be building for more group placements and bests for Standard Schnauzers. Momentum is an elusive process, but it definitely exists. Group placements were much rarer in the 1960s and 1970s. That does not mean that the dogs weren't as good by any means. Every win makes it easier for the next dog.

Leading Producers

The SSCA has designated as a leading producer a dog that has sired six champions or a bitch that has produced four champions. In addition, the SSCA initiated the Hall of Fame in 1982. To be included in the Hall of Fame, a sire must have twenty champions, and a dam must have ten.

The leading producer of all time is Ch. Katahdin Kon-Tiki, CD, the sire of seventy-six champions. Max was bred by Gail Mackiernan and owned by her and Carol Davis. According to Carol Davis-Earl, nineteen of the champions came from three litters out of her bitch Ch. Katahdin Tsunami, and seventeen from four litters out of Ch. Yamada's Heidi Belle, CD.

Other Hall of Fame sires are the following: Ch. Allex Von Freudenberg, CD; Ch. Erik Von Hahlweg; Ch. Andy v. d. munteren Gesellen; Ch. Bayerischen Wind Von Holz; Ch. Drehil Phantom, CD; Ch. Katahdin Meteor; Ch. Ricknpat's Royal Rogue, CDX; Ch. Charisma Cafe Diable; Ch. Geistvoll Bonanza, Ch. Morganwald's Buccaneer; Ch. Oakwood Phantom Phlyer, UD, Can. CD; Ch. Pepper Tree Victor's Vanity, CD; Ch. Uhlan Lieutenant Kije; and Ch. Yamada's Star of Taurus.

The Hall of Fame dams include the top-producing Ch. Bardwood's Lady Dulcinea, the dam of twenty-two champions. Bred and owned by Ron and Pat Lombardi, she was also the SSCA dog of the year of opposite sex in 1982.

Other Hall of Fame dams are the following: Ch. Baenz Von Holz, CD; Ch. Jimay's Princess Pooka, CD; Ch. Karestesco's Augusta, CD; Ch. Katahdin Tsunami, CD; Ch. Mardan's Mistal v. Hartzheidi; Ch. Stone Pine Nickel; Ch. Tonsa Von Hahlweg, CD; Ch. Toxi Von Hahlweg; Ch. Tru-Lov's Seidlog Pampers, CD; Ch. Yamada's Heidi Belle, CD; Ch. Yamada's Kato's Belle Star; Ch. Asgard Kithara Von Holz, CD; Ch. Carabella Angelica; Ch. Charisma Cappucino; Ch. Dulcinea Von Holz, CD; Ch. Geistvoll Amethyst; Ch. Holzgeist Von Kaiserbart, UD, Can. CDX; Ch. Klemmen

Ajan, UD, Can. CD; Ch. Liebevoll's Pfennig Von Geld; Ch. Pepper Tree Love Song; Ch. Princess Schatzi of Tanterra; Ch. Tsunami Checkmate; and Ch. Tu-B's Brandy Von Schonheit.

In terms of percentages, the girls outnumber the boys in having attained obedience degrees to go with their championships. It is worth noting that all of the Hall of Fame sires and dams are champions of record.

Obedience and Other Activities

Standard Schnauzers often seem to have more talent for obedience than their owners. Certainly when their owners have trained them, the dogs' performances have ranked with the best, though a Standard Schnauzer is never a small machine that is just turned on to do obedience work. While it is true that a dog must be shown to win, it is equally true that the dog needs a trainer to compete in obedience. When given the opportunity, Standard Schnauzers shine in obedience. When the owners have the interest, it is also true that a Standard Schnauzer can compete successfully for many years.

The first obedience trial champion of the breed was Ch./O.T.Ch. Hodgendell's Frieda Houdini, UD, Can. UD, owned by Sharon Hodgens. Frieda was the SSCA obedience dog of the year for six years, 1974–1980.

After Frieda came the all-time top obedience dog Am./Can. O.T.Ch. Artaxerxes Von Molloy, UD, Can. UD. Artaxerxes earned his obedience championship in just ten weeks after attaining his UD title. He was the SSCA obedience dog of the year for seven straight years, from 1981–1987. He had attained the elusive perfect 200 score early in his career, and he was a very consistent worker. He was owned by Bob and Cathy Knight and shown by Bob.

Both of these dogs were sired by Pat Korn's Ch. Drehil Whiplash of Williams. Other obedience dogs in the same line include Whiplash's dam Ch. Indi Von Volken, UD, his brother Vortac Von Williams, UD, and his niece Puff's Phanfare Von Edwards, all of which were SSCA obedience dog of the year once and all of which competed before the AKC instituted the obedience championship title.

In 1986, the SSCA presented a special award to Jane Mayo and Ch. Barnaba von Krumchen for their search-and-rescue work. The two traveled all over the country to help in the search for disaster victims.

In 1993, the SSCA voted another special award to Dwayne Pickel and Ch. Tailgates George Vonpickel, UD. George is a full-time K-9 on the Tallahassee Police Department's bomb squad with Sgt. Pickel. A very talented dog, he achieved his UD within 6 months of his first obedience lesson with scores above 190 all the way. While other dogs have earned all three obedience titles within 6 months, they generally train for a much longer period before being exhibited. George is fully trained in all police work, showing that a Standard Schnauzer can do it all.

Ch. OTCh. Hodgendell's Frieda Houdini, owned by Sharon Hodgens-Wood, was the breed's first OTCh. She was SSCA's Obedience Dog of the Year for six years.

FIGURE 16-14

Other Standard Schnauzers have proved their usefulness in tracking and in assistance dog work, and many are therapy dogs.

The Standard

Over the years, the Standard Schnauzer standard has changed several times, with revisions in 1929, 1939, 1968, and 1991.

The proportions of the dog's body have changed. In the 1929 standard, the height of the dog was to equal the length of the back (from withers to set on of tail), but it also specified they were to be built squarely. The height was given as 15¾ to 19¾ inches.

By 1939, the description is much closer to the contemporary understanding of the dog. The height is different for the two sexes—from 17 to 19 inches for bitches and from 18 to 20 inches for the dog, the same as it is now. The proportions are the same as in the 1929 standard, however. A fault listed in this standard is a too-narrow head; today, narrow heads are

preferred by most breeders.

The 1968 revision calls for a dog that is square in proportion of body length to height, which is consistent with the 1991 standard. One would think that several inches of dog disappeared in 1968. In fact, pictures of the dogs from the early days show that they were just as square as today's dogs, with some longer-bodied dogs then as now. Evidently, the judges never did judge from the standard!

There are differences between the German standard (used by FCI clubs all over the world) and the AKC standard. In some instances, the qualities preferred by the European breeders differ from the qualities preferred by American judges and, hence, breeders. The AKC standard allows a size of 16–19 inches for bitches and 18–20 inches for dogs. The German standard has one size for dogs and bitches, 45–50 cm (about 17¾ to 19½ inches).

The German standard calls for an overall medium salt-and-pepper color, disallowing white on chest, legs, or head. Furnishings are expected to be close to the color of the rest of the dog. In the United States and Canada, contrasting furnishings and cheeks—the whiter the better—are preferred. The German standard requires a darker facial mask, but the AKC standard merely says it is desirable. The German standard is specific in specifying evenly distributed pigment of a medium shade, but the AKC standard specifies that the color may fade out in certain areas: eyebrows, whiskers, cheeks,

Ch. Arjo's Siegfried Von Erivic. Owned by Arnold and Joan McCullough. Winner of three best-in-show awards in a short show career.

under throat, across chest, under tail, leg furnishings, under body, and inside legs. As a consequence, some people feel that lack of pigment is a problem in some of today's Standard Schnauzers in the United States.

The quality of furnishings has been changing as well. Most people feel that a dog with a very hard coat and sparse furnishings has a very difficult time in the ring, whereas a dog with a faulty coat and profuse furnishings does well. Whether coats have actually changed or grooming techniques have improved to make sparse furnishings look like more as some people contend, the look of winning dogs has definitely changed in America.

Perhaps the differences are mainly cosmetic and related to grooming. Certainly as one looks at pictures of schnauzers of the early 1900s, the basic dog—ignoring the ear crop and grooming—looks very similar to today's schnauzer. A full range of desirable features and faults may be seen in both groups.

Ch. Morganwald's Izod. Bred by Bill and Penny Duffee; owned by Christa Duffee. Winner of four bests in show in 1992, Izod was handled throughout his career by Christa or by Penny.

Ch. Heidi's Christmas Bell. Bred and owned by Joan and Jeff Hodges. A best-in-show winning bitch.

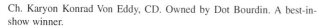

Ch. Karyon Konrad Von Eddy, CD. Owned by Dot Bourdin. A best-in-show winner.

Am./Can. O.T.Ch. Artaxerxes Von Molloy. Owned by Bob and Cathy Knight. SSCA's obedience dog of the year for seven years.

Ch. Blythewood Tell It Like It Is. Owned by Joan Huber. A specialty-show winner.

Ch. Blythewood Star Player. Owned by Joan Huber.

Ch. Blythewood Storm Damage. Owned by Joan Huber. One of the top winners in 1991 and 1992.

17

The Miniature Schnauzer in the United States

by Marcia Feld

Emergence

In the summer of 1924, Rudolph Krappatsch exported four little dogs from Germany to Mrs. Marie E. Lewis (better known as Marie Slattery, "Marienhof") at the Zeitgeist Kennels in Massachusetts. These four animals were the foundation of what would become one of the most popular breeds in the United States, the Miniature Schnauzer.

Initially, these small schnauzers as well as their larger cousins, the Standard Schnauzers, were shown as Wirehaired Pinschers—a direct reflection of their heritage—and competed in the working group. After moving to the terrier group and renamed Schnauzers in 1926, separate varieties were recognized in 1927, with two representatives in the group. From 1931 to 1933, however, they were again classified as a single breed.

The division of the two as separate breeds became final in 1933, when the AKC ruled that breed clubs could represent only one breed, and the Miniature Schnauzer Club of America was founded. Both breeds competed in the terrier group until 1945, when the Standard Schnauzer moved back to the working group.

During the schnauzer's first ten years in the United States—from 1925 to 1935—108 dogs were imported, most from Germany. Today's schnauzers, with rare exception, trace back to about 40 of these imports.

Evolution

The placement of the Miniature Schnauzer in the terrier group is unique to the United States and has had a profound influence on the evolving appearance of the breed. Successful competition in the terrier group required a breed that more closely resembled a terrier. The Miniature Schnauzer is now a "high-maintenance" breed requiring as many hours for grooming as any other terrier, if not more. In addition, the breed has two definite types. One reflects the working heritage—well laid back shoulders, slightly longer body, and very efficient movement that is tireless and agile. The other type reflects the terrier influence—straighter shoulders, square (or shorter than square) body, pleasing terrier-type outline, and more typical terrierlike movement.

The first Miniature Schnauzer standard, written in 1934, was revised in 1957 and again in 1991. A comparison of the 1934 and 1957 standards in Table 17–1 lends insight into the evolving breed.

Although both cropped and natural ears are equally acceptable in the U.S. show ring, very few natural ears are seen in competition, and how natural ears should look is a subject of controversy. England allows only natural ears and has, therefore, definite opinions as to their placement. In 1982, the American export Ch. Travelmore's from U.S. to You (bred by William and Olive Moore, Trenton, New Jersey) was England's top schnauzer (all sizes), and apparently his lovely ears are what the English consider just right.

Table 17-1. Comparison of the 1934 and 1957 standards

Feature	1934	1957
Skull	Moderately broad, width not exceeding ⅔ of length of the head; too long and narrow a skull is a fault	Width not exceeding ½ of length of head; fault deleted
Eyes	Medium sized	Small, expression should be keen
Tail	Moderately high, carried erect	Set high, carried erect
Coat	Wiry whiskers, hard and wiry coat, slightly rough appearance, harsh to the touch	Wiry whiskers accentuating the rectangular shape of the head
	Trimmed only enough to accentuate body outline	No mention of grooming restrictions
	No mention of furnishings	Furnishings to be fairly thick but not silky
Size	Dogs 10½ to 13½ inches	From 12 to 14 inches
	Bitches 10 to 12½ inches	
	Disqualification—dogs over 14 inches and bitches over 13 inches	Disqualification—dogs or bitches under 12 or over 14 inches

Colors

Unlike its larger relatives, the Miniature Schnauzer standard recognizes three colors. In addition to the salt-and-pepper and black colors of the Giant and Standard Schnauzers, the Miniature comes in black-and-silver, indicating presence of the gene for black-and-tan markings and the possible infusion of smaller breeds to reduce size. The order of genetic dominance from most to least is as follows: black, salt-and-pepper, black-and-silver.

American Miniature Schnauzers differ from those on the Continent in the manner of breeding and showing the three colors. Elsewhere, each of the colors is shown independently, resulting in three best-of-breed winners and three entries to the group; in the United States, all three colors compete for a single breed win and one representative in the group. In most countries, the colors may not be interbred, whereas American breeders frequently cross the three colors.

Since the first imports, the salt-and-pepper color has been prevalent. By 1990, salt-and-pepper accounted for 75 percent of the registered Miniature Schnauzers.

As mentioned earlier, most of today's Miniature Schnauzers decend from a small portion of the 108 prewar imports, all of which were salt-and-pepper and formed the genetic base of the breed in the United States. The evolution toward a more terrier-like appearance occurred in the salt-and-pepper Miniatures. The other two colors had little show success until the 1970s and 1980s, and indeed, those successes were possible because of the freedom to cross them with salt-and-pepper Miniatures of the desired show type.

The crosses that have been of great benefit to the black and black-and-silver colors have also affected the quality of the salt-and-pepper color. For example, the salt-and-pepper coat is sometimes too dark because of reduced banding on a portion of the dog, especially in a puppy, and undercoats are sometimes black. The vast majority of the salt-and-pepper

Ch. Feldmar Night Reveler. Bred by M. Feld (United States); owned by M. Brick (New Zealand). His show record is unequaled by any other black-and-silver Miniature Schnauzer in the United States.

Ch. Blythewood Shooting Sparks. Owned by Joan Huber. Specialty and all-breed best-in-show winner; sire of more than twenty-five champions.

Ch. Blythewood National Acclaim. Owned by Joan Huber. Shown winning best in show.

Ch. Blythewood Be My Guest. Owned by Joan Huber.

dogs now have other colors in their ancestry. The one noted exception to this is the Penlan Kennel (Penny and Lanny Hirstein of Washington, Illinois), which has avoided crossing with other colors. Their breeding program began in the early 1960s and has done much to preserve the color in its original form.

It is important to remember that black is the most dominant color. A schnauzer that carries the gene for black will always be black; a schnauzer of any other color cannot produce black offspring.

Although some blacks were imported in the 1920s, they were mated to salt-and-peppers, and only salt-and-pepper descendents remain. The first serious attempt to breed blacks was made in the 1930s by Willia Maguire (Bambivin). At that time, crosses between Standards and Miniatures were allowed, and she obtained her black Miniatures from crosses with black Standards. Indeed, she produced the first black Miniature champion (a bitch) in 1935. It was not until 1969 that a second American-bred black (another bitch) completed an AKC title.

After World War II, few blacks could be found in the U.S., and there was almost no interest in breeding them. In Germany, however, blacks rapidly gained in popularity, and a number of them brought back as pets were bred to salt-and-pepper show stock.

Ch. Woodhaven's Black Gough Drops finished in 1972. The first black male champion, he was the first to have any significant impact on American bloodlines. He was also the first to achieve a group first and did so twice. A second male finished in 1973.

Ch. Aljamar Tommy Gun finished in 1974. He influenced black-and-silver lines as well as blacks, having inherited the black-and-silver gene from his imported Italian father.

Twelve blacks obtained their titles in 1984, the first "bumper" year, bringing the total of black champions to 65. In 1987, that total climbed to 99, and by 1992, the number had almost doubled with a total of 193.

Blacks climbed to the top in 1986 and 1987 with Ch. Sibehil's Dark Shadows, the culmination of many years of breeding effort on the part of Beverly Pfaff (Jebema) of Suisun, California. Barnabus broke all show records for Miniature Schnauzers of any color, and he was the first black to top a national specialty. His record as a producer was equally outstanding, with twenty-two champions in a limited period of time at stud. Although he was not affected, Barnabus retired from stud when he was found to carry the gene for progressive retinal atrophy. An interesting item of note is that Mrs. Pfaff has established another excellent line of blacks, this time using a black-and-silver as a foundation and picking up the black gene from the remnants of a kennel best known for intense black color.

The black-and-silver color has been unpopular for most of the breed's history in this country. It usually cropped up in litters from salt-and-pepper or black parents in which both parents carried the recessive gene, and the puppies were usually sold as pets.

The first serious attempt to produce the color was made in 1955 by Jackie Walsh Olsen (Walsh's). Although she produced no AKC champions, Mrs. Walsh's line met with success under the continued efforts of Joanna Griggs of Canada (Sylva Sprite) in the 1960s.

The first two black-and-silver champions (a dog and a bitch) finished in 1938 and 1940. The third black-and-silver champion, Ch. Tiger Bo Von Riptide, finished in 1967. Again, he was a black-and-silver produced by chance. He left no progeny of note, but he did generate interest in the color.

To appreciate the development of the black-and-silver Miniature, it is necessary to understand the difficulty of working with it. First, it is a recessive trait; second, to improve the quality of black-and-silver Miniatures, it was necessary to breed them to one of the other colors, usually salt-and-pepper. Unless the other parent already carried the recessive black-and-silver gene, all puppies in the litter would be of the dominant black or salt-and-pepper color and would have to be bred back to a black-and-silver mate to recover the color. By that time, the desired qualities might have been lost or greatly reduced, and the puppies that exhibited the desired structural traits might not be the desired black-and-silver color. After many years and two or three generations, all effort may have been futile.

During the 1970s, the Bo-Nanza and Sycamore kennels made great strides with the black-and-silver color, but it was not until the 1980s that they came into their own.

In rapid succession, three midwestern dogs of differing lineage completed their titles and became a firm foundation for the black-and-silver color: Ch. Sercatep Strut N Proud, 1982 (Debra Herrell, Grasslake, Michigan); Ch. Rampage's Waco Kid, 1983 (Janice Ramel, St. Francis, Wisconsin); and Ch. Feldmar Nightshade, 1985 (Marcia Feld, Libertyville, Illinois). All three became top producers and have top-producing offspring. Ch. Feldmar Night Reveler (a Nightshade son) was the first black-and-silver to top a national specialty, and Ch. Blythewood Amara on the Move (a Reveler daughter) was the first to top a national sweepstakes. Reveler enjoyed a show career unrivaled by any other of his color.

In 1982, the year that Rampage's Waco Kid finished, the total black-and-silver champions was 35. By 1987, that had risen to 86, and in 1992, the total was 209, surpassing that of black champions (193).

The freedom of American breeders to cross with the salt-and-pepper color to improve the black and both colors to improve the black-and-silver has given them an advantage not enjoyed by the majority of the dog world. American black-and-silver schnauzers are now spreading their influence through exports to the rest of the world.

AMERICAN MINIATURE SCHNAUZER CLUB
MONTGOMERY COUNTY KENNEL CLUB
BEST OF BREED

1960 Ch. Phil-Mar Lugar
1961 Ch. Luvemal's Master Copy
1962 Ch. Magic of Sparks
1963 Ch. Phil-Mar Dark Knight GR4
1964 Ch. Mankit's Signal Go GR2
1965 Ch. Mankit's Signal Go
1966 Ch. Mankit's Signal Go
1967 Ch. Travelmor's Witchcraft
1968 Mankit's To The Moon, BIS
1969 Ch. Mankit's To The Moon, BIS
1970 Ch. Marcheim Helza Poppin GR4
1971 Ch. Sky Rocket's Uproar
1972 Ch. Kazel's Favorite GR3
1973 Ch. Sky Rocket's Bound to Win GR3
1974 Ch. Sky Rocket's Bound to Win
1975 Ch. Skyline's Blue Spruce
1976 Ch. Penlan Peter's Son
1977 Ch. Skyline's Star Spangled Banner GR2
1978 Ch. Blythewood National Acclaim
1979 Ch. R-Bo's Victory Flash
1980 Ch. Irrenhaus Stamp of Approval
1981 Ch. Richlene's Top Billing
1982 Ch. Blythewood National Newsman
1983 Ch. Skyline's Storm Signal GR4
1984 Ch Skyline's Storm Signal
1985 Ch. Sathgate Breakaway
1986 Ch. Galaxy's Victory Promise
1987 Ch. Haybrook's Shooting Match (B)
1988 Ch. Sathgate Breakaway
1989 Ch. Blythewood Dream Chaser
1990 Ch. Time's Man of the Hour
1991 Ch. Rampage's Representative
1992 Dynasty's Title Page (B)
1993 Ch. Das Feder's Drivin Miss Daisy (B)
1994 Ch. Das Feder's Drivin Miss Daisy (B)
1995 Ch. Gough's Class Act O' Pickwick

(B) = Bitch

Ch. Sibehil's Dark Shadows,
owned by Beverly Pfaff.

Right: Brickmark Louie (Miniature), bred and owned by M. Brick (New Zealand).

Above: Ch. Jasper van de Semshoeve—*ISPU Sieger* and champion in the Netherlands (Miniature). Owned by M Rulkens (Netherlands).

Ch. Feldmar-Lovejoy Trigger Happy at Tamarack (Miniature), Best Miniature Schnauzer in South Africa, 1995. Bred by N. Banas (USA) and owned by M. and B. Gale (South Africa).

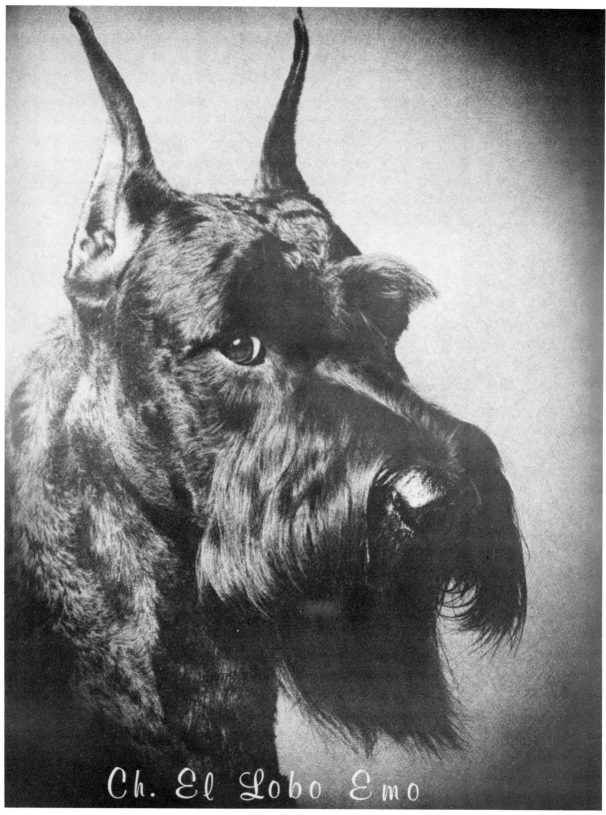

Ch. El Lobo Emo

BIS Ch. El Lobo Emo. The first American-bred AKC All-breed Best-in-Show Giant, and winner of the 1972 National Specialty, Emo left a great legacy of many champions including two more Best-in-Show winners.

18

The Giant Schnauzer in the United States

by Sylvia Hammarstrom

The first Giant Schnauzers reached the United States during the 1930s and 1940s, but the breed did not attract much attention until Ch. Terry v. Krayenrain was imported in the 1950s from Krayenrain Kennel, the most famous of that time. Terry was the first Giant Schnauzer to win an American best in show, which brought much-needed attention to the breed.

The dog who made the greatest impact was Ch. Quedame de la Steingasse. Also an import, Quedame came from the same kennel as Terry, and his sire, Ch. M'Tambo v. Krayenrain, was Terry's brother. The kennel had the unusual idea of using one prefix for their show dogs (Krayenrain) and another for their working dogs (de la Steingasse). Quedame was the first top-winning dog in the United States, with several best-in-show wins, and he also won the 1970 and 1971 Giant Schnauzer National Specialty. Quedame became an influential sire, and his record of fifty champions stood for many years.

Another highly influential dog was Ch. Ebenholtz Bobi Deluxe v. Deberic, who won six all-breed bests in show as well as the 1975, 1976, and 1978 Giant Schnauzer National Specialty. A grandson of Terry v. Krayenrain, Bobi became a most popular stud and produced thirty-three champions. Almost all top-winning and top-producing Giants trace back to Quedame and Bobi and, of course, their sires Terry and M'Tambo. Bobi was a magnificent dog, and his grooming was beautiful. His handler-groomers introduced the

Ch. Skansen's I Have a Dream. Bred by Sylvia Hammerstrom; owned by Marcia Nanci.

Ch. Neger v. Denlinger, the first American-bred Giant Schnauzer champion. Owned by Mr. and Mrs. Milo G. Denlinger; bred by J. M. Hoyt of Ago Farms. Neger was whelped February 20, 1932, sired by Ch. and Sieger Carlo v. Saldern. His dam was Bella v. Fuchspark-Potzhaus.

Ch. Skansen's Gentleman Thief, number one stud dog in the Giant Scnauzer breed with eighty champion sons and daughters.

Ch. Faust van de Havenstad—*Weltsieger* (1983, 1985, 1986), *Bundessieger* (1983, 1984, 1985), *Klubsieger PSK, Europasieger,* Amsterdam Winner (1983, 1984, 1985), and a champion in Germany, Luxemberg, United States, and the Netherlands. Bred and owned by Mr. and Mrs. C. de Meulenaer (Belgium).

Ch. Camoli's Gemini of the East (Giant). Owned by Donald L. and Marilyn K. Garlisch (USA).

Minaco Inki and Minaco Katja (Giants) in wintry Sweden.

grooming technique for longer leg hair on Giant Schnauzers, which gave a more attractive, balanced appearance. The style was not as severe as the German practice of trimming off all the leg hair. This grooming, which looked more like a Miniature Schnauzer is probably one of the reasons the Giant Schnauzer became more popular as a family pet in the late seventies and eighties.

In the 1990s, the most Giant Schnauzers are groomed with much of the leg hair intact. In fact, all but one of the dogs that have won the national specialty since Bobi have been presented in the so-called American style.

One of the best-known recent imports is Ch. Lillemark's Kobuch, a Danish dog from German parents. From litters produced during the nine months Kobuch was in the United States, he has twenty-six champions. His most famous son, of course, is Ch. Skansen's Debonair v. Kobuch, winner of the 1982 National Specialty and two all-breed bests in show. Another son, Ch. Skansen's der Figaro v. Kobuch, became his most influential son, with twenty-five champions. Figaro produced the breed's top-producing sire, Ch. Skansen's Gentleman Thief, the sire of eighty champions and is still producing at the age of ten years. Thief's most famous son is Ch. Skansen's I Have a Dream.

Ch. Skansen's I Have a Dream was the first since Bobi to win three national specialties. He has set many breed records: thirty-three all-breed best-in-show wins; won the working group at the 1990 Westminster Kennel Club show (a breed first); top-winning working dog in 1990 (breed first). Dreamer is developing into one of the breed's top sires, with about forty champion offspring by 1990.

The top-winning salt-and-pepper Giant in the world is Ch. Faust van de Havenstad, a Belgian dog. In 1987, Faust was brought to the United States to be used at stud. Today, there are about two-hundred salt-and-pepper Giants in the US, all descendents of Faust. The most common color is, of course, black, and the salt-and-pepper color is quite rare worldwide.

During the 1970s, interest in the Giant Schnauzer as a show breed gradually increased, but the entries were so low that dogs and bitches competed against each other for the points. Because of Dreamer's spectacular wins, the public became aware of the Giant Schnauzer as both a family companion and show breed, and the Giant Schnauzer is now represented with good entries at almost all shows. The Giant Schnauzer is, without question, one of the most regal, handsome breeds in the American working group.

In 1990, one of the top-working obedience dogs was a Giant Schnauzer bitch, Sherborn's One Hundred Proof, UD, so the breed can be excellent precision workers if in the right hands.

Schutzhund work is not highly popular in the United States. Emphasis on breeding a sharp dog, capable of attack work is almost frowned on in the United States. In fact, the AKC does not have any events that includes attack work. The incidence of dog bites has soared, and the average schnauzer owner only wants a sound, reliable family companion that will bark and scare off intruders, attacking only if necessary.

The American Giant Schnauzer is mainly bred and kept as a family guardian and companion. The breed's natural protectiveness without extensive training is one reason for its popularity. This trait is so strong in the German dogs that American breeders maintain this by importing European dogs with regularity.

GIANT SCHNAUZER CLUB OF AMERICA TOP WINNERS

1991 Ch. Skansen's Mordecai Siegal
1992 Ch. Skansen's Sheba Beucinder
1993 Ch. Skansen's Sheba Beucinder
1994 Ch. Skansen's Popcorn
1995 Ch. Ruster's Your Cheating Hearts

GIANT SCHNAUZER NATIONAL SPECIALTY WINNERS SINCE 1979

1979 Ch. Lovewind's Happy New Year (Quedame grandson)
1980 Ch. J-Starr's Thunderation (Quedame grandson)
1981 Ch. Echo of Erin Howard Quay Hughes (Quedame grandson)
1982 Terresta's Hallmark von Gesi (Quedame great, great grandson)
1983 Ch. Skansen's Debonair v. Kobuch (Bobi great grandson)
1984 Von Gestern's Violent Affair (first bitch, Bobi great granddaughter)
1985 Ch. Skansen's Great Expectations
1986 Ch. Skansen's I Have a Dream (Bobi and Quedame great, great grandson)
1987 Ch. Skansen's I Have a Dream
1988 Ch. Homested's Cast a Giant Shadow (Bobi great, great grandson)
1989 Ch. Skansen's I Have a Dream
1990 Ch. Skansen's Katchina Dancer (second bitch, Bobi and Quedame great, great, great granddaughter)
1991 Ch. Skansen's Notorious K.O.V. Thief
1992 Ch. Skansen's I Have A Dream
1993 B.O.B. Ch. Lucas De Campos De Oro   B.O.S. Ch. Blueship Show Phisticate
1994 B.O.B. Ch. Homesteads Cast A Giant Shadow B.O.S. Ch. Valefsa's Blue Valor
1995 B.O.B. Ch. DeBussy V.D. Norderenk   B.O.S. Ch. Skansen's Sixty Minutes

Left: Ch. Iwan v. d. Lederhecke, FH, SchH I, WMZ-3--*Klubsieger PSK, Eurosg,* and champion in Germany (Giant). Bred and owned by W. Büschel, (Germany).

Below: Ch. Ike v. d. Lederhecke, AD, FH, SchH III, and champion in Germany (Giant). Bred by W. Büchel; owned by R. Tupat (Germany).

Doug Suffel takes a full bite from Lee Pullis's Jago v. Scharfenwind TDX, SchH III, AD, FH, during the courage test at the 1993 AWDF.

19

The Working Schnauzer Federation

by Storm Bergin

The Working Schnauzer Federation (WSF) was officially launched on 12 May 1991.[1] The new club has the following objectives:

- To preserve and protect the Giant Schnauzer and its heritage as a working dog
- To maintain the character and form of the Giant Schnauzer in North America according the international standard as adhered to by the Giant Schnauzer member clubs of the FCI
- To advance the interests of the breed by educating members about temperament, conformation, health, breeding, training, and maintenance of the total Giant Schnauzer
- To maintain an open dialogue with all clubs sharing similar objectives, including membership in the American Working Dog Federation
- To conduct events that promote the Giant Schnauzer as a working breed, and to record and issue titles for such events
- To publish an official publication to promote the objectives of the club

Since its founding, the WSF has held three national conventions, each offering a Schutzhund trial, a conformation match, and a working seminar. The 1993, the club had ninety members.

Critical to the international scope of the WSF was acceptance into the American Working Dog Federation (AWDF), which was founded in January 1991 to strengthen a common interest and enthusiasm for Schutzhund and to preserve the working character of the respective breeds. The following organizations had joined the AWDF by 1993: the North American Working Bouvier Association, the United Doberman Club, the United States Rottweiler Club, the United Schutzhund Clubs of America (German Shepherd Dogs), the United Belgian Shepherd Dog Organization, and the Working Schnauzer Federation, which was accepted as a full member in January 1993. One condition of membership was that the WSF be a single-breed organization; although Standard Schnauzers may participate in some events, it is basically a Giant Schnauzer organization.

The AWDF has applied for FCI membership, and if membership is approved, the AWDF will be the only U.S. dog club with membership in this largest international dog organization. In 1992, the AWDF was invited to send a team to the FCI World Championship held in Slovenia. It was the first time that a team from the United States—or even North America—was invited to this very prestigious competition.

The AWDF sponsors an annual team championship in which each breed club is invited to send its best representatives from the SchH I, SchH II, and SchH III categories. The WSF fielded its first team to compete in the March 1992 AWDF Team Championship held in Birmingham, Alabama. Five breed clubs vied for the highest combined team score. The schnauzers gave a very spirited performance and placed second, only 6 points behind the United Schutzhund Club of America's German Shepherd team. In the 1993 Team Championship held in Phoenix, Arizona, the schnauzers again placed second overall, just 10 points behind the dominating German Shepherd team. This is really an outstanding accomplishment for the breed, considering that there may be a thousand German Shepherd Dogs to each Giant Schnauzer competing in the sport of Schutzhund.

In 1992, the WSF was invited to send two teams to compete in the ISPU World Championship (IPO trial) to be held near Dresden, Germany. Furthermore, the WSF was also invited to send one team to the PSK's *Bundesleistungssiegerprüfung* to be held in Mannheim, Germany. The international door has been opened for the WSF, and Giant Schnauzers representing the United States will be seen for the first time in international championships.

The WSF has a comprehensive registration program in the implementation stage as well as plans to award conformation championships and other worthy titles.

---

[1] For information about the WSF, contact Martha Galuszka, Membership Secretary, 324 Oakwood Avenue, West Hartford, Connecticutt 06110.

Klaux v. Eichenbaum, SchH I, owned by Pete Ciesiolka.

Ch. Enak van't Wareheim (I.P.O. III) demonstrates how to stop, guard, and escort an escaping "criminal" (J. Chelin).

1. Enak Leaps for the arm.

2. He takes a firm grasp.

3. Enak brings the runner to a complete halt.

4. Keeping a vigilant eye on the immobile "suspect."

5. Enak still watches alertly while escorting the prisoner.

Iro v. Sandokan, SchH II, owned by Storm Bergin, on a track.

Iro v. Sandokan, SchH II, attack training with helper John Kunie.

Jago v. Scharfenwind, TDX, SchH III, AD, FH, owned by Lee Pullis, takes the jump at the AWDF competition in Phoenix.

During the retrieve over an A-frame the judge will look for a dog that does not anticipate, but at the command quickly executes the jump and the retrieve and brings the object nicely in front of his handler.

Appendix—
International Working Regulations

1. SCHEDULE AND DESCRIPTION OF EXERCISES FOR GRADE I

1.1 GROUP A: TRACKING (Maximum 100 marks)
(See Figure 1)

Track = 80 marks

Two articles (10 + 10) = 20 marks

Command allowed: "Track" or equivalent.

1.1.1 The track is between 350 and 400 paces long, must be at least 20 minutes old and laid by the handler. There are two articles on the track. The track must have two corners of 90 degrees. The judge must be present at the area of the track to decide how it will be laid. The start of the track must be well indicated by means of a stake which the handler plants in the ground at his left side. After the handler has stood at the start stake for some time, he proceeds to lay the track as indicated by the judge and drops the first article in the middle of the first or second leg, without changing his pace.

The second article must be dropped at the end of the track. After placing the last article, the handler must continue for several more paces in the same direction of the last leg and then return via a detour to the judge. The handler may choose to work the track with the dog either on the 10 metre lead or free. Both cases are marked equally. If the end of the track has not been reached 15 minutes from the starting time, the track must be abandoned at the command of the judge.

1.1.2 Procedure:

The handler must show the articles to the judge before he proceeds to lay the track. Only articles in everyday use with a length of 150mm, a width of 50 to 60mm and a thickness of 20 to 30mm may be used. They must be handed to the handler 15 minutes before the track has to be laid.

Whilst the track is being laid, the dog must be placed out of sight. If possible, the scent of the track must not be disturbed whilst the articles are being placed. The handler may not shuffle or trample the place where the articles are dropped nor may he stop when placing the articles. The articles must be placed on the track and not beside it.

The handler proceeds to his dog and prepares it for the working of the track. When called, he proceeds to the judge with his dog and informs him whether his dog retrieves or indicates the articles. Indicating and retrieving on the same track is incorrect.

At a command from the judge, the dog is taken slowly and calmly to the start and is commanded to begin. Here the dog must be given sufficient time to take scent. Before the commencement of the track, at the commencement as well as during the entire tracking procedure any pressure on the dog or anything which could awaken the dog's desire to rush onto the track must be avoided. The dog should take scent calmly with the nose close to the ground. As soon as the dog begins to track, the handler remains on the spot and allows the 10m long tracking lead to glide through his hand up to the end. He then follows his dog strictly at this distance which in the case of a free tracking dog, must also be maintained. The tracking lead may hang slack during the performance of the track while it has not been dropped on the ground by the handler.

As soon as the dog has found an article, he must, without any influence from the handler, immediately pick it up or indicate it convincingly. After having picked up the article, the dog may stand, sit or return to the handler. It is incorrect to continue on the track whilst carrying the article. It is incorrect to pick up the article whilst in the down position. Indication of the article is by standing, sitting or lying down. The handler drops the tracking lead, immediately walks to the dog and by raising the article shows that the dog has found it. Thereafter, the handler and dog continue to track. After the completion of the track the handler shows the found articles to the judge. It is permissible for the handler to walk to his dog after it has picked up the article. It is incorrect for the dog to walk forwards whilst carrying the article.

1.1.3 Evaluation:

False starting, dawdling, repeated circling at the corners, constant encouragements, incorrect indication or picking up or dropping an article must be penalized by up to 4 marks. Reset on track, persistent dawdling, consistently tracking with a high nose, rushing onto the track, voidance of bowels and bladder whilst on track and hunting or similar behavior will be penalized up to 8 marks.

For incorrectly indicated or picked up articles up to 4 marks may be deducted. For each article not found, 10 marks will be deducted. For indicating or picking up articles not placed by the handler, 4 marks will be deducted.

1.2 GROUP B: OBEDIENCE (Maximum 100 marks)

Every separate exercise begins and ends with the "start position" i.e. with the handler standing still with his dog in correct heel position.

The command to commence each exercise is given by the judge. The sequence of each exercise such as turns, halts, changes of pace etc. are carried out without commands from the judge. A handler is, however, entitled to ask the judge to give commands for the exercise.

Figure 20-1. Tracking—breakdown of total marks.

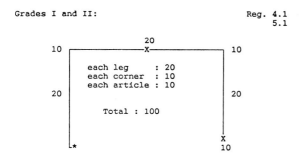

Grades I and II: Reg. 4.1
                                                          5.1

```
              20
        10 ─────X───── 10
        10            10

           each leg     : 20
           each corner  : 10
        20 each article : 10     20

              Total : 100

        └★               X
                         10
```

Grade III: Reg. 6.1

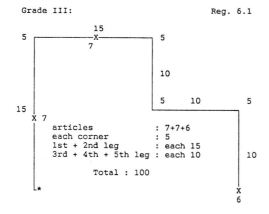

```
              15
         5 ───X──── 5
              7
                           10

              5    10     5

        15
         X 7
           articles              : 7+7+6
           each corner           : 5
           1st + 2nd leg         : each 15
           3rd + 4th + 5th leg   : each 10     10

              Total : 100

        └★                      X
                                6
```

Figure 20-2. Fixed and moveable hedges.

FIXED HEDGE: 1.5m wide and 1m high, mounted between 2 solid poles, linked by 3 double cross-slats and filled with twigs or thatch.

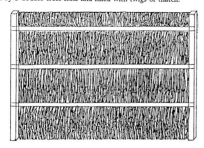

MOVEABLE HEDGE, mounted on a galvanised frame, with height adjustable from 0.5m to 1m.

Figure 20-3. Sloping stockade.

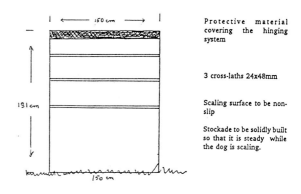

Protective material covering the hinging system

3 cross-laths 24x48mm

Scaling surface to be non-slip

Stockade to be solidly built so that it is steady while the dog is scaling.

150 cm

191 cm

150 cm

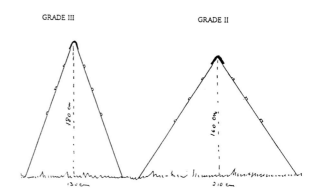

GRADE III   GRADE II

180 cm   140 cm

130 cm   210 cm

Figure 20-4. Pattern for heel exercise.

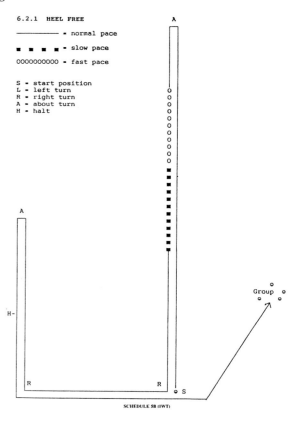

```
6.2.1  HEEL FREE

──────────── = normal pace
■ ■ ■ ■      = slow pace
0000000000   = fast pace

S = start position
L = left turn
R = right turn
A = about turn
H = halt
```

SCHEDULE 5B (IWT)

1.2.1 HEEL ON LEAD (15 marks)
Command allowed: "heel"

From the start position, the dog on lead and neckchain must, on the command to "heel" follow his handler in a happy workmanlike manner. At the start of the exercise, the handler and his dog must proceed in normal pace for a distance of 40 to 50 paces in a straight line without stopping and then execute an about turn and after a further 10 or 15 paces, execute the fast pace and slow pace, each for not less than 10 paces.

Thereafter at least one right, one left and one about turn must be carried out at a normal pace. The dog must have its shoulder next to the left knee of the handler and may not stray in front, behind or to the side. The about turns carried out by the handler must be left-about turns. The command "heel" is allowed only at the beginning of the exercise and at the changes of pace. When the handler comes to a halt, the dog has to sit promptly without any influence from the handler. The handler may not change his position and especially not move towards a dog which is sitting wide. The lead must be held in the left hand during the exercise and must hang slack between the dog and handler. Upon order from the judge the handler with the dog must then proceed through a group of at least four (4) persons. The handler must halt at least once within the group. The persons in the group must mingle. Lagging, moving in front, swerving to the side by the dog, as well as the handler adjusting to the position of the dog at the turns is incorrect.

1.2.2 HEEL FREE (20 marks)
Command allowed: "heel"

Upon order from the judge, the dog is unleashed after taking up the start position. The handler then hangs the lead over his shoulder or puts it in his pocket and proceeds with his dog at heel, "off lead" into the group of people and halts there at least once. After leaving the group, the handler assumes the start position for a moment and commences the same sequence of exercises as described in "heel on lead." Whilst this exercise is in progress (although not when the dog is in the group), two shots must be fired (calibre 6–9mm). The dog must be indifferent to the gunshot. If at the gunshot, the dog demonstrates a tendency to attack but remains under control of the handler he is to be penalized. Shot-shy dogs must immediately be excluded from further participation in the trial. The full allotment of marks can only be awarded to a dog which appears completely indifferent to shot.

Procedure:

Considerable value must be placed on indifference to shot. Two shots at an interval of five (5) seconds, must be fired from a distance of fifteen (15) paces. Should the dog run away during the firing of the shots, he has to be excluded from the remainder of the trial.

Should the judge be of the opinion that the dog is sensitive to gunshot he is free to ask that the gunshot test be repeated.

Indifference to shot may only be tested during the "heel off lead" and the "down stay with diversion" exercises.

1.2.3 SIT ON THE MOVE (10 marks)
Command allowed: "sit"

From the start position, the handler with his dog off lead, moves forward in a straight line. After at least ten (10) paces, the dog must sit quickly at the handler's command, "sit," given without a change in pace and without looking back. After a further thirty (30) paces, the handler halts, turns around immediately and faces his dog. Upon order from the judge, the handler returns to the right hand side of his dog and takes up the start position. If the dog takes up an incorrect position (down or stand) during the exercise, up to 5 marks are to be deducted.

1.2.4 DOWN ON THE MOVE WITH RECALL (10 marks)
Commands allowed: "down," "come," "heel"

From the start position and on the command "heel," the handler with his dog off lead moves forward in a straight line. After at least ten (10) paces the dog must assume the "down" position quickly at the handler's command. Without looking back or influencing the dog in any way, the handler must continue for at least thirty (30) paces in a straight line and then turn around immediately to face his dog and stand still.

Upon order from the judge, the handler must recall his dog. The dog should return willingly at a brisk pace and sit closely in front of his handler. At the "heel" command, the dog must assume the heel position briskly. Should the dog take up an incorrect position (sit or stand) but thereafter return correctly to his handler, up to 5 marks are to be deducted.

1.2.5 RETRIEVING ON LEVEL GROUND AN OBJECT BELONGING TO THE HANDLER (10 marks)
Commands allowed: "fetch," "leave," "heel"

The dog should be sitting off lead, next to the handler. Upon a single command from the handler to "fetch" the object, which was previously thrown over a distance of approximately ten (10) paces, the dog must proceed briskly to the object, pick it up immediately and return it to his handler in the same manner. The dog must sit closely in front of the handler retaining the article, until, after a short pause, the handler commands the dog to "leave" and takes the object.

At the command "heel," the dog must proceed quickly to the heel position. Besides an object belonging to the handler, a dumbbell may also be used. The handler must remain in the start position until such time as the dog has delivered the object and has assumed the heel position.

Evaluation:

Up to 4 marks may be deducted for dropping, chewing or playing with the object. Up to 3 marks may be deducted should the handler move from the start position. All marks must be lost if the dog does not retrieve the object.

1.2.6 RETRIEVING OF AN OBJECT BELONGING TO THE HANDLER WITH CLEAR JUMP OVER A 1 METRE HIGH BY 1.5 METRES WIDE HEDGE JUMP (15 marks) (See Figure 2)

Commands allowed: "over," "fetch," "leave," "heel"

The handler places himself at a suitable distance from the jump with his dog sitting off lead next to him. An object belonging to the handler or a dumbbell may be thrown over the jump. At the handler's command: "over," "fetch," the dog must jump over the hedge without touching it, immediately pick up the object and after jumping back with it, return to sit closely in front of his handler whilst retaining the object. After a short pause, the handler commands the dog to "leave" and takes the object. Upon the command "heel," the dog must briskly assume the heel position. The command "fetch" must be given before the dog reaches the object.

Evaluation:

Up to 2 marks to be deducted for slightly grazing the jump, up to 3 marks to be deducted for touching the jump more heavily or for slight support on jump. Up to 4 marks to be deducted for taking heavy support on jump and for dropping the object, chewing or playing with it.

Award 15 marks for: correct jump over and back with correctly retrieved object.

Award 8 marks for: correct jump over, no return jump, object correctly retrieved.

Award 8 marks for: no jump over, return jump correct and object correctly retrieved.

Award 8 marks for: jump over and back without retrieve.

Award 0 marks for: no jumps executed but object correctly retrieved.

Award 0 marks for: jump over correct but no return jump and no retrieve.

In the event that the object has, as a result of being clumsily thrown or because of a strong wind, fallen far to one side, the handler may, after having requested permission from the judge, collect the object so as to throw it again. No marks will be lost because of this. Should the handler, without leaving his start position, give assistance to the dog during the jump, marks must be deducted accordingly.

Should the handler leave his start position in order to encourage his dog to jump, then the marks for either the jump over or the return jump must be deducted.

Banging on the jump, which requires the handler to leave his start position, must be considered as such a strong help to the dog, that the forward and return jumps cannot be assessed.

The handler must remain in his start position until such a time as the dog has, after having delivered the object and having received the "heel" command, returned to the heel position briskly.

In the event that more than one hedge is present, all dogs must jump the same one.

1.2.7 SEND AWAY WITH DOWN (10 marks)
Commands allowed: "away," "down," "sit"

Upon order from the judge, the handler with the dog off lead proceeds in the indicated direction for several paces. With the audible command "away," the handler simultaneously raises his arm forward and stands still. Hereupon, the dog must proceed in fast pace in the direction indicated for at least twenty-five (25) paces. At the command "down," the dog must obey instantly. The handler's arm may remain raised, indicating the direction, until the dog has assumed the down position. Upon order from the judge the handler proceeds to his dog, takes up a position at the dog's right hand side and gives the command to sit.

Procedure:

Repeated raising of the handler's arm is not permitted. The dog must proceed forward in a straight line although a slight deviation is not incorrect. Marks must be deducted for severe deviation, too short a distance, hesitance to assume the down position, anticipation of the down command, or getting up at the handler's approach.

1.2.8 DOWN STAY WITH DIVERSION (10 marks)
Commands allowed: "down," "sit"

This exercise is carried out whilst another dog is carrying out exercises 1.2.1 to 1.2.6. Before commencement of another dog's obedience exercise, the handler places his dog in the down-stay position at a distance of approximately forty (40) paces without leaving any object or lead near the dog. Remaining in sight of the dog the handler takes up a position some forty (40) paces away without looking back and stands still with his back towards his dog. The dog must remain lying there without any influence from the handler until the other dog has completed exercises 1.2.1 to 1.2.6. After exercise 1.2.6, the handler returns to his dog and follows the instructions given for the end of exercise 1.2.7.

Procedure:

The handler must remain in the position on the field, as indicated by the judge, with his back to the dog, standing quietly until the judge orders him to proceed to his dog. A restless attitude of the handler, attempts at concealed help to the dog or anticipated getting up by the dog upon the handler's return are incorrect.

Should the dog stand or sit but remain on the spot, then he only receives part of the marks.

Should the dog leave his position by more than three (3) metres before the end of exercise 1.2.3 as performed by the other dog, then no marks will be awarded.

Should the same occur after exercise 1.2.3, then only part of the marks can be awarded.

Should the dog leave his position to go to his handler during the return of the latter, then three (3) marks must be deducted.

1.3 GROUP C: DEFENSE WORK - GRADE 1 - Total marks 100

1.3.1 QUARTERING FOR THE ASSISTANT (5 marks)

On suitable grounds of about 100m long and 80m wide, 6 hides are placed staggered, 3 on either side of the field.

A defense work Assistant (A) in complete defense outfit with padded armguard and soft stick is out of the dog's (D) sight, concealed in the last hide.

The dog Handler (H) with his D off lead and sitting at heel place themselves on the imaginary centre line level with the fifth hide. By raising his arm the H indicates that he is ready.

Upon order from the officiating Judge (J) the H commences the Defense Work. With short audible commands and signals given with the left or right arm, all of which can be repeated, the D must leave the H at a brisk pace and explore around the hides in sequence. The H must move along an imaginary centre line, from which he may not deviate whilst the D is quartering.

Whenever the D has rounded a hide, the H may recall him with a short audible command and whilst the D is on the move, with another command, send him in the other direction. The command to recall the D may be combined with the dog's call name. The D must always remain in front of the H. When the D has arrived at the last hide, the H must stop moving and commands are no longer permitted.

1.3.2. Confrontation and Barking (10+10=20 Marks)

The D must confront the A with attention and bark continuously. The D may not jump against the A nor may he take hold of him. Upon order from the J the H returns to his D. Upon an additional order from the J, the H with his D take up a heel position at a distance of 1 pace from the A. The H thereupon orders the A to come 5 paces out of the hide.

1.3.3 Attempt to Escape (25 Marks)

Upon order from the J the H proceeds with his free heeling dog from the hide to halt at a distance of 5 paces from the A. He leaves his D sitting in a guarding position and returns into the hide.

Upon order from the J the A attempts to escape at fast pace. Upon a verbal command from the H, the D must, immediately and without hesitation, endeavor to prevent the escape by an energetic action and by taking a firm hold of the A.

Upon order from the J the A stands still. The D must release the A on a single command and guard the A close and attentively.

1.3.4 Defense during the Guard (25 Marks)

After a guarding period of about five seconds, and upon order from the J the A launches an attack on the D. Without assistance from the H, and D must without hesitation, defend itself by energetically and forcefully taking hold of the A.

Upon order from the J the A stands still. The D must upon a single audible command release its hold and guard the A closely and attentively. Thereupon the H goes to his D to take it to heel. The A is not disarmed.

1.3.5 Attack on Dog on the move (25 Marks)

The H with his D is ordered to go in the middle of the field approximately level with the third hide. The D must sit next to his H and may be restrained by the collar. Upon order from the J the A, armed with a stick, comes out of the 6th hide and heads directly toward the D at normal pace.

As soon as the A is within 30 paces of the H and his in heel sitting D, the H will upon order from the J release his D. The H may not leave his position. The A attacks the D from the front while making loud verbal threats and exercising considerable physical threat. Without hesitation the D must counter the attack with an energetic and forceful bite. Once the D has taken hold he receives two stick blows. The blows are permitted on the flanks, the withers and the thighs.

Upon order from the judge the A stands still. The D must then upon a single short command release its hold and guard the A closely and attentively.

Upon order from the J the H goes to his D, takes the stick from the A, and takes up a position in preparation for the escort by side.

The A is escorted by side towards the J over a distance of about 20 paces. A short command is allowed to start the escort. The H must walk at the right hand side of the A, so that the D is between the A and the H. During the escort the D is not allowed to jump against the A or to take hold of him. The escort terminates in front of the J and the H delivers the stick. The A leaves the area.

On the way to, and during the announcement of the grading, the D must be heeled off lead and sit free. Once the announcement is completed the H leaves the field with his D off lead.

1.3.6 Procedures:

- The A must wear a complete outfit (jacket, pants and armguards).
- Only a padded stick covered with soft material may be used.
- If more than 6 dogs are entered a second A is required. He will carry out exercise 5.
- An attentive and close circling of the A, including when he is inside the hide, is not incorrect.
- If during exercise 3 the D leaves his place before or without the verbal command from his handler, the exercise has to be graded insufficient.
- If during exercise 5 the D leaves his place before the judge's signal, the exercise has to be graded insufficient.
- If during the defense exercises the D has not released its hold after a third short verbal command, the exercise must be graded insufficient. In the event that the D does not release its hold, an additional (fourth) command, may be allowed by the J from a distance of 10 paces. If the D does not let go on this command the defense work has to be discontinued.
- In order for the A to maintain full view of the D, he need not remain standing absolutely stationary. However the

A may not assume any further threatening attitudes or make any defensive movements. He has to hold the arm-guard as to protect his body.

- The defense work has to be discontinued and qualification can not be awarded:
  — if the D is not under full control of the H,
  — if the D does not let go after the 4th command to leave,
  — if the D releases because of physical intervention by the H,
  — if the D fails any defense exercise (including the escape) or allows himself to be chased aside,
  — if the D during any guarding phase, attacks and firmly bites the A.
- Barking is only permitted at the hide and during other guarding exercises.

2. SCHEDULE AND DESCRIPTION OF EXERCISES FOR GRADE II

2.1 GROUP A: TRACKING (Maximum 100 marks)
(See Figure 1)

Track = 80 marks

Two articles (10 + 10) = 20 marks

Command allowed: "Track" or equivalent.

2.1.1 The track is approximately 600 paces long and must be at least 30 minutes old and laid by a tracklayer unfamiliar to the dog. There are two articles on the track. The track must have two corners of 90 degrees. The judge decides upon the format of the track, taking into consideration the topography of the land. The start of the track must be well indicated by means of a stake which the tracklayer plants in the ground at his left side. After the tracklayer has stood at the start stake for some time, he proceeds to lay the track as prescribed and drops the first article in the middle of the second leg, (halfway between the first and second corners) without changing his pace.

The second article must be dropped at the end of the track. After placing the article, the tracklayer must continue for several more paces in the same direction of the last leg and then return via a detour.

The handler may choose to work the track with the dog either on the 10 metre lead or free. Both cases are marked equally. If the end of the track has not been reached 15 minutes from the starting time, the track must be abandoned at the command of the judge.

2.1.2 Procedure:

The tracklayer must show the articles to the judge before he proceeds to lay the track. Only well scented articles which were carried in his pockets for at least 30 minutes may be used by the tracklayer. Only articles in everyday use with a length of 150mm, a width of 50 to 60mm and a thickness of 20 to 30mm may be used.

Whilst the track is being laid, handler and dog must remain out of sight. If possible, the scent of the track must not be disturbed whilst the articles are being placed. The track-layer may not shuffle or trample the place where the articles are dropped nor may he stop when placing the articles. The articles must be placed on the track and not beside it.

In the meantime, the handler prepares his dog for the working of the track. When called, he proceeds to the judge with his dog and informs him whether his dog retrieves or indicates the articles. Indicating and retrieving on the same track is incorrect.

At a command from the judge, the dog is taken slowly and calmly to the start and is commanded to begin. Here the dog must be given sufficient time to take scent. Before the commencement of the track, at the commencement as well as during the entire tracking procedure any pressure on the dog or anything which could awaken the dog's desire to rush onto the track must be avoided. The dog should take scent calmly with the nose close to the ground. As soon as the dog begins to track, the handler remains on the spot and allows the 10m long tracking lead to glide through his hand up to the end. He then follows his dog strictly at this distance which in the case of a free tracking dog, must also be maintained.

The tracking lead may hang slack during the performance of the track while it has not been dropped on the ground by the handler. As soon as the dog has found an article, he must, without any influence from the handler, immediately pick it up or indicate it convincingly. After having picked up the article, the dog may stand, sit or return to the handler. It is incorrect to continue on the track whilst carrying the article. It is incorrect to pick up the article whilst on the down position. Indication of the article is by standing, sitting or lying down. The handler drops the tracking lead, immediately walks to the dog and by raising the article shows that the dog has found it.

Thereafter, the handler and dog continue on the track. After the completion of the track, the handler shows the found articles to the judge. It is permissible for the handler to walk to his dog after it has picked up the article. It is incorrect for the dog to walk forward whilst carrying the article.

2.1.3 Evaluation:

False starting, dawdling, repeated circling at the corners, constant encouragements, incorrect indication or picking up or dropping an article must be penalized by up to 4 marks. Reset on track, persistent dawdling, voidance whilst on track and hunting or similar behavior will be penalized up to 8 marks.

For incorrectly indicated or picked up articles up to 4 marks may be deducted. For each article not found, 10 marks will be deducted. For indicating or picking up articles not placed by the tracklayer, 4 marks will be deducted.

2.2 GROUP B: OBEDIENCE (Maximum 100 marks)

Every separate exercise begins and ends with the "start position" i.e. with the handler standing still with his dog in correct heel position. The command to commence each exercise is given by the judge. The sequence of each exercise such as turns, halts, changes of pace etc. are carried out without commands from the judge. A handler is, however, entitled to ask the judge to give commands for the exercise.

2.2.1 HEEL ON LEAD (10 marks)
Command allowed: "heel"

From the start position, the dog on lead and neckchain must, on the command to "heel," follow his handler in a happy workmanlike manner. At the start of the exercise, the handler and his dog must proceed at normal pace for a distance of 40 to 50 paces in a straight line without stopping and then execute an about turn and after a further 10 to 15 paces, execute the fast pace and slow pace, each for not less than 10 paces.

Thereafter at least one right, one left and one about turn must be carried out at normal pace. The dog must have its shoulder next to the left knee of the handler and may not stray in front, behind or to the side. The about turns carried out by the handler must be left-about turns. The command "heel" is allowed only at the beginning of the exercise and at changes of pace. When the handler comes to a halt, the dog has to sit promptly without any influence from the handler. Here the handler may not change his position and especially not move towards a dog which is sitting wide. The lead must be held in the left hand during the exercise and must hang slack between the dog and handler. Upon order from the judge the handler with the dog must then proceed through a group of at least four (4) persons. The handler must halt at least once within the group. The persons in the group must mingle. Lagging, moving in front, swerving to the side by the dog, as well as the handler adjusting to the position of the dog at the turns is incorrect.

2.2.2 HEEL FREE (15 marks)
Command allowed: "heel"

Upon order from the judge, the dog is unleashed after taking up the start position. The handler then hangs the lead over his shoulder or puts it in his pocket and proceeds with his dog at heel, off lead into the group of people and halts there at least once. After leaving the group, the handler assumes the start position for a moment and commences the same sequence of exercises as described in "heel on lead." Whilst this exercise is in progress (although not when the dog is in the group), two shots must be fired (calibre 6–9mm). The dog must behave in an "indifferent to shot" manner. If at the gunshot, the dog demonstrates a tendency to attack but remains under control of the handler he is to be penalized. Shot-shy dogs must immediately be excluded from further participation in the trial. The full allotment of marks can only be awarded to a dog which appears completely indifferent to shot.

Procedure:

Considerable value must be placed on indifference to shot. Two shots at an interval of five (5) seconds, must be fired from a distance of 15 paces. Should the dog run away during the firing of the shots, he has to be excluded from the remainder of the trial.

Should the judges be of the opinion that the dog is sensitive to gunshot he is free to ask that the gunshot test be repeated. Indifference to shot may only be tested during the "heel off lead" and the "down stay with diversion" exercises.

2.2.3 SIT ON THE MOVE (5 marks)
Command allowed: "sit"

From the start position, the handler with his dog off lead, moves forward in a straight line. After at least ten (10) paces, the dog must sit quickly at the handler's command, "sit," given without a change in pace and without looking back. After a further thirty (30) paces, the handler halts, turns around immediately and faces his dog. Upon order from the judge, the handler returns to the right hand side of his dog and takes up the start position. If the dog, at the command "sit," takes up an incorrect position (down or stand), up to 3 marks are to be deducted.

2.2.4 DOWN ON THE MOVE WITH RECALL (10 marks)
Commands allowed: "down," "come," "heel"

From the start position and on the command "heel," the handler with his dog off lead moves forward in a straight line. After at least ten (10) paces the dog must assume the "down" position quickly at the handler's command. Without looking back or influencing the dog in any way, the handler must continue for at least thirty (30) paces in a straight line and then turn around immediately to face his dog and stand still.

Upon order from the judge, the handler must recall his dog. The dog should return willingly at a brisk pace and sit closely in front of his handler. At the "heel" command, the dog must assume the heel position briskly. Should the dog, at the command, "down" sit or stand, but thereafter return correctly to his handler, up to 5 marks are to be deducted.

2.2.5 RETRIEVING OF A DUMBBELL WITH A MASS OF 1Kg ON THE LEVEL GROUND (10 marks)
Commands allowed: "fetch," "leave," "heel"

The dog should be sitting off lead, next to the handler. Upon a single command from the handler to "fetch" the dumbbell, which was previously thrown over a distance of approximately ten (10) paces, the dog must proceed briskly to the dumbbell, pick it up immediately and return it to his handler in the same manner. The dog must sit closely in front of the handler retaining the dumbbell, until, after a short pause, the handler commands the dog to "leave" and takes the dumbbell. At the command "heel," the dog must proceed briskly to the heel position. The handler must remain in the start position until such time as the dog has assumed the heel position.

Evaluation:

Up to 4 marks may be deducted for dropping, chewing or playing with the dumbbell. Up to 3 marks may be deducted should the handler move from the start position. All marks must be lost if the dog does not retrieve the dumbbell.

2.2.6 RETRIEVING OF A DUMBBELL WITH A MASS OF 650g WITH CLEAR JUMP OVER A 1

METRE HIGH BY 1.5 METRES WIDE HEDGE JUMP (15 marks) (See Figure 2)

Commands allowed: "over," "fetch," "leave," "heel"

The handler places himself at a suitable distance from the jump with his dog sitting off lead next to him. Now he throws a dumbbell with a mass of 650g over the obstacle. At the handler's command: "over," "fetch," the dog must jump over the hedge without touching it, immediately pick up the dumbbell and after jumping back with it, return to sit closely in front of his handler while retaining the dumbbell. After a short pause, the handler commands the dog to "leave" and takes the dumbbell. Upon the command "heel," the dog must briskly assume the heel position.

The command "fetch" must be given before the dog reaches the dumbbell.

Evaluation:

Up to 2 marks to be deducted for slightly grazing the jump. Up to 3 marks to be deducted for touching the jump more heavily or for slight support on jump. Up to 4 marks to be deducted for taking heavy support on the jump, for dropping the dumbbell, chewing it or playing with it.

Award 15 marks for: correct jump over and back with correctly retrieved dumbbell.

Award 8 marks for: correct jump over, no return jump, dumbbell correctly retrieved.

Award 8 marks for: no jump over, return jump correct and dumbbell correctly retrieved.

Award 8 marks for: jump over and back without retrieve.

Award 0 marks for: no jump executed but object correctly retrieved.

Award 0 marks for: jump over correct but no return jump and no retrieve.

In the event that the dumbbell has, as a result of being clumsily thrown or because of a strong wind, fallen far to one side, the handler may, after having requested permission from the judge, collect the dumbbell so as to throw it again. No marks will be lost because of this.

The handler must remain in his start position until such a time as the dog has, after having delivered the dumbbell, returned to the heel position. Should the handler, without leaving his start position, give assistance to the dog during the jump, marks must be deducted accordingly.

Should the handler leave his start position in order to encourage his dog to jump, then the marks for either the jump over or the return jump must be deducted.

Banging on the jump, which requires the handler to leave his start position, must be considered as such a strong help to the dog, that the forward and return cannot be assessed.

In the event that more than one hedge is present, all dogs must jump the same one.

2.2.7 SCALING A SLOPING STOCKADE, 1.6 METRES HIGH AND 1.5 METRES WIDE, WITH THE RETRIEVAL OF AN OBJECT BELONGING TO THE HANDLER (15 marks)

Commands allowed: "over," "fetch," "leave," "heel"

The sloping stockade consists of two board faces, each with a height of 1.9m and a width of 1.5m, connected at the top. At ground level these boards are separated by such a distance that the vertical height of the stockade is 1.6m. Each board of the stockade is fitted with three climbing ledges of 24 x 48mm. (See Figure 3)

The handler places himself at a suitable distance from the stockade with the dog sitting off lead next to him. Either an object belonging to the handler or a dumbbell may be thrown over the stockade. At the handler's command, "over," "fetch," the dog must scale the stockade, immediately pick up the object and after scaling back with it, return to sit closely in front of the handler whilst retaining the object. After a short pause, the handler commands the dog to "leave" and takes the object. Upon the command "heel," the dog must briskly assume the heel position.

The command "fetch" must be given before the dog reaches the object.

Evaluation:

Up to four marks to be deducted for dropping the object or playing with it or chewing it.

Award 15 marks for: correct jump over and back with correctly retrieved object.

Award 8 marks for: correct jump over, no return jump, object correctly retrieved.

Award 8 marks for: no jump over, return jump correct and object correctly retrieved.

Award 8 marks for: jump over and back without retrieve.

Award 0 marks for: no jumps executed but object correctly retrieved.

Award 0 marks for: jump over correct but no return jump and no retrieve.

In the event that the object has, as a result of being clumsily thrown or because of a strong wind, fallen to one side, the handler may, after having requested permission from the judge, collect the object so as to throw it again. No marks will be lost because of this.

The handler must remain in his start position until such a time as the dog has, after having delivered the object, returned to the heel position. Should the handler, without leaving his start position, give assistance to the dog during the scaling, marks must be deducted accordingly. Should the handler leave his start position in order to encourage his dog to scale, then the marks for either the jump over or the return jump must be deducted.

Banging on the stockade, which requires the handler to leave his start position, must be considered as such a strong help to the dog, that the forward and return jumps cannot be assessed. In the event that more than one stockade is present, all dogs must use the same one.

2.2.8 SEND AWAY WITH DOWN (10 marks)

Commands allowed: "away," "down," "sit"

Upon order from the judge, the handler with the dog off lead proceeds in the indicated direction for several paces. With the audible command "away," the handler simultaneously raises his arm forward and stands still. Hereupon the dog must proceed in fast pace in the direction indicated for at least thirty (30) paces. At the command "down," the dog must obey instantly. The handler's arm may remain raised, indicating the direction, until the dog has assumed the down position. Upon order from the judge the handler proceeds to his dog, takes up a position at the dog's right hand side and gives the command to sit.

Procedure:

Repeated raising of the handler's arm is not permitted. The dog must proceed forward in a straight line although a slight deviation is not incorrect. Marks must be deducted for severe deviation, too short a distance, hesitance to assume the down position, anticipation of the down command, or getting up at the handler's approach.

2.2.9 DOWN STAY WITH DIVERSION (10 marks)
Commands allowed: "down," "sit"

This exercise is carried out whilst another dog is carrying out exercises 2.2.1 to 2.2.7. Before commencement of the other dog's obedience exercise, the handler places his dog in the down-stay position at a distance of approximately forty (40) paces without leaving any object or lead near the dog. Remaining in sight of the dog the handler takes up a position some forty (40) paces away without looking back and stands still with his back towards his dog. The dog must remain lying there without any influence from the handler until the other dog has completed exercises 2.2.1 to 2.2.7. After exercise 2.2.7, the handler returns to his dog and follows the instructions given for the end of exercise 2.2.8.

Procedure:

The handler must remain in the position on the field, as indicated by the judge, with his back to the dog, standing quietly until the judge orders him to proceed to his dog. A restless attitude of the handler, attempts at concealed help to the dog or anticipated getting up by the dog upon the handler's return are incorrect.

Should the dog stand or sit but remain on the spot, then he only receives part of the marks.

Should the dog leave his position by more than three (3) metres before the end of exercise 2.2.4 as performed by the other dog, then no marks will be awarded.

Should the same occur after exercise 2.2.4, then only part of the marks can be awarded.

Should the dog leave his position to go to the handler at the return of the latter, then three (3) marks must be deducted.

2.3 GROUP C: DEFENSE WORK - GRADE II - Total marks 100

2.3.1 Quartering for the Assistant (5 marks)

On suitable grounds of about 100m long and 80m wide, 6 hides are placed staggered, 3 on either side of the field.

A defense work Assistant (A) in complete defense outfit with padded armguard and soft stick is out of the dog's (D) sight, concealed in the last hide.

The dog Handler (H) with his D off lead and sitting at heel place themselves on the imaginary centre line level with the third hide. By raising his arm the H indicates that he is ready.

Upon order from the officiating Judge (J) the H commences the Defense Work. With short audible commands and signals given with the left or right arm, all of which can be repeated, the D must leave the H at a brisk pace and explore around the hides in sequence. The H must move along an imaginary centre line, from which he may not deviate whilst the D is quartering.

Whenever the D has rounded a hide, the H may recall him with a short audible command and whilst the D is on the move, with another command, send him in the other direction. The command to recall the D may be combined with the dog's call name. The D must always remain in front of the H. When the D has arrived at the last hide, the H must stop moving and commands are no longer permitted.

2.3.2 Confrontation and Barking (5+5=10 Marks)

The D must confront the A with attention and bark continuously. The D may not jump against the A nor may he take hold of him. Upon order from the J the H returns to his D. Upon an additional order from the J, the H with his D take up a heel position at a distance of 1 pace from the A. The H thereupon orders the A to come 5 paces out of the hide.

2.3.3 Attempt to Escape (20 Marks)

Upon order from the J the H proceeds with his free heeling D from the hide to halt at a distance of 5 paces from the A. He leaves his D sitting in a guarding position and returns into the hide.

Upon order from the J the A attempts to escape at fast pace. Upon a verbal command from the H, the D must, immediately and without hesitation, endeavor to prevent the escape by an energetic action and by taking a firm hold of the A.

Upon order from the J the A stands still. The D must release the A on a single command and guard the A close and attentively.

2.3.4 Defense during the Guard (20 Marks)

After a guarding period of about five seconds, and upon order from the J, the A launches an attack on the D. Without assistance from the H, and D must without hesitation, defend itself by energetically and forcefully taking hold of the A.

Upon order from the J the A stands still. The D must upon a single audible command release its hold and guard the A closely and attentively. Thereupon the H goes to his D and takes up a position as to start the escorting at rear. The H does not disarm. The A has to carry the stick in such a manner that it remains invisible to the dog until exercise 6.

2.3.5 Escorting at rear (5 Marks)

Following on the A is escorted at rear over a distance of about 30 paces. The H commands the A to go forward and follows with his heeling D at a distance of 5 paces. A brief command at the start is permitted.

2.3.6 Attack on the dog during the escorting at rear (20 Marks)

During the escorting at rear, the A will without stopping launch a sudden attack on the D. Without intervention by the H and without hesitation the D must defend itself by energetically and forcefully taking hold of the A. At that moment the H may not move from his position.

Upon order from the J the A ceases his action and stands still. The D must then upon a single short command release its hold and guard the A close and attentively.

Upon order from the J, the H returns to his D, takes the stick from the A and prepares for the escort by side.

The A is escorted by side towards the J over a distance of about 20 paces. A short command is allowed to start the escort. The H must walk at the right hand side of the A, so that the D is between the A and the H. During the escort the D is not allowed to jump against the A or to take hold of him. The escort terminates in front of the J and the H delivers the stick. The A leaves the area or proceeds to hide 6.

2.3.7 Attack on Dog on the Move (20 Marks)

The H with his D take up a position in the middle of the field approximately level with the third hide. The D must sit free next to his H.

Upon order from the J, the A armed with a stick, comes out of the 6th hide and proceeds, in fast pace, heading directly toward the D.

As soon as the A is within 30 paces of the H with his still free in heel sitting D, the H will upon order from the J send his D to attack. The H may not leave his position. The A attacks the D from the front while making loud and verbal threats and exercising considerable physical threat. Without hesitation the D must counter the attack with an energetic and forceful bite. Once the D has taken hold he receives 2 stick blows. Blows are permitted on flanks, withers and thighs.

Upon order from the J the A stands still. The D must then upon a single short command release its hold and guard the A closely and attentively.

Upon order from the J the H goes to his D, takes the stick from the A, and takes up a position in preparation for the escort by side.

The A is escorted by side towards the J over a distance of about 20 paces. A short command is allowed to start the escort. The H must walk at the right hand side of the A, so that the D is between the A and the H. During the escort the D is not allowed to jump against the A or to take hold of him. The escort terminates in front of the J and the H delivers the stick. The A leaves the area.

On the way to, and during the announcement of the grading, the D must be heeled off lead and sit free. Once the announcement is completed the H leaves the field with his D off lead.

2.3.8 Procedures:

- the A must wear a complete outfit (jacket, pants and arm-guard)

- only a padded stick covered with soft material may be used.
- If more than six dogs are entered a second A is required. He will carry out exercise 7.
- an attentive and close circling of the A, including when he is inside the hide, is not incorrect.
- If during exercise 3 the D leaves his place before or without the verbal command from his handler, the exercise has to be graded insufficient.
- if during exercise 7 the D leaves his place before the judge's signal, the exercise has to be graded insufficient.
- If during the defense exercises the D has not released its hold after a third short verbal command, the exercise must be graded insufficient. In the event that the D does not release its hold, an additional (fourth) command, may be allowed by the J from a distance of 10 paces. If the D does not let go on this command the defense work has to be discontinued.
- In order for the A to maintain full view of the D, he need not remain standing absolutely stationary. However the A may not assume any further threatening attitudes or make any defensive movements. He has to hold the arm-guard as to protect his body.
- The defense work has to be discontinued and qualification can not be awarded:
  — if the D is not under full control of the H,
  — if the D does not let go after the 4th command to leave,
  — if the D releases because of physical intervention by the H,
  — if the D fails any defense exercise (including the escape) or allows himself to be chased aside,
  — if the D during any guarding phase, attacks and firmly bites the A.
- Barking is only permitted at the hide and during other guarding exercises.

3. SCHEDULE AND DESCRIPTION OF EXERCISES FOR GRADE III

3.1 GROUP A: TRACKING (Maximum 100 marks)
(See Figure 1)

Three articles (7 + 7 + 6) = 20 marks

Track = 80 marks

Command allowed: "track" or equivalent.

3.1.1 The track is approximately 800 paces long and must be at least 60 minutes old and laid by a tracklayer unfamiliar to the dog. There are three articles on the track. The track must have four corners of 90 degrees. The judge decides upon the format of the track, taking into consideration the topography of the land. Different tracking patterns must be used. This means that corners and articles may not be in the same position for each track.

The start of the track must be well indicated by means of a stake which the tracklayer plants in the ground at his left side. After the tracklayer has stood at the start for some time, he proceeds to lay the track as prescribed and drops the first article after about 100 paces, the second article in the middle of the second or third leg, without changing his pace.

The third article must be dropped at the end of the track. After placing the last article, the tracklayer must continue for several more paces in the same direction of the last leg and then return via a detour.

The handler may choose to work the track with the dog either on the 10 metre lead or free. Both cases are marked equally. If the end of the track has not been reached 20 minutes from the starting time, the track must be abandoned at the command of the judge.

3.1.2 Procedure:

The tracklayer must show the articles to the judge before he proceeds to lay the track. Only well scented articles which were carried in his pocket for at least 30 minutes may be used by the tracklayer. Only articles in everyday use with a length of 100mm, a width of 20 to 30mm and a thickness of 5 to 10mm may be used. All articles must carry a number which corresponds with the number of the track.

Whilst the track is being laid, handler and dog must remain out of sight. If possible, the scent of the track must not be disturbed whilst the articles are being placed. The track-layer may not shuffle or trample the place where the articles are dropped nor may he stop when placing the articles. The articles must be placed on the track and not beside it.

In the meantime, the handler prepares his dog for the working of the track. When called, he proceeds to the judge with his dog and informs him whether his dog retrieves or indicates the articles. Indicating and retrieving on the same track is incorrect.

At a command from the judge, the dog is taken slowly and calmly to the start and is commanded to begin. Here the dog must be given sufficient time to take scent. Before the commencement of the track, at the commencement, as well as during the entire tracking procedure any pressure on the dog or anything which could awaken the dog's desire to rush onto the track must be avoided. The dog should take scent calmly with the nose close to the ground. As soon as the dog begins to track, the handler remains on the spot and allows the 10m long tracking lead to glide through his hand up to the end. He then follows his dog strictly at this distance, which in the case of a free tracking dog, must also be maintained.

The tracking lead may hang slack during the performance of the track while it has not been dropped on the ground by the handler. As soon as the dog has found an article, he must, without any influence from the handler, immediately pick it up or indicate it convincingly. After having picked up the article, the dog may stand, sit or return to the handler. It is incorrect to continue on the track whilst carrying the article. It is incorrect to pick up the article whilst in the down position. Indication of the article is by standing, sitting or lying down. The handler drops the tracking lead, immediately walks to the dog and by raising the article he shows that the dog has

found it. Thereafter the handler and dog continue on the track. After the completion of the track, the handler shows the found articles to the judge.

It is permissible for the handler to walk to his dog after it has picked up the article. It is incorrect for the dog to walk forwards whilst carrying the article.

3.1.3 Evaluation:

False starting, dawdling, repeated circling at the corners, constant encouragements, incorrect indication or picking up or dropping an article must be penalized by up to 4 marks. Reset on track, persistent dawdling, voidance whilst on track and hunting or similar behavior will be penalized by up to 8 marks.

For incorrectly indicated or picked up articles up to 4 marks may be deducted. For either the first and second article not found, 7 marks will be deducted; for the third article not found, 6 marks are deducted.

For indicating or picking up articles not placed by the tracklayer, 4 marks will be deducted.

3.2 GROUP B: OBEDIENCE (Maximum 100 marks)
(See Figure 4)

Every separate exercise begins and ends with the start position i.e. with the handler standing with his dog in correct heel position.

The command to commence each exercise is given by the judge. The sequence of each exercise such as turns, halts, changes of pace etc. are carried out without commands from the judge. A handler is, however, entitled to ask the judge to give commands for the exercise.

3.2.1 HEEL FREE (10 marks)
Command allowed: "heel"

The handler reports to the judge with his dog off lead. The lead must not be visible to the dog. From the start position the dog must, on the command to heel, follow his handler in a happy workmanlike manner.

At the start of the exercise, the handler and his dog must proceed at normal pace for a distance of 40-50 paces in a straight line without stopping and then execute an about turn and after a further 10 to 15 paces, execute the fast pace and slow pace, each for not less than 10 paces.

Thereafter at least one right, one left and one about turn must be carried out at normal pace. The about turns carried out by the handler must be left-about-turns. The dog must have its shoulder next to the left knee of the handler and may not stray in front, behind or to the side. The command "heel" is allowed only at the beginning of the exercise and at the changes of pace. When the handler comes to a halt, the dog has to sit promptly without any influence from the handler. Here the handler may not change his position and especially not move towards a dog which is sitting wide. Upon order from the judge the handler with his dog must then proceed through a group of at least four (4) persons. The handler must halt at least once in the group. The persons in the group must mingle. Lagging, moving in front, swerving to the side by the dog, as well as the handler adjusting to the position of the dog at the turns is incorrect. Whilst the handler with his dog executes the exercise "heel off lead," (but not while moving through the group), two shots must be fired (calibre 6–9mm). The dog must behave in an indifferent to shot manner. If at the gunshot, the dog demonstrates tendency to attack but remains under control of the handler, he is to be penalized.

Shot-shy dogs must immediately be excluded from further participation in the trial.

The full allotment of marks can only be awarded to a dog which appears completely indifferent to shot.

Evaluation:

Considerable value must be placed on indifference to shot. Two shots at an interval of five (5) seconds, must be fired from a distance of fifteen (15) paces. Should the dog run away during the firing of the shots, he has to be excluded from the remainder of the trial.

Should the judge be of the opinion that the dog is sensitive to gunshot, he is free to ask that the gunshot test be repeated. Indifference to shot may only be tested during the "heel off lead" and the "down stay with diversion" exercises.

3.2.2 SIT ON THE MOVE (5 marks)
Command allowed: "sit"

From the start position, the handler with his dog off lead, moves forward in a straight line. After at least ten (10) paces, the dog must sit quickly at the handler's command, "sit," given without a change in pace and without looking back. After a further thirty (30) paces, the handler halts, turns around immediately and faces his dog. Upon order from the judge, the handler returns to the right hand side of his dog and takes up the start position. If the dog takes up an incorrect position (down or stand) during the exercise, up to 3 marks are to be deducted.

3.2.3 DOWN ON THE MOVE WITH RECALL (10 marks)
Commands allowed: "down," "come," "heel"

From the start position, the handler with his dog off lead moves forward, at normal pace, in a straight line for ten (10) paces and then goes over into fast pace. After at least ten (10) further paces, the dog must assume the "down" position quickly at the handler's command. Without interrupting his fast pace, looking back or influencing the dog in any way, the handler must continue for at least thirty (30) paces in a straight line and then turn around immediately to face his dog and stand still.

Upon order from the judge, the handler must recall his dog. The dog should return willingly at a brisk pace and sit closely in front of his handler. At the "heel" command, the dog must assume the heel position briskly. Should the dog at the command "down," either sit or stand, and thereafter return correctly to his handler, up to 5 marks are to be deducted.

3.2.4 STAND STAY, AT NORMAL PACE (5 marks)
Commands allowed: "stand," "sit"

From the start position, the handler with his dog off lead moves in a straight line. After at least ten (10) paces, the dog must, at the handler's command, stand promptly.

Without interrupting his pace, looking back or influencing the dog in any way, the handler continues for a further thirty (30) paces, halts, turns around immediately and faces his dog. Upon order from the judge, the handler returns to the right hand side of his dog. The exercise is complete when the dog, after the command to "sit," has assumed the sit position.

3.2.5 STAND STAY, AT FAST PACE WITH RECALL (10 marks)
Commands allowed: "stand," "come," "heel"

From the start position, the handler with his dog off lead, moves forward at fast pace. After at least ten (10) paces, the dog must, at the handler's command, stand promptly. Without looking back or influencing the dog in any way, the handler must continue for at least thirty (30) paces in a straight line and then turn around immediately to face his dog and stand still. Upon order from the judge, the handler must recall his dog. The dog should return willingly at a brisk pace and sit closely in front of his handler. At the heel command the dog must assume the heel position briskly.

Evaluation:

Should the dog, at the command "stand," assume the sit or down position, up to 5 marks are to be deducted. It is incorrect for the dog to move forward after the command to stand. Looking back by the handler and slowing down by the dog at its return are also incorrect.

3.2.5 RETRIEVING OF A DUMBBELL WITH A MASS OF 2Kg ON LEVEL GROUND (10 marks)
Commands allowed: "fetch," "leave," "heel"

The dog should be sitting off lead, next to the handler. Upon a single command from the handler to "fetch" the dumbbell, which was previously thrown over a distance of approximately ten (10) paces, the dog must proceed briskly to the dumbbell, pick it up immediately and briskly return it to his handler. The dog must sit closely in front of the handler retaining the dumbbell until, after a short pause, the handler commands the dog to "leave" and takes the dumbbell.

At the command "heel," the dog must proceed briskly to the heel position. The handler must remain in the start position until such time as the dog has assumed the heel position.

Evaluation:

Up to 4 marks may be deducted for dropping, chewing or playing with the dumbbell. Up to 3 marks may be deducted should the handler move from the start position. All marks must be lost if the dog does not retrieve the dumbbell.

3.2.6 RETRIEVING OF A DUMBBELL WITH A MASS OF 650g, WITH CLEAR JUMP OVER A 1 METRE HIGH BY 1.5 METRES WIDE HEDGE JUMP (15 marks) (See Figure 2)
Commands allowed: "over," "fetch," "leave," "heel"

The handler places himself at a suitable distance from the jump with his dog sitting off lead next to him. Now he throws a dumbbell with a mass of 650g over the obstacle. At the handler's command: "over," "fetch," the dog must jump over the hedge without touching it, immediately pick up the dumbbell and after jumping back with it, return to sit closely in front of his handler whilst retaining the dumbbell. After a short pause, the handler commands the dog to "leave" and takes the dumbbell. Upon the command "heel," the dog must briskly assume the heel position. The command "fetch" must be given before the dog reaches the dumbbell.

Evaluation:

Up to 2 marks to be deducted for slightly grazing the jump.

Up to 3 marks to be deducted for touching the jump more heavily or for slight support on jump.

Up to 4 marks to be deducted for taking heavy support on jump or dropping the dumbbell, chewing it or playing with it.

Award 15 marks for: correct jump over and back with correctly retrieved dumbbell.

Award 8 marks for: correct jump over, no return jump, dumbbell correctly retrieved.

Award 8 marks for: no jump over, return jump correct and dumbbell correctly retrieved.

Award 8 marks for: jump over and back without retrieve.

Award 0 marks for: no jumps executed but object correctly retrieved.

Award 0 marks for: jump over correct but no return jump and no retrieve.

In the event that the dumbbell has, as a result of being clumsily thrown or because of a strong wind, fallen far to one side, the handler may, after having requested permission from the judge, collect the dumbbell so as to throw it again. No marks will be lost because of this.

The handler must remain in his start position until such a time as the dog has, after having delivered the dumbbell, returned to the heel position. Should the handler, without leaving his start position, give assistance to the dog during the jump, marks must be deducted accordingly.

Should the handler leave his start position in order to encourage his dog to jump, then the marks for either the jump over or the return jump must be deducted.

Banging on the jump, which requires the handler to leave his start position, must be considered as such a strong help to the dog, that the forward and return jumps cannot be assessed.

In the event that more than one hedge is present, all dogs must jump the same one.

3.2.8 SCALING A SLOPING STOCKADE, 1.8 METRES HIGH AND 1.5 METRES WIDE, WITH THE RETRIEVAL OF AN OBJECT BELONGING TO THE HANDLER (15 marks) (see Figure 3)

Commands allowed: "over," "fetch," "leave," "heel"

The sloping stockade consists of two board faces, each with a height of 1.9m and a width of 1.5m, connected at the top. At ground level these boards are separated by such a

distance that the vertical height of the stockade is 1.8m. Each board of the stockade is fitted with three climbing ledges of 24 x 48mm.

The handler places himself at a suitable distance from the stockade with the dog sitting off lead next to him. An object belonging to the handler or a dumbbell may be thrown over the stockade. At the handler's command, "over," "fetch," the dog must scale the stockade, immediately pick up the object and after scaling back with it, return to sit closely in front of the handler whilst retaining the object. After a short pause, the handler commands the dog to "leave" and takes the object. Upon the command "heel," the dog must assume the heel position.

The command "fetch" must be given before the dog reaches the object.

Evaluation:

Up to four marks to be deducted for dropping the object or playing with it or chewing it.

Award 15 marks for: correct jump over and back with a correctly retrieved object.

Award 8 marks for: correct jump over, no return jump, object correctly retrieved.

Award 8 marks for: no jump over, return jump correct, object correctly retrieved.

Award 8 marks for: jump over and back without retrieve.

Award 0 marks for: no jumps executed but object correctly retrieved.

Award 0 marks for: jump over correct but no return jump and no retrieve.

In the event that the object has, as a result of being clumsily thrown or because of a strong wind, fallen far to one side, the handler may, after having requested permission from the judge, collect the object so as to throw it again. No marks will be lost because of this.

The handler must remain on his start position until such a time as the dog has, after having delivered the object, returned to the heel position. Should the handler, without leaving his start position, give assistance to the dog during the scaling, marks must be deducted accordingly.

Should the handler leave his start position in order to encourage his dog to scale, then the marks for either the jump over or the return jump must be deducted.

Banging on the stockade, which requires the handler to leave his start position, must be considered as such a strong help to the dog, that the forward and return jumps cannot be assessed.

In the event that more than one stockade is present, all dogs must use the same one.

3.2.9 SEND AWAY WITH DOWN (10 marks)
Commands allowed: "away," "down," "sit"

Upon order from the judge, the handler with the dog off lead proceeds in the indicated direction for several paces. With the audible command "away," the handler simultaneously raises his arm forward and stands still. Hereupon the

Defense Work

Escape of the suspect (R. Weingartz), followed by an attack on the dog.

dog must proceed in fast pace in the direction indicated for at least forty (40) paces. At the command "down," the dog must obey instantly. The handler's arm may remain raised, indicating the direction, until the dog has assumed the down position. Upon order from the judge the handler proceeds to his dog, takes up a position at the dog's right hand side and gives the command to sit.

Procedure:

Repeated raising of the handler's arm is not permitted. The dog must proceed forward in a straight line although a slight deviation is not incorrect. Marks must be deducted for severe deviation, too short a distance, hesitance to assume the down position, anticipation of the down command, or getting up at the handler's approach.

3.2.10 DOWN STAY WITH DIVERSION (10 marks)
Commands allowed: "down," "sit"

This exercise is carried out whilst another dog is carrying out exercises 3.2.1 to 3.2.8.

Before commencement of the other dog's obedience exercise, the handler places his dog in the down-stay position at a distance of approximately forty (40) paces without leaving any object or lead near the dog. Now the handler, without looking back, takes up an out of sight position some forty (40) paces away from the dog but within the perimeter of the obedience grounds.

Upon order from the judge, the handler returns to his dog and gives the command to "sit."

Evaluation:

The handler must remain quietly out of sight, until the judge orders him to return to his dog.

A restless attitude of the handler, attempts at concealed help to the dog or anticipated getting up by the dog upon the handler's return are incorrect.

Should the dog stand or sit but remain on the spot, then he only receives part of the marks.

Should the dog leave his position by more than 3 metres before the end of exercise 3.2.5 as performed by the other dog, then no marks will be awarded. Should the same occur after exercise 3.2.5, then only part of the marks can be awarded.

Should the dog leave his position to go to the handler at the return of the latter, then 3 marks must be deducted.

3.3 GROUP C: DEFENSE WORK - GRADE III Total marks 100

3.3.1 Quartering for the Assistant (10 marks)

On suitable grounds of about 100m long and 80m wide, 6 hides are placed stagged, 3 on either side of the field.

A defense work Assistant (A) in complete defense outfit with padded armguard and soft stick is out of the dog's (D) sight, concealed in the last hide.

The dog Handler (H) with his D off lead and sitting at heel place themselves on the imaginary centre line level with the first hide. By raising his arm the H indicates that he is ready.

Upon order from the officiating Judge (J) the H commences the Defense Work. With short audible commands and signals given with the left or right arm, all of which can be repeated, the D must leave the H at a brisk pace and explore around the hides in sequence. The H must move along an imaginary centre line, from which he may not deviate whilst the D is quartering.

Whenever the D has rounded a hide, the H may recall him with a short audible command and whilst the D is on the move, with another command, send him in the other direction. The command to recall the D may be combined with the dog's call name. The D must always remain in front of the H. When the D has arrived at the last hide, the H must stop moving and commands are no longer permitted.

3.3.2 Confrontation and Barking (5+5=10 Marks)

The D must confront the A with attention and bark continuously. The D may not jump against the A nor may he take hold of him. Upon order from the J the H returns to his D. Upon an additional order from the J, the H with his D take up a heel position at a distance of 1 pace from the A. The H thereupon orders the A to come 5 paces out of the hide.

3.3.3 Attempt to Escape(15 Marks)

Upon order from the J the H proceeds with his free heeling D from the hide to halt at a distance of 5 paces from the A. He leaves his D sitting in a guarding position and returns into the hide.

Upon order from the J the A attempts to escape at fast pace. Upon a verbal command from the H, the D must, immediately and without hesitation, endeavor to prevent the escape by an energetic action and by taking a firm hold of the A.

Upon order from the J the A stands still. The D must release the A on a single command and guard the A close and attentively.

3.3.4 Defense during the Guard (15 Marks)

After a guarding period of about five seconds, and upon order from the J, the A launches an attack on the D. Without assistance from the H, the D must without hesitation, defend itself by energetically and forcefully taking hold of the A. Once the D has taken hold he receives 2 stick blows. The blows are permitted on the flanks, the withers and the thighs.

Upon order from the J the A stands still. The D must upon a single audible command release it's hold and guard the A closely and attentively. Thereupon the H goes to his D and takes up a position as to start the escorting at rear. The H does not disarm. The A has to carry the stick in such a manner that it remains invisible to the D until exercise 6.

3.3.5 Escorting at rear (5 Marks)

Following on the A is escorted at rear over a distance of about 30 paces. The H commands the A to go forward and follows with his heeling D at a distance of 5 paces.A brief command at the start is permitted.

Escorting at Rear

Followed by an attack on the handler and concluded with escorting by side.

These photos illustrate the test of courage in defense work.

1. Bastian goes for the suspect (G. Chantrie) in the test of courage.

2. Bastian counters this test of his courage without hesitation.

3. Bastian holds the suspect securely.

4. The suspect attacks vigorously.

5. When the suspect stops moving, Bastian releases his hold and assumes a guarding stance.

3.3.6. Attack on the dog during the escorting at rear (15 Marks)

During the escorting at rear, the A will without stopping launch a sudden attack on the D. Without intervention by the H and without hesitation the D must defend itself by energetically and forcefully taking hold of the A. At that moment the H may not move from his position.

Upon order from the J the A ceases his action and stands still. The D must then upon a single short command release its hold and guard the A close and attentively.

Upon order from the J, the H returns to his D, takes the stick from the A and prepares for the escort by side.

The A is escorted by side towards the J over a distance of about 20 paces. A short command is allowed to start the escort. The H must walk at the right hand side of the A, so that the D is between the A and the H. During the escort the D is not allowed to jump against the A or to take hold of him. The escort terminates in front of the J and the H delivers the stick. The A leaves the area or proceeds to hide 6.

3.3.7. Attack on Dog on the Move (15 Marks)

The H with his D take up a position in the middle of the field approximately level with the third hide. The D must sit free next to his H.

Upon order from the J, the A armed with a stick, comes out of the 6th hide and proceeds, in fast pace, in the direction of the centre line of the field. Arrived there, and without changing pace, he now turns and heads directly toward the dog.

As soon as the A is within 30 paces of the H with his still free in heel sitting D, the H will upon order form the J send his D to attack. The H may not leave his position. The A attacks the D from the front while making loud verbal threats and exercising considerable physical threat. Without hesitation the D must counter the attack with an energetic and forceful bite. Upon order from the J the A stands still. The D must then upon a single short command release its hold and guard the A closely and attentively.

3.3.8. Defense during the Guard (15 Marks)

After a guarding period of about five seconds, and upon order from the J, the A launches an attack on the D. Without assistance from the H, the D must without hesitation, defend itself by energetically and forcefully taking hold of the A.

Once the D has taken hold, he receives two stick blows. The blows are permitted on the flanks, the withers and the thighs.

Upon order from the J the A stands still. The D must upon a single audible command release its hold and guard the A closely and attentively.

Upon order from the J the H goes to his D, takes the stick from the A, and takes up a position in preparation of the escort by side.

The A is escorted by side towards the J over a distance of about 20 paces. A short command is allowed to start the escort. The H must walk at the right hand side of the A, so that the D is between the A and the H. During the escort the D is not allowed to jump against the A or to take hold of him. The escort terminates in front of the J and the H delivers the stick. The A leaves the area.

On the way to, and during the announcement of the grading the D must be heeled off lead and sit free. Once the announcement is completed the H leaves the field with his D off lead.

3.3.9. Procedures:

- The A must wear a complete outfit (jacket, pants and armguard).
- Only a padded stick covered with soft material may be used.
- If more than six dogs are entered a second A is required. He will be put in action as from exercise 7.
- An attentive and close circling of the A, including when he is inside the hide, is not incorrect.
- If during exercise 3 the D leaves his place before or without the verbal command from his handler, the exercise has to be graded insufficient.
- If during exercise 7 the D leaves his place before the judge's signal, the exercise has to be graded insufficient.
- If during the defense exercises the D has not released its hold after a third short verbal command, the exercise must be graded insufficient. In the event that the D does not release its hold, an additional (fourth) command, may be allowed by the J from a distance of 10 paces. If the D does not let go on this command the defense work has to be discontinued.
- In order for the A to maintain full view of the D, he need not remain standing absolutely stationary. However the A may not assume any further threatening attitudes or make any defensive movements. He has to hold the armguard as to protect his body.
- The defense work has to be discontinued and qualification can not be awarded:
  — if the D is not under full control of the H,
  — if the D does not let go after the 4th command to leave,
  — if the D releases because of physical intervention by the H,
  — if the D fails any defense exercise (including the escape) or allows himself to be chased aside,
  — if the D during any guarding phase, attacks and firmly bites the A.
- Barking is only permitted at the hide and during other guarding exercises.

From Kommission für Gebrauchshunde der F.C.I., *Leitfaden für das Internationale Gebrauchshundewesen der F.C.I.: Internationale Prüfungsordnung Klasse I, II und III (I.P.O.).* Gultig ab 1990. Translated by J. Gallant, J. Princen, and M. Pieper.

Bibliography

American Kennel Club. *The Complete Dog Book.* 18th ed. Howell, 1992.

Baumeister, Johann Wilhelm. *Die Jagd- und Andere Hunde in Allen Ihren Verhaltnissen.* Ulm, 1832.

Bazille, F. *Die Kennzeichen Unserer Rassehunde.* Bielefeld: Grundlach, 1926.

Berta, Josef. "Foreword." *Pinscher Zuchtbuch.* Vol. 1. Erfurt: N.p., 1902.

Brockhaus, H. A. *Brockhaus' Konversations-Lexikon.* 16 vols. Leipzig: Brockhaus, 1892.

Bungartz, Jean. *Handbuch zur Beurteilung der Rassenreinheit des Hundes.* 1884.

Campbell, William E. *Behavior Problems in Dogs.* Santa Barbara: American Veterinary Publications, 1975.

Canadian Kennel Club. *The Canadian Kennel Club Book of Dogs.* Toronto: Canadian Kennel Club, 1982.

Chastel, J. *Le Bouvier des Flandres Hier et Aujourd'hui.* Londoz-Gilly, 1976.

Compton, Herbert. *The Twentieth Century Dog.* 4 vols. London: Grant Richards, 1904.

Corbett, T. M. *The Dog Owners Guide.* London: Watmoughs.

Ebner, Felix. *Schnauzer und Pinscher,* Hamburg: Otto Meissners, 1937.

Fiorenzo, Fiorone. *Le Schnauzer.* Paris: Editions de Vecchi, 1979.

Fitzinger, Leopold Joseph. *Der Hund und Seine Rassen.* Tübingen: H. Laupp, 1876.

Fogle, Bruce. *The Dog's Mind.* New York: Penguin, 1990.

Fox, Michael W. *Understanding Your Dog.* New York: Coward, McCann & Geoghegan, 1972; reprinted., New York: St. Martin, 1992.

Gallant, Johan. *Schnauzers.* Lisse: Zuid Boekprodukties, 1980.

Gaston Phoebus. *Le Livre de Chasse.* Manuscript, circa 1387.

Götz, Theodor. Monographie des Hundes, Gotha: Hennings & Hopf, 1834.

_____. *Hunde-Gallerie.* Weimar: Eduard Lobe, 1838.

Hertz, Hamilton, and Hertz, Joan. *How to Raise and Train a Standard Schnauzer.* Jersey City, N.J.: TFH Publications, 1965.

Hirschfelder, Herbert. "(article)." *Pinscher-Schnauzer Zeitung,* Number 1, 5, 1985.

Höhn, Alfred. *Schnauzer und Pinscher.* Stuttgart: Kosmos, 1977.

Höller, Heinz. *Schnauzer und Pinscher.* Stuttgart: Ulmer, 1986.

Hubbard, C. H. B. *The Observer's Book of Dogs.* London: F. Warne, 1932.

Humphrey, Elliot, and Warner, Lucien. *Working Dogs.* Baltimore: Johns Hopkins, 1934; reprint ed., Palo Alto: National Press, 1974.

Isabell, Jackie. *Genetics: A Handbook for Dog Breeders.* (In preparation.)

Jahn, Conrad. *Das Werk von Johann Adam Klein.* Munich: Montmorillon'sche Kunsthandlung, 1863.

Jesse, George R. *Researches into the History of the British Dog.* 2 vols. London: R. Hardwicke, 1866.

Judy, William Lewis. *The Dog Encyclopedia.* Chicago: Judy Publishing Co., 1925.

Jung, W. *Standard Buch der Schnauzer- und Pinscherrassen.* Cologne: PSK, 1956.

Kiedrowsky, Dan. *The New Miniature Schnauzer.* New York: Howell, 1986.

Lee, Rawdon B. *A History and Description of the Modern Dogs of Great Britain and Ireland.* 3d ed. London: Horace Cox, 1899.

Leighton, Robert. *The New Book of the Dog.* London: Cassell & Co., 1907.

_____. *Dogs and All about Them.* London: Cassell & Co., 1910.

Lockley, Arthur S. *How to Raise and Train a Giant Schnauzer.* Jersey City, N.J.: TFH Publications, 1964.

Lorenz, Konrad. *Das Sogenannte Böse. Zur Naturgeschichte der Aggression.* Vienna: Borotha-Schoeler, 1965.

MacDonald, Daly. *Odd Dogs.* London: W. & R. Chambers, 1955.

Marx, P. *Der Zwergschnauzer.* Butzbach: Gratzfeld, 1982.

Meunier, Theo. *Chasse et Pêche* 34 (21 January 1922): 36, 720.

Nussbaumer, Marc, and Althaus, Thomas. *Vom Torfhund zum Heutigen Rassehund.* Bern: SKG, 1979.

Pfaffenberger, Clarence J. *The New Knowledge of Dog Behavior.* New York: Howell, 1963.

Pinscher–Schnauzer Klub 1895 e.V. *1895–1970 75 Jahre PSK.* Cologne: PSK, 1970.

_____. *1895–1985 90 Jahre PSK.* Alsdorf: PSK, 1985.

_____. *Zuchtbuch.* Vols. 1 to 11, 1902–1933.

Reichenbach, H. *Der Hund in Seinen Haupt-und Nebenrassen.* 1834.

Reul, A. *Cynotechnie, Les Races de Chiens.* 8 vols. Brussels: 1891–1894.

Robson, Phyllis. *Popular Dogs.* Popular Dogs Publishing Co., 1934.

Schmiedeberg, R. von. *"Was ist ein Pinscher?"* Der Hund, 17 July 1879.

_____. *Rassekenzeichen von Pinschern.* 1884.

Scott, John Paul, and Fuller, John L. *Genetics and the Social Behavior of the Dog.* Chicago: University of Chicago Press, 1965.

Seiferle, Eugen. *Kleine Hundekunde.* Zurich: Albert Müller, 1949.

Smith, A. Croxton *Dogs Since 1900.* London: Andrew Dakers, 1950.

_____. *About Our Dogs.* London: Ward, Lock & Co., 1931.

Stone, B, and Migliorini, M. *Clipping and Grooming Your Terrier.* London: John Gifford, 1968.

Strebel, Richard. *Die Deutsche Hunde und Ihre Abstammung.* Munich: Ertel, 1905.

Studer, Theodor. *"Beiträge zur Geschichte unserer Hunderassen" Naturwissenschaftliche Wochenschrift,* 11 July 1897, 1.

Tchudy, W. *Geschichte des Hundes.* Bern: Grunau, 1926.

Toman, J. R. *De Politiehond in Dienst van de Mens.* Antwerp: Helios, 1982.

Trumler, Eberhard. *Mit dem Hund auf Du.* Munich: R. Piper & Co., 1971.

_____. *Your Dog and You.* Seabury Press, 1973.

_____. *Hunde Ernst Genommen.* Munich: R. Piper & Co., 1974.

Turner, J. Sidley. *Kennel Encyclopedia.* London: The Exhibitor's Supply Assoc., 1910.

Van Bylandt, Henri. *Les Races de Chiens.* Brussels: Vanbuggenhoudt, 1897.

Verband für das Deutsche Hundewesen. *80 Jahre Deutsches Hundewesen.* Dortmund, Germany: VDH, 1986.

Walsh, J. H. *The Dogs of the British Isles.* 2d ed. London: H. Cox, 1862.

Other Sources of Information

CLUBS

American Kennel Club
51 Madison Avenue, New York, NY 10010

Canadian Kennel Club,
Commerce Park, Etobicoke,
Ontario, Canada M9W 6R4

Federation Cynologique Internationale
13 Place Albert I,
B-6530 THUIN, Belgium

Kennel Union of Southern Africa,
P. O. Box 2659, 8000 Cape Town
Republic of South Africa

TheKennel Club,
1-4 Clarges St.,
London W1Y 8AB England

Pinscher-Schnauzer Klub, e. V. 1895 (PSK),
Barmer StraBe 80
D-42899 Remscheid, Germany

Verband fur das, Deutsche Hundewesen, e. V. (VDH),
Postfach 10 41 54
D-44041 Dortmund, Germany

Standard Schnauzer Club of America
Liz Hansen, Secretary
P. O. Box 153, Kampsville, IL 62053

North American Working Dog Assn
7318 Brennans Dr., Dallas, TX 75214

Canine Eye Registration Inc. (CERF)
South Campus Courts, Bldg. C
Purdue University, West Lafayette, IN 47907

Orthopedic Foundation for Animals (OFA)
University of Missouri
2300 Nifong Blvd., Columbia, MO 65211

PERIODICALS

AKC Gazette, 5580 Centerview Dr., Raleigh, NC 17606

Dog Fancy, P. O. Box 53264, Boulder, CO 80322

Dogs in Canada, 43 Railside Rd., Don Mills, Ontario
Canada M3A 3L9

Dog Sports, Journal of the Working Dog, 940 Tyler St.,
Benecia, CA 94510

Dog World, 29 Wacker Dr., Chicago, IL 60606

Ch. Klondaike's Diplomat (Miniature), bred by B. and
N. Jordal (Denmark).